International Studies: Perspectives on a Rapidly Changing World

Preliminary Edition

Edited by Greta Uehling

University of Michigan, Ann Arbor

cognella® | ACADEMIC PUBLISHING

Bassim Hamadeh, CEO and Publisher
Kassie Graves, Director of Acquisitions
Jamie Giganti, Senior Managing Editor
Miguel Macias, Senior Graphic Designer
Jennifer Codner, Acquisitions Editor
Michelle Piehl, Project Editor
Alexa Lucido, Licensing Coordinator
Berenice Quirino, Associate Editor

Printed in the United States of America

ISBN: 978-1-5165-1377-2 (pbk) / 978-1-5165-1378-9 (br)

Perspectives on International Studies

International Studies:

Perspectives on a Rapidly Changing World

WHAT IS INTERNATIONAL STUDIES?

In the past few decades, global interdependence has been increasing. This volume explores some of the many ways that people, ideas, capital, and technology have flowed across political, economic, and cultural borders, as well as perspectives on those flows. The interconnected quality of the world we live in suggests a strict disciplinary approach may no longer be ideal for understanding complex global problems. The field of international studies has developed to meet this challenge. It has evolved from being a subtopic within political science into an interdisciplinary and comparative approach to questions of global significance. There is a closely related field you may have heard of, global studies, which focuses more on the role of race, class, and gender in international affairs. This closely related field places less emphasis on the importance of the nation-state. Both international and global studies are inspired by looking at the world from the perspective of different geographical areas and academic disciplines and both fields are designed to nurture the development of global citizens.

International studies is a relatively new field of study. The International Studies Association (ISA) has played a crucial role in the field's rapid growth and development. The ISA was formed in 1959 when scholars and practitioners saw a need for greater international and interdisciplinary dialogue (http://www.isanet.org). The association continues to connect scholars and practitioners around the world and even has nongovernmental consultative status at the United Nations (http://www.isanet.org). The seven journals that the association publishes are valuable sources of information for students of international studies.[1] This is a great time to be interested in this field: individuals have never been as affected by events far from their homes as they are today.

International Studies is a very broad field and this volume can only provide an introduction. In spite of this breadth, there are some connecting themes that readers will find throughout the selections. First, globalization, as a central and organizing concept, is explored from a different angle in each module. Human rights, human security, and human development are other key concepts you will take with you from the readings and links that follow. The first chapter on globalization will give readers a sense of the main debates about this central topic. Chapter two will explore international organizations and relations and relies predominantly on the discipline of political science. In chapter three, we consider two responses to the shortcomings of the state system: human rights and humanitarianism. Chapter four includes readings from the sciences as we consider global health and environment. Human development, the topic of chapter five, came about in part to help solve issues of global health and environment.

---

[1] The journals students at the undergraduate level will find most helpful are The International Studies Review, International Studies Perspectives and Foreign Policy Analysis http://www.isanet.org/Publications/ISP

The field of human development aspires to reduce inequalities and enhance health and well being for all people. The sixth and last chapter brings us back to central problematic of globalization with which we began the course: understanding continued cultural heterogeneity in spite of the homogenizing forces of globalization. In this chapter, we consider these tendencies from the perspective of refugees and indigenous peoples. As a whole, the volume aims to give students a clearer appreciation of an increasingly interdependent world; a better understanding of a selection of important international issues; and some conceptual tools for analyzing events long after Introduction to International Studies.

Globalization: what's in a word?

While the adjective "global" has been used at least since 1892, the word "globalization" only found its way into dictionaries in 1961 (MacGillivray 2006: 11). MacGillivray traces the first use of the adjective "global" all the way back to 1892, when a Frenchman named Monsieur de Vogue was described in Harper's Magazine as having "global ambitions." The magazine describes him as a person who is hungry to experience colors, tastes, and ideas from all over the world, a person whose interests were "as wide as the universe" (McGillivray 2006: 10).

In his book on globalization, McGillivray suggests that a necessary prerequisite to the globalization we see today was the intent at first to know, and then to circumnavigate the globe (2006: 26). The history of globalization is in many ways the history of competition for the knowledge and power to encompass the world. Distinguishing the global from the international, and zeroing in on a precise definition is helpful because the word "global" is too often used casually, as a synonym for "great." For the purpose of this volume, globalization will be defined as the processes through which regions have become more interdependent through intensified communication, transportation, and trade. It can be studied by following the transnational movement of ideas, people, goods, and capital.

A useful tool for exploring the usage of particular words is the google Ngram[3] viewer. Google Ngram viewer is a free, online search engine that measures the frequency of a given word (or words) in published sources. It is possible to perform searches in eight different languages: American English, British English, French, German, Spanish, Russian, Hebrew, and Chinese. What is visible in the screen capture of a search for American English sources using globalization is the precipitous rise of the term in the 1990s and first decade of the twenty-first century. You can see from figure one just how rapidly use of the term expanded.

---

[2]http://www.merriam-webster.com/dictionary/globalization.
[3]You can access the google Ngram viewer to perform your own searches here https://books.google.com/ngrams

Google Books Ngram Viewer

Graph these comma-separated phrases: | globlisation,globalization,Globalisation,Globalization | ▾ | ☐ case-insensitive

between 1900 and 2008 from the corpus English (2009) ⬍ with smoothing of 0 ⬍. Search lots of books

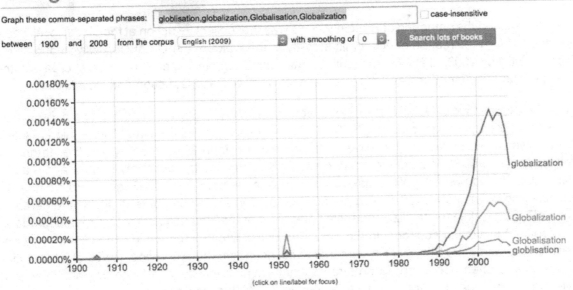

(click on line/label for focus)

When sifting through titles of books on globalization, some interesting patterns appear. One tendency is to make normative assessments about whether globalization is good or bad. This often entails painting globalization in a stark way using opposites. *McWorld vs Jihad* (Barbar 1995) and *The World is Flat* (Friedman 2005) are two titles that are typical of the unequivocal way that many people talk about globalization. This may be a reflection of the insecure place the topic holds in contemporary scholarship. Another strong tendency is to see the phenomenon as negative, and to fear globalization. In fact, throughout the late 1990s, the word was most often seen in print with the "anti-" prefix (McGillivray 2006). Globalization has vocal critics. Although the media has characterized these critics as "anti-globalization," few among them would be against globalization itself. After all, protesters benefit from the same communication and transportation networks as people who see globalization as a beneficial process. What they object to is the specific ways that international institutions have promoted globalization to the detriment of

the world's most vulnerable people.

The United Nations Monetary and Financial Conference at Bretton Woods

Globalization has a long history, which may be studied in a number of excellent books.[4] Since this course is primarily focused on events in the second half of the twentieth century, it is sufficient for now to understand how institutions created after World War II shaped the processes of globalization, and hence the political and economic systems we see today. A key moment in this progression was when delegates from the Allied nations convened a meeting in Bretton Woods, New Hampshire. The conference was officially called the United Nations Monetary and Financial Conference, but most people use "Bretton Woods" as an abbreviated way of referring to the pivotal decisions made at the Mount Washington Hotel in July 1944. Bretton Woods is central to the

[4] *Globalization: A Very Short Introduction* by Manfred Steger, *Globalization and Its Discontents* by Joseph E. Stiglitz, and *Globalization: A Basic Text* (second edition) by George Ritzer and Paul Dean are recommended.

process of globalization because it established the institutions that have been instrumental in integrating previously separated economies.

The spirit behind the gathering at Bretton Woods was that collective action at the global level would be required for the creation of economic stability in the wake of the Great Depression and World War II (Stiglitz 2003: 12). As a result of the gathering, two institutions were created: the International Monetary Fund and the International Bank of Reconstruction and Development.

From the perspective of Nobel Prize winning economist Joseph Stiglitz, the IMF had a difficult task: prevent another global depression (2003: 10). Economists noticed the Great Depression resulted in massive unemployment. The thinking on the part of John Maynard Keynes, the "father" of economics, was that boosting aggregate demand would cause the economy to grow again and it was within the power of policy makers to stimulate demand. The IMF aimed to do this by encouraging countries who had weak economies to do more to contribute to aggregate demand. The IMF also worked to stabilize currencies and prevent the kind of volatility that had jeopardized a smoothly functioning economy in the past. The dollar became the world's global currency and was backed with gold. Stiglitz points out that at its inception, the IMF recognized that intervention in markets is often necessary to protect national economies (2003: 12), an approach that was eventually set aside. The IMF became famous in the 1990s for unwavering support for the idea that markets are best left to regulate themselves.

The International Bank for Reconstruction and Development (IBRD) is another institution that was created at the conference. This organization was tasked with administering grants and loans to countries (primarily European) whose economies were damaged by the war. Stiglitz suggests the word "development" was tacked on at the end of the name without a great deal of reflection (2003: 11). This was a time when most of the countries in the developing world were still colonies. Very little development was foreseen because these countries were thought to be the responsibility of their colonizers. That changed dramatically with time.

A third institution was planned but failed to materialize at the Bretton Woods conference. Organizers of the conference envisioned an international trade organization to promote equitable rules. While they were not able to agree on the establishment of this organization, a less comprehensive agreement was signed, called the General Agreement on Tariffs and Trade (GATT). Decades passed before a round of negotiations, the Uruguay Round in 1995, founded the World Trade Organization (WTO). Together, these three organizations provided the basic economic institutions or "architecture" that led to greater economic interdependence.

Additional Works Cited

Barbar, Benjamin. 1996. "Jihad vs. Mc World: How Globalization and Tribalism are Shaping the World." New York: Times Books.

Freidman, Thomas. 2005. The World is Flat: A Brief History of the Twenty-First Century. New York: Farrar, Straus and Giroux.

Mac Gillivray, Alex. 2006. *A Brief History of Globalization, the Untold Story of Our Incredible Shrinking Planet*. New York: Carroll and Graf.

McNeill. W. 1989. *The age of gunpowder empires, 1450-1800: Essays on global and comparative history*. Washington, D.C: American Historical Association.

Stiglitz, Joseph. 2003. *Globalization and its Discontents*. New York: Norton.

I. MODULE ONE:

Globalization

While the term "globalization" has become one of the most widely used terms in the contemporary international studies lexicon, scholars still disagree about when the process began, what drives it, and whether or not it is making the world a more peaceful or prosperous place.

There are many debates about the significance of globalization. One has to do with how the process is understood historically. Just how long has globalization been going on? This is a thought-provoking question because setting the start date at human migration out of the African continent, as some do, equates globalization with migration and dilutes the concept – perhaps to the point of rendering it useless. The word "globalization" is best reserved for efforts that aim to be global, and for the processes that bring parts of the world into greater interdependence.

Another common debate is about the extent to which globalization fosters economic prosperity. Champions of the phenomenon like Thomas Friedman suggest globalization offers poor countries an opportunity to develop economically and achieve greater well-being. Opponents of this view counter that the specific ways in which the global economy is organized have primarily benefitted multinational corporations based in the Western world, not the world's poor. The best way to set this debate to rest is to avoid overly broad generalizations and engage in a detailed and country-by-country analysis – something many scholars, including Pankaj Ghemawat, are endeavoring to do. He discusses the Global Connectedness Index, which was designed to measure the various impacts of globalization.[5]

A third debate has to do with the extent to which globalization facilitates democracy. There is no question that waves of democratization have been facilitated by globalization. As scholars Leeson and Deen point out (2009) the factors are complex. One influential dynamic is that when people travel or use communication technology, they can quickly become aware of how their lives might be different. In some cases, this may cause them to become less willing to tolerate leaders that abuse their power. It is also true, however, that advances in globalization have made terrorism more possible (Hoffman 2002: 111) and there are equally complex dynamics at work here. Hoffman emphasizes that when marginalized and economically destitute people become more aware of the chances they are missing, the feelings of exclusion and resentment can inspire social and political movements that seek change (2002: 3).

A fourth debate is whether globalization is leading to cultural homogenization or not. A closely related argument has to do with whether or not globalization essentially entails Americanization. There are certainly some striking trends that point to a loss of diversity. For example, the United Nations Educational, Scientific and Cultural Organization (UNESCO) states on its website that of the approximately 6,000 languages that are spoken today, as many as half will disappear by the end of this century.[6] But more often than not, global trends acquire unique local expressions, as these readings will explore.

---

[5] https://www.youtube.com/watch?v=5YHZna0ENLY
[6] http://www.unesco.org/new/en/culture/themes/endangered-languages/

Readings

In "What's in a Dumpling" **Seanon Wong** gives the example of fast food in China to show how globalization does not always lead to homogenization. Rather than devastating local business, the arrival of American-style fast food, in Wong's estimation, inspired local entrepreneurs to innovate.

Hoffman's essay titled "Clashing Globalizations" provides a brief tour of key debates about globalization. This article appeared in a leading journal of international relations: *Foreign Affairs*. Hoffman wrote the article in response to the terrorist attacks of September 11, 2001, but his observations concerning the debates about globalization, what he calls "the sound and the fury" remain relevant today. He suggests that globalization presents a challenge to the study of international relations, which had previously contented itself with studying inter-state relations.

Hoffman explores the weaknesses of various models of globalization that gained currency in the 1990s. He takes issue with Francis Fukuyama's idea that we witnessed the end of ideological conflicts, and Samuel Huntington's idea that "civilizational" conflicts are likely to erupt. Both Fukuyama and Huntington see globalization affecting politics in such a way that the nation-state is becoming less important. Hoffman suggests that this fails to take into account the continued relevance of nationalism and national identity. Hoffman explores significant effects of globalization on politics, as well as globalization's connection to terrorism.

Friedman is one of the more outspoken optimists about globalization. His classic article "It's Flat World After All" is included in the volume not because Friedman provides a particularly accurate view of globalization, but because he represents the views of a "hyper-globalist." In fact, the metaphors he uses and the tone he strikes demonstrate the attitude that people outside the United States find troubling. Hyper-globalists argue that globalization is bringing about sweeping changes in the world today. They believe that the power of governments is waning and that the process has gone far enough to undermine the ability of governments to regulate their economies. They are particularly interested in the importance of organs of transnational governance. For example, Held (1999) et al think that with time, the world will embrace a more unified set of principles with regard to economic and political organization, making a truly global civilization possible.

Pankaj Ghemawat disagrees with Freidman and provides economic data to refute some of Freidman's more sweeping generalizations. One useful take-away from Ghemawat's talk is that the world is not as globalized as we often think. He provides quantitative evidence that international trade, migration, and communication are limited. Thus overstatements, when they lead to irrational fears of globalization are counterproductive. Whereas Freidman is a hyper-globalist, Ghemawat is a skeptic. Skeptics acknowledge that globalization is occurring, but see it as a more regionalized phenomenon. They emphasize that industrialized nations have built regionalized trading blocks (Schiff and Winters 2003: 209) rather than a truly global economy. Skeptics suggest that the endurance of the nation-state system is evidence that globalization has not resulted in anything resembling the decline of the nation state and therefore emphasize the distinct limits of globalization.

In "Victim or Criminal: The Experiences of a Human-Trafficking Survivor in the U.S. Immigration System" **Letica Saucedo** follows the story of an individual trafficking victim, Mae. This piece is included in the volume because while theories are helpful to analyzing trends, the story of a single individual can make the subjective world of a trafficking survivor more understandable. Saucedo demonstrates how it is possible to be a victim and a criminal at the same time: even though Mae won her trafficking case, the victory has not (yet) absolved her of her unauthorized border crossing. While Saucedo uses the term "victim" to describe Mae, actual trafficking survivors do not typically use this term. Survivors of human trafficking usually see themselves as people who have made unfortunate choices. This is a vital distinction to make because the words and images used to describe survivors can help restore the dignity that was undermined by human traffickers.

Alice Hill and **Ramona Carey** wrote "Precious Commodity: The Trade in Human Lives" to underscore the value of focusing on protection for the survivors of human trafficking. While this might seem like common sense, their emphasis represents a departure from anti-trafficking efforts in the past. Human trafficking rose in importance on the international agenda because of its association with transnational terrorism and crime (Gallagher 2013). Therefore, initial efforts were disproportionately concentrated on prosecution of the perpetrators. These authors describe United States legislations pertaining to human trafficking. International law on human trafficking is found under the United Nations Convention on Transnational Organized Crime (2000). The United Nations supplemented this convention with two protocols that address smuggling and trafficking in 2003 and 2004 respectively. While Hill and Carey refer to human trafficking as "modern day slavery" this metaphor has limited utility. Considering slavery was legal in the past, there are considerable differences between human rights abuses then and now.

What's in a Dumpling?

by Seanon Wong

University of Chicago

Critics of globalization who bemoan the corruptive e! ects of McDonald's and KFC on fragile local cuisines often overlook the interesting corollary that globalization also serves to export local cuisines, stimulating instead of stifling cultural diversity. Taking as her major example Chinese fast-food, Wong makes a strong case that, far from being subsumed, local cultures have thrived in today's globalized environment by benefiting from enlarged markets and modern business management.

The impact of globalization on indigenous cultures has been hotly debated in recent years. Proponents of globalization celebrate it as the ultimate order of humanity. David Rothkopf, an international trade scholar, for example, argues that the "homogenizing influences of globalization… [are] positive; globalization promotes integration and the removal not only of cultural barriers but of many of the negative dimensions of culture." Being the primary sponsors of globalization, Americans should not hesitate to promote their culture worldwide because it is "fundamentally different" and provides "the best model for the future."[1] On the other hand, critics condemn globalization as a new form of domination. The cultural imperialism thesis claims that "authentic, traditional and local culture in many parts of the world is being battered out of existence by the indiscriminate dumping of large quantities of slick commercial and media products, manly from the United States."[2] Regardless of one's take on this debate, one common assumption prevails: Indigenous cultures, as Barber famously proclaims, are giving way to the uniform culture of "McWorld."

Commentators have rightly observed that in China, as in other countries opening up to global exchanges, the entry of Western fast food (American in particular) has altered the dietary habits of many Chinese. However, it would be a grave oversight to conclude that Chinese culinary practices are in peril on the course towards cultural homogenization. In this article, I take a revisionist standpoint on the cultural effects of globalization. Using the culinary cultures of China as illustration, I refute the claim that globalization is simply cultural homogenization by highlighting that globalization has provided for the promotion and exportation of certain local cuisines; it can thus be understood as a means of propagating elements of traditional cultures in novel ways. The increasing awareness of Chinese culinary cultures worldwide offers a case in point: thanks to the proliferation of Chinese fast food establishments globally, Australians, Europeans and Americans can savor Chinese dumplings, Mongolian hotpots, Cantonese *dimsum* and northwestern Chinese noodles – cuisines that were mostly unheard of in the West before China lifted the "bamboo curtain" and resumed foreign contact in the 1970s – with as much convenience as hamburgers and pizzas are found in China nowadays.

My arguments are presented in three sections. First, I provide an overview of past discussions on China's experience with cultural globalization. Second, I argue that the extant literature is flawed by a theoretical misconception about globalization. As the experience of other developing countries confirms, globalization allows indigenous cultures to grow through participation in one important institution of modernity – the global market. To conclude, I discuss the origin and evolution of China's fast food industry. I select several notable chains to illustrate how China is contributing to global cultural diversity by reviving and exporting its culinary cultures abroad.

The Advent of McWorld?

As recently as two to three decades ago, it was assumed that hamburgers, French fries, pizza and other fast food products would never succeed in China. When McDonald's opened its first restaurant in Hong Kong in 1975, "few thought it would survive more than a few months."[3] American fast food chains brought products and services that bore little resemblance to the local culinary interests. In a region where rice is the traditional staple, fast food was largely perceived as a snack rather than a proper meal.[4] Besides, fast food table manners typically oppose traditional eating etiquette. For example, in Japan, eating while standing or with one's bare hands were social taboos.[5] Chinese societies shared similar attitudes, as formal meals are traditionally consumed with chopsticks and other utensils. How could Western companies such as KFC market its "finger-lickin'" chicken in such an adverse environment?

As a result, many were surprised when Western fast food became an enormous success in China. The industry expanded into mainland China in 1987 when KFC set up its first franchise in downtown Beijing. At that time, the restaurant was the world's largest fast food outlet, drawing up to 3,000 customers daily during its first year of operation and subsequently setting numerous company records.[6] The Golden Arches first appeared when McDonald's arrived at Shenzhen in 1990, and American fast food chains experienced a spectacular boom thereafter. When Beijing's first McDonald's opened in 1992, the restaurant – equipped with 700 seats and 29 cash registers – served 40,000 customers on its first day.[7] Currently, there are approximately 700 McDonald's all over mainland China. Hong Kong alone boasts over 200 with more than 10,000 employees. The company proudly declares on its website that in 2003, "McDonald's Hong Kong cracked 32.5 million U.S.A. Grade A eggs, prepared over 25 million pounds of French fries, and grilled over 4.4 million pounds of beef patties to serve its customers." KFC has been even more ambitious. From 2001 to 2003, the number of KFC franchises in the mainland doubled from 400 to over 800. Today, it has 1,400 in more than 200 Chinese cities, with a presence in every province save Tibet.

What does this phenomenal success of Western fast food reveal about cultural globalization? As anthropologist James Watson points out, Chinese cuisines "are not small-scale cultures under imminent threat of extinction; we are dealing with... societies noted for their haute cuisines. If McDonald's can make inroads in these societies... it may indeed be an irresistible force for world culinary change."[8] Indeed, at first glance, the introduction of American-style fast food in China may suggest that indigenous cultures will soon be tossed into the trash heap of history. In Beijing, people reacted with a mixture of surprise and anxiety. Some Chinese restaurants, including ones that have been local favorites for generations, were soon driven out of business as customers opted for Western food. The "invasion" was seen as "an alarming threat to both the local food industry and the national pride of Chinese culinary culture."[9]

This viewpoint is echoed by other academics: humanity, as some suggest, is on an irreversible track towards cultural homogenization. Benjamin Barber, for instance, foresees the future as "a busy portrait of onrushing economic, technological, and economic forces that demand integration and uniformity and that mesmerize peoples everywhere with fast music, fast computers, and fast food – MT, Macintosh, and McDonald's – pressing nations into one homogeneous global theme park, one McWorld tied together by communications, information, entertainment, and commerce."[10] In his international bestseller, *Fast Food Nation*, journalist Eric Schlosser claims that the end of the Cold War "has led to an unprecedented 'Americanization' of the world, expressed in the growing popularity of movies, CDs, music videos, television shows, and clothing from the United States."[11]

The Western media has also sided with academic wisdom. According to the *Washington Post*, "China's cuisine is increasingly being altered by the growing consumption of fast food, with Chinese now more likely than Americans to eat takeout meals." Ironically, as China strives to assert its stature as an autonomous and distinctive power, it finds itself being integrated into the "Filet-O-Fish-eating, Pepsi-drinking cosmos."[12] Globalization has made the country susceptible to foreign ideas, and culinary preferences have shifted accordingly. For example, cheese traditionally had been too pungent to be palatable for many Chinese. But in recent years, aggressive marketing by multinational suppliers of dairy products – along with their allies in the supermarket and fast food industries – are gradually recasting Chinese tastes. The demand for cheese is growing.[13]

Chinese lifestyle has changed so dramatically that some even call into question the meaning of being Chinese. The *New York Times* notes that "ordinary people in China's cities have found much common ground with Americans, with the way they live converging rapidly in the marketplace… Europeans may be wont to view every Big Mac as a terrifying sign of American cultural imperialism, but Chinese have mostly welcomed the invasion – indeed they ha e internalized it."[14] Studies show that receptiveness to American fast food has little to do with the taste of the food itself. Rather, most Chinese visit the Golden Arches or KFC because the experience satisfies their curiosity about, if not yearning for, American culture. The Big Mac, in the words of Yunxiang Yan, is "a Symbol of Americana." Especially to the younger generations, eating fast food is "an integral part of their new lifestyle, a way for them to participate in the transnational cultural system."[15]

Globalization and the Spread of Indigenous Cultures

Has the extant literature aptly described and explained the dynamics of globalization and its impact on the culinary cultures of China?[16] Those who lament the end of cultural diversity base their reasoning on two assumptions. The first is that globalization on the one hand and the persistence of indigenous cultures on the other are inherently antithetical; as Barber puts it, their relationship constitutes the "dialectic of McWorld".[17] The second assumption is that local identities exist *a priori*. A culture must already be recognized by both members within and without a community before being brought under the impact

13

of globalization. For instance, to make the case that KFC is uprooting Beijing's native identity by ousting the city's famed roast duck from its restaurant menus, one must argue that people were conscious of a Beijing identity in the first place, and that Beijing delicacies are an essential component of this identity. Identity erosion would not be an issue if this identity never existed.

Both of these assumptions are flawed, as cultural identities are more a modern creation than a primordial conception. "Globalization," according to Tomlinson,

> is really the globalization of modernity, and modernity is the harbinger of identity… Modernity… means, above all, the *abstraction* of social and cultural practices from contexts of local particularity… [It] institutionalizes and regulates cultural practices, including those by which we imagine attachment and belonging to a place or a community. The *mode* of such imagination it promotes is what we have come to know as 'cultural identity'. (italics in original)[18]

Contrary to popular belief, globalization is not a unilateral process in which a "McWorld" culture spreads, erodes and ultimately supplants indigenous cultures. Globalization produces – rather than victimizes – people's consciousness of their cultural environment. As in the case of Chinese culinary cultures, by successfully incorporating an important institution of modernity – a market economy – "globalizing" societies are empowered to repackage and promote their cultures beyond their geographical confines.

The experiences of Japan and India are instructive. According to Tulasi Srinivas, while the forces of "cultural globalization… do enter India, cultural models are also increasingly emitted *from* India." The most prominent example is the rise of New Age culture, as reflected by the widespread practice of meditation, yoga and spiritual healing, and by the consumption of Indian cultural artifacts all over the world.[19] Furthermore, the "entry of multinational food companies has been widely reported… but the concurrent boom in local foods and indigenous cuisine has been ignored." Inspired by the efficiency of Western management, the Indian catering sector "takes Indian recipes, simplifies them for quick production, and decreases time and cost to the consumer."[20] Indian society, as Srinivas succinctly posits, is experiencing "a restructuring of cultural concepts and institutions, incorporating the global and modern with the traditional and local."[21]

In addition, a culture's influence abroad has less to do with its inherent "strength" – a notion Huntington adopts in his famous analysis of civilization conflict – than with a society's level of economic development and integration with the global order. According to Tamotsu Aoki, the success of American fast food in Japan since the 1960s only in part reflected a dietary revolution that transformed Japanese society. As the number of foreign restaurants grew exponentially, "a simultaneous process of fast-foodization of traditional Japanese food was occurring."[22] Nowadays, hamburgers have to compete with sushi in many Western countries.

Economic development also enabled Japanese corporations to promote their native cultures internationally. Suntory, for instance, pioneered "the penetration of Japanese mass culture and Japan's image in Asia" through the aggressive marketing of its beverages. Shiseido managed to infiltrate the saturated European market and compete on par with the European cosmetic giants because the company highlighted its Japanese origin. The exoticism associated with Japanese aesthetics bolstered Shiseido's popularity among European consumers. The case of Japan shows that globalization "progresses in accordance with the degree of development in each society, and the traditions and culture of each country and society are reflected in the process."[23]

Similar observations can be made for other Asian societies. For example, economic prosperity has provided the material foundation for Hong Kong and Taiwan to develop their entertainment sectors. Combining traditional Chinese with modern elements, Hong Kong and Taiwanese popular cultures have been enormously influential in mainland China[24] and also globally. Despite its history as a British colony and its cosmopolitan outlook, Hong Kong retained its Chinese roots. The city became an exemplar of Chinese culture as it became the chief producer and exporter of products ranging from Chinese *qipao* (cheongsams) to movies glorifying Shaolin martial arts.

Noodles vs. Sesame Seed Buns

Considering the omnipresence of McDonald's, KFC and Pizza Hut, American fast food has been a revolutionary force in China's everyday culture. They have yet to become the most popular dining locations, however. Indigenous cultures, including culinary traditions, are on the rise in China. Paradoxically, globalization is responsible for their revival.

The evolution of Hong Kong's culinary scene offers an ideal starting point for discussion, since the city has been on the forefront of global integration for a much longer time than mainland China. As American fast food chains have boomed in Hong Kong over the last three decades, the demand for fast food – American or otherwise – has grown

even faster. Currently, Hong Kong ranks first in the world for frequency of fast food consumption. Over 60 percent of the city's denizens eat at takeway restaurants at least once a week, compared to only 41 percent and 35 percent in mainland China and the United States respectively.[25] Hong Kong's fast food industry, nevertheless, is dominated by Chinese companies such as Café de Coral, Fairwood and Maxim. Chinese dishes accounted for over 70 percent of fast food supplied in Hong Kong in 2002.

Just as India underwent a trend of "fast-foodization" as it joined the global economy, the success of Café de Coral in Hong Kong epitomized the mass commoditization of Chinese cuisines. Before the company was established in 1969, Hong Kong already had a long history of eating out. Café de Coral, however, was among the first to put Chinese food into large-scale production and consumption. Its initial strategy was simple: "It moved Hong Kong's street foods indoors, to a clean, well-lighted cafeteria that o' ered instant services and moderate prices…",[26] and business expanded steadily thereafter. Ironically, the real boost for Café de Carol came when the Golden Arches arrived in 1975. According to Michael Chan, the company's current chairman, "McDonald's landing… inspired [Café de Coral's] confidence in self-service catering."[27] In the late-1970s, Café de Coral started using television commercials for mass advertising, and learning from McDonald's production model, established its first central food processing plant. Café de Coral is now Hong Kong's largest supplier of fast food.

Recently, Café de Coral extended its ambition beyond Hong Kong. ' e company's mission is to become "a distinguished corporation in the food and catering industry as the world's largest Chinese quick service restaurant group…"[28] In 2000, it acquired Manchu Wok, Canada's largest Chinese fast food supplier and second largest in the United States. With over 200 restaurants throughout North America and the number rising constantly, Café de Coral prides itself "as a menu innovator specializing in fast and fresh Chinese cuisine, ranging in style from Cantonese to Szechwan." Chan boasts that eventually, "Chinese [food] will displace the burger and the pizza". The future of fast food, as *The Economist* predicts, "may be congee, tofu and roast duck."[29]

The recent flourish of local fast food restaurants in mainland China is reminiscent of Hong Kong's experience, as challenges posed by American fast food since the late-1980s have compelled many Chinese restaurateurs to react and innovate. It was against this backdrop of foreign competition that the genesis of Chinese fast food occurred. The industry's nascent phase – which lasted until the early-1990s – was marked by constant attempts by local entrepreneurs to imitate their foreign challengers. Numerous copycat restaurants, with names such as "McDuck's," "Mcdonald's" and "Modormal's", appeared in the major cities. Most of them have posed little threat to the Western fast food giants. One outstanding exception, however, is Ronghuaji, or "Glorious China Chicken".

Ronghuaji was founded in 1989 after two Shanghai entrepreneurs were inspired by KFC's business model. Since its inception, emulating KFC has been Ronghuaji's *modus operandi*. Franchises were set up in downtown Beijing and Shanghai, usually right next to existing KFC restaurants, selling chicken products prepared with a wide variety of Chinese recipes. Although all of its Beijing outlets failed to be consistently profitable and eventually went out of business, Ronghuaji's moment of success "demonstrated that Chinese entrepreneurs could

employ Western technology and create an industry with 'Chinese characteristics.'"[30]

Throughout the 1990s, Chinese entrepreneurs learned that reinvention of Chinese cuisine in the form of fast food – rather than blind imitation of foreign recipes – provided a better path to business success. Alarmed by the popularity of the American chains, the Chinese government promulgated state policy in 1996 to foster a local fast food industry.[31] As Yan observes, the "fast-food fever" jumpstarted by the Western restaurants in Beijing "has given restaurant frequenters a stronger consumer consciousness and has created a Chinese notion of fast food and an associated culture."[32] By the end of 1996, over 800 local fast food companies were doing business in China, operating over 4,000 restaurants. The annual revenue was over RMB40 billion, accounting for one-fifth of the catering industry's total revenue. By 1999, annual revenue surged to RMB75 billion, 20 percent higher than the previous year, and accounted for one-third of the industry's total. The growth rate for fast food was 7 percent higher than the average growth rate of the catering industry as a whole. Furthermore, contrary to the myth of foreign domination, Chinese-style fast food occupied a much larger portion of the market. As of 2002, four out of five fast food operators are Chinese restaurants. Business turnover of fast food restaurants serving Western dishes in 2000 accounted for only one-third of the industry's total volume.[33]

The extraordinary growth of the Chinese fast food market is the direct result of rising consumerism. As in Café de Coral's success in Hong Kong, however, the real impetus to growth was the introduction of fast food management to aspiring Chinese entrepreneurs. Several of the industry's leading figures were former employees of McDonald's and KFC – an experience which equipped them with

Western management concepts and techniques. The success of their business owed much to their ability to combine "modern methods of preparation and hygiene with traditional Chinese cuisine…" Beijing's most famous restaurant, Quanjude Roast Duck Restaurant, even sent its management team to McDonald's in 1993. A year later, it introduced its own roast duck fast food.[34]

An important business concept that helped Chinese chains to proliferate is franchising. Today, nearly all fast food restaurants in China publicize telephone hotlines for franchise information. With the friendly denomination of *jiameng rexian* (literally, "the hotline to join the league") these numbers are usually posted in prominent places, such as restaurant entrances. For instance, in 1996, Daniang Dumplings was merely a community restaurant in Changzhou in Jiangsu province with only six employees selling arguably the most prototypical of northern Chinese food – *shuijiao* (boiled dumplings). Within the next nine years, it expanded into an empire of over 150 franchises throughout the country and as far as Indonesia and Australia.

The phenomenal success of Café de Coral, Daniang Dumplings and others is of great significance not only to the preservation of Chinese culinary cultures at home, but also their influence abroad. When a new restaurant is established in a foreign territory, not only is its food consumed, but its associated culture is also propagated among the host community. The case of Mongolian hotpot illustrates how a culture that was once found in a restricted geographical region can spread through market expansion. In the past, Mongolian hotpot was found mostly in northern China; it was considered an exotic cuisine even to Chinese of other regions. In the past six years, however, Xiaofeiyang – a chain enterprise started at the turn of the century with just one outlet in Inner Mongolia – transformed hotpot into a regular repast throughout the country. Today, the chain owns franchises in as far south as Guangdong and Hong Kong – the geographical opposite of the cuisine's origin in China. It has an aggressive plan to expand overseas, with outlets already set up in North America.

Another remarkable example is Malan Hand-Pulled Noodles. The company opened its first restaurant in 1993, serving traditional dishes from northwestern China in a fast food setting. By the end of 2002 it had multiplied into 436 outlets nationwide. By 2004, it had expanded outside of China, into Singapore, Western Europe, and California.[35] On the opening day of its first restaurant in the United States, company manager Frank Wang declared that by "inheriting the essence of traditional beef noodles, and maintaining the original taste of Chinese food culture, Malan Noodle achieves further development by applying the modern fast food concept, thus making the national snack flourish."[36]

Conclusion

The primary lesson one can learn from the thriving Chinese fast food sector is that globalization is facilitating the spread of cultural diversity, rather than – as the word "globalization" so misleadingly suggests – a tendency towards cultural homogeneity. The opening up of Chinese society cultivated a population curious about outside ideas, values and cultures. A taste for foreign lifestyle, however, is not the same as cultural submission. As the Chinese learned to become "modern," globalization also nurtured a class of outward-looking entrepreneurs who extracted elements of Chinese culture and combined them with modern business management to compete in the global economy.

The arguments presented in this article serve to rectify the misconception of cultural homogenization that underpinned intellectual exchanges in the past. The case of Chinese culinary cultures, however, represents only the tip of the iceberg of China's contribution to global cultural trends. Other areas of Chinese traditions are also experiencing a revival. The production, research and development of Chinese medicine, for example, have been modernized; its practice is gaining wide acceptance in many Western countries. Various types of *qigong* – the Chinese art of self-healing that combines meditation and body movements – are also proliferating. To truly understand the fate of indigenous cultures under globalization, analysts should pay more attention to China as a cultural emitter, rather than simply labeling it a passive follower of a purported global culture.

ENDNOTES

1 David Rothkopf, "In Praise of Cultural Imperialism? Effects of Globalization on Culture," *Foreign Policy*, June 22, 1997, 39, 48-49.
2 John Tomlinson, *Cultural Imperialism: A Critical Introduction* (Baltimore: Johns Hopkins University Press, 1991), 8.
3 James L. Watson, "McDonald's in Hong Kong: Consumerism, Dietary Change, and the Rise of a Children's Culture," in James L. Watson, ed., *Golden Arches East: McDonald's in East Asia* (Stanford: Stanford University Press, 1997), 78.
4 Ibid., 84.
5 Emiko Ohnuki-Tierney, "McDonald's in Japan: Changing Manners and Etiquette," in James L. Watson, ed., *Golden Arches East: McDonald's in East Asia* (Stanford: Stanford University Press, 1997), 175-180.
6 Eriberto P. Lozada, Jr., "Globalized Childhood?: Kentucky Fried Chicken in Beijing," in Jun Jing, ed., *Feeding China's Little Emperors: Food, Children, and Social Change* (Stanford: Stanford University Press, 2000), 117.
7 Yunxiang Yan, "McDonald's in Beijing: The Localization of Americana," in James L. Watson, ed., *Golden Arches East: McDonald's in East Asia* (Stanford: Stanford University Press, 1997), 39.
8 James L. Watson, "Introduction: Transnationalism, Localization, and Fast Foods in East Asia," in James L. Watson, ed., *Golden Arches East: McDonald's in East Asia* (Stanford: Stanford University Press, 1997), 6.
9 Yunxiang Yan, "Of Hamburger and Social Space: Consuming McDonald's in Beijing," in Deborah S. Davis, ed., *The Consumer Revolution in Urban China* (Berkeley and Los Angeles: University of California Press, 2000), 205.
10 Benjamin Barber, *Jihad vs. McWorld* (New York: Ballantine Books, 1995), 4.
11 Eric Schlosser, *Fast Food Nation: The Dark Side of the All-American Meal* (New York: Perennial, 2002), 239-240.
12 Peter S. Goodman, "Fast Food Takes a Bit Out of Chinese Culture," *Washington Post*, December 26, 2004.
13 Rebecca Buckman, "Let Them Eat Cheese," *Far Eastern Economic Review*, December 11, 2003.
14 Elisabeth Rosenthal, "Buicks, Starbucks and Fried Chicken. Still China?," *New York Times*, February 25, 2002.
15 Yan, "McDonald's in Beijing: The Localization of Americana," 40-53.
16 Watson and his team have proposed a rebuttal to the cultural homogenization thesis. They claim that albeit its popularity in East Asia, McDonald's has been more or less detached from its American root. In order to cater to the particular needs of local markets, the food and services of McDonald's have changed so much that the company has ceased to be a fast food supplier in the American sense. For further details, see James L. Watson, ed., *Golden Arches East: McDonald's in East Asia* (Stanford: Stanford University Press, 1997).
17 Barber, op.cit., 6.
18 John Tomlinson, "Globalization and Cultural Identity," in David Held and Anthony McGrew, eds., *The Global Transformations Reader: An Introduction to the Globalization Debate* (Cambridge: Polity Press, 2003), 60.
19 Tulasi Srinivas, "'A Tryst with Destiny': The Indian Case of Cultural Revolution," in Peter L. Berger and Samuel P. Huntington, eds., *Many Globalizations: Cultural Diversity in the Contemporary World* (New York: Oxford University Press, 2002), 90.
20 Ibid., 94-99.
21 Ibid., 106.
22 Tamotsu Aoki, "Aspects of Globalization in Contemporary Japan," in Peter L. Berger and Samuel P. Huntington, eds., *Many Globalizations: Cultural Diversity in the Contemporary World* (Oxford University Press, 2002), 68-80.
23 Ibid., 74.
24 Thomas Gold, "Go With Your Feelings: Hong Kong and Taiwan Popular Culture in Greater China," *China Quarterly*, vol. 136 (December 1993), 907-925.
25 ACNielsen, *Consumers in Asia Pacific – Our Fast Food/Take Away Consumption Habits*, 2nd Half, 2004.
26 Watson, "McDonald's in Hong Kong: Consumerism, Dietary Change, and the Rise of a Children's Culture," 81.
27 Café de Coral company profile, Hong Kong Chamber of Commerce, available online at <www.chamber.org.hk/info/member_a_week/member_profile.asp?id=80>.
28 Company website, <www.cafedecoral.com.>.
29 "Fast Chinese Cuisine: Junk Food?," *The Economist*, December 7, 2002.
30 Lozada, Jr., op. cit., 125.
31 Yan, "Of Hamburger and Social Space," 207.
32 Ibid., 201.
33 *Fast Food Market Report* (Friedl Business Information, 2002)
34 Yan, "McDonald's in Beijing," 74-75.
35 Malan Noodle Corporate Website, "Introduction," <http://www.malan.com.cn/introduce_en.htm>
36 Malan Noodle Corporate Website, "Grand Opening of Malan Noodle Outlet Restaurant in Monterey Park, USA," <http://www.malan.com.cn/news/73147200312264325_en.htm>

Clash of Globalizations

by Stanley Hoffmann

A NEW PARADIGM?

WHAT IS THE STATE of international relations today? In the 1990s, specialists concentrated on the partial disintegration of the global order's traditional foundations: states. During that decade, many countries, often those born of decolonization, revealed themselves to be no more than pseudostates, without solid institutions, internal cohesion, or national consciousness. The end of communist coercion in the former Soviet Union and in the former Yugoslavia also revealed long-hidden ethnic tensions. Minorities that were or considered themselves oppressed demanded independence. In Iraq, Sudan, Afghanistan, and Haiti, rulers waged open warfare against their subjects. These wars increased the importance of humanitarian interventions, which came at the expense of the hallowed principles of national sovereignty and nonintervention. Thus the dominant tension of the decade was the clash between the fragmentation of states (and the state system) and the progress of economic, cultural, and political integration—in other words, globalization.

Everybody has understood the events of September 11 as the beginning of a new era. But what does this break mean? In the conventional approach to international relations, war took place among states. But in September, poorly armed individuals suddenly challenged, surprised, and wounded the world's dominant superpower. The attacks also showed that, for all its accomplishments, globalization makes an awful form of violence easily accessible to hopeless fanatics. Terrorism is the bloody link between interstate relations and global society. As

Stanley Hoffmann, "Clash of Globalizations," Foreign Affairs, vol. 81, no. 4, pp. 104-115. Copyright © 2002 by Council on Foreign Relations, Inc. Reprinted with permission.

countless individuals and groups are becoming global actors along with states, insecurity and vulnerability are rising. To assess today's bleak state of affairs, therefore, several questions are necessary. What concepts help explain the new global order? What is the condition of the interstate part of international relations? And what does the emerging global civil society contribute to world order?

SOUND AND FURY

TWO MODELS made a great deal of noise in the 1990s. The first one—Francis Fukuyama's "End of History" thesis—was not vindicated by events. To be sure, his argument predicted the end of ideological conflicts, not history itself, and the triumph of political and economic liberalism. That point is correct in a narrow sense: the "secular religions" that fought each other so bloodily in the last century are now dead. But Fukuyama failed to note that nationalism remains very much alive. Moreover, he ignored the explosive potential of religious wars that has extended to a large part of the Islamic world.

Fukuyama's academic mentor, the political scientist Samuel Huntington, provided a few years later a gloomier account that saw a very different world. Huntington predicted that violence resulting from international anarchy and the absence of common values and institutions would erupt among civilizations rather than among states or ideologies. But Huntington's conception of what constitutes a civilization was hazy. He failed to take into account sufficiently conflicts within each so-called civilization, and he overestimated the importance of religion in the behavior of non-Western elites, who are often secularized and Westernized. Hence he could not clearly define the link between a civilization and the foreign policies of its member states.

Other, less sensational models still have adherents. The "realist" orthodoxy insists that nothing has changed in international relations since Thucydides and Machiavelli: a state's military and economic power determines its fate; interdependence and international institutions are secondary and fragile phenomena; and states' objectives are imposed by the threats to their survival or security. Such is the world described by Henry Kissinger. Unfortunately, this venerable model has trouble integrating change, especially globalization and the rise of

nonstate actors. Moreover, it overlooks the need for international cooperation that results from such new threats as the proliferation of weapons
of mass destruction (WMD). And it ignores what the scholar Raymond
Aron called the "germ of a universal consciousness": the liberal, pro-
market norms that developed states have come to hold in common.

Taking Aron's point, many scholars today interpret the world in
terms of a triumphant globalization that submerges borders through
new means of information and communication. In this universe, a
state choosing to stay closed invariably faces decline and growing
discontent among its subjects, who are eager for material progress.
But if it opens up, it must accept a reduced role that is mainly limited
to social protection, physical protection against aggression or civil war,
and maintaining national identity. The champion of this epic without
heroes is *The New York Times* columnist Thomas Friedman. He contrasts
barriers with open vistas, obsolescence with modernity, state control
with free markets. He sees in globalization the light of dawn, the
"golden straitjacket" that will force contentious publics to understand
that the logic of globalization is that of peace (since war would interrupt
globalization and therefore progress) and democracy (because new
technologies increase individual autonomy and encourage initiative).

BACK TO REALITY

THESE MODELS come up hard against three realities. First, rivalries
among great powers (and the capacity of smaller states to exploit such
tensions) have most certainly not disappeared. For a while now,
however, the existence of nuclear weapons has produced a certain
degree of prudence among the powers that have them. The risk of
destruction that these weapons hold has moderated the game and
turned nuclear arms into instruments of last resort. But the game
could heat up as more states seek other WMD as a way of narrowing
the gap between the nuclear club and the other powers. The sale of
such weapons thus becomes a hugely contentious issue, and efforts to
slow down the spread of all WMD, especially to dangerous "rogue"
states, can paradoxically become new causes of violence.

Second, if wars between states are becoming less common, wars
within them are on the rise—as seen in the former Yugoslavia, Iraq,

much of Africa, and Sri Lanka. Uninvolved states first tend to hesitate to get engaged in these complex conflicts, but they then (sometimes) intervene to prevent these conflicts from turning into regional catastrophes. The interveners, in turn, seek the help of the United Nations or regional organizations to rebuild these states, promote stability, and prevent future fragmentation and misery.

Third, states' foreign policies are shaped not only by realist geopolitical factors such as economics and military power but by domestic politics. Even in undemocratic regimes, forces such as xenophobic passions, economic grievances, and transnational ethnic solidarity can make policymaking far more complex and less predictable. Many states—especially the United States—have to grapple with the frequent interplay of competing government branches. And the importance of individual leaders and their personalities is often underestimated in the study of international affairs.

For realists, then, transnational terrorism creates a formidable dilemma. If a state is the victim of private actors such as terrorists, it will try to eliminate these groups by depriving them of sanctuaries and punishing the states that harbor them. The national interest of the attacked state will therefore require either armed interventions against governments supporting terrorists or a course of prudence and discreet pressure on other governments to bring these terrorists to justice. Either option requires a questioning of sovereignty—the holy concept of realist theories. The classical realist universe of Hans Morgenthau and Aron may therefore still be very much alive in a world of states, but it has increasingly hazy contours and offers only difficult choices when it faces the threat of terrorism.

At the same time, the real universe of globalization does not resemble the one that Friedman celebrates. In fact, globalization has three forms, each with its own problems. First is economic globalization, which results from recent revolutions in technology, information, trade, foreign investment, and international business. The main actors are companies, investors, banks, and private services industries, as well as states and international organizations. This present form of capitalism, ironically foreseen by Karl Marx and Friedrich Engels, poses a central dilemma between efficiency and fairness. The specialization and integration of firms make it possible to increase aggregate wealth, but the logic of pure capitalism does not favor social justice. Economic globalization has thus become a formidable cause of inequality among and within states, and the concern for global competitiveness limits the aptitude of states and other actors to address this problem.

Next comes cultural globalization. It stems from the technological revolution and economic globalization, which together foster the flow of cultural goods. Here the key choice is between uniformization (often termed "Americanization") and diversity. The result is both a "disenchantment of the world" (in Max Weber's words) and a reaction against uniformity. The latter takes form in a renaissance of local cultures and languages as well as assaults against Western culture, which is denounced as an arrogant bearer of a secular, revolutionary ideology and a mask for U.S. hegemony.

Finally there is political globalization, a product of the other two. It is characterized by the preponderance of the United States and its political institutions and by a vast array of international and regional organizations and transgovernmental networks (specializing in areas such as policing or migration or justice). It is also marked by private institutions that are neither governmental nor purely national—say, Doctors Without Borders or Amnesty International. But many of these agencies lack democratic accountability and are weak in scope, power, and authority. Furthermore, much uncertainty hangs over the fate of American hegemony, which faces significant resistance abroad and is affected by America's own oscillation between the temptations of domination and isolation.

The benefits of globalization are undeniable. But Friedmanlike optimism rests on very fragile foundations. For one thing, globalization is neither inevitable nor irresistible. Rather, it is largely an American creation, rooted in the period after World War II and based on U.S. economic might. By extension, then, a deep and protracted economic crisis in the United States could have as devastating an effect on globalization as did the Great Depression.

Second, globalization's reach remains limited because it excludes many poor countries, and the states that it does transform react in different ways. This fact stems from the diversity of economic and social conditions at home as well as from partisan politics. The world is far away from a perfect integration of markets, services, and factors of production. Sometimes the simple existence of borders slows down and can even paralyze this integration; at other times it gives integration the flavors and colors of the dominant state (as in the case of the Internet).

Third, international civil society remains embryonic. Many non-governmental organizations reflect only a tiny segment of the populations of their members' states. They largely represent only modernized countries, or those in which the weight of the state is not too heavy. Often, NGOs have little independence from governments.

Fourth, the individual emancipation so dear to Friedman does not quickly succeed in democratizing regimes, as one can see today in China. Nor does emancipation prevent public institutions such as the International Monetary Fund, the World Bank, or the World Trade Organization from remaining opaque in their activities and often arbitrary and unfair in their rulings.

Fifth, the attractive idea of improving the human condition through the abolition of barriers is dubious. Globalization is in fact only a sum of techniques (audio and videocassettes, the Internet, instantaneous communications) that are at the disposal of states or private actors. Self-interest and ideology, not humanitarian reasons, are what drive these actors. Their behavior is quite different from the vision of globalization as an Enlightenment-based utopia that is simultaneously scientific, rational, and universal. For many reasons—misery, injustice, humiliation, attachment to traditions, aspiration to more than just a better standard of living—this "Enlightenment" stereotype of globalization thus provokes revolt and dissatisfaction.

Another contradiction is also at work. On the one hand, international and transnational cooperation is necessary to ensure that globalization will not be undermined by the inequalities resulting from market fluctuations, weak state-sponsored protections, and the incapacity of many states to improve their fates by themselves. On the other hand, cooperation presupposes that many states and rich private players operate altruistically—which is certainly not the essence of international relations—or practice a remarkably generous conception of their long-term interests. But the fact remains that most rich states still refuse to provide sufficient development aid or to intervene in crisis situations such as the genocide in Rwanda. That reluctance compares poorly with the American enthusiasm to pursue the fight against al Qaeda and the Taliban. What is wrong here is not patriotic enthusiasm as such, but the weakness of the humanitarian impulse when the national interest in saving non-American victims is not self-evident.

IMAGINED COMMUNITIES

AMONG the many effects of globalization on international politics, three hold particular importance. The first concerns institutions. Contrary to realist predictions, most states are not perpetually at war with each other. Many regions and countries live in peace; in other cases, violence is internal rather than state-to-state. And since no government can do everything by itself, interstate organisms have emerged. The result, which can be termed "global society," seeks to reduce the potentially destructive effects of national regulations on the forces of integration. But it also seeks to ensure fairness in the world market and create international regulatory regimes in such areas as trade, communications, human rights, migration, and refugees. The main obstacle to this effort is the reluctance of states to accept global directives that might constrain the market or further reduce their sovereignty. Thus the UN's powers remain limited and sometimes only purely theoretical. International criminal justice is still only a spotty and contested last resort. In the world economy—where the market, not global governance, has been the main beneficiary of the state's retreat—the network of global institutions is fragmented and incomplete. Foreign investment remains ruled by bilateral agreements. Environmental protection is badly ensured, and issues such as migration and population growth are largely ignored. Institutional networks are not powerful enough to address unfettered short-term capital movements, the lack of international regulation on bankruptcy and competition, and primitive coordination among rich countries. In turn, the global "governance" that does exist is partial and weak at a time when economic globalization deprives many states of independent monetary and fiscal policies, or it obliges them to make cruel choices between economic competitiveness and the preservation of social safety nets. All the while, the United States displays an increasing impatience toward institutions that weigh on American freedom of action. Movement toward a world state looks increasingly unlikely. The more state sovereignty crumbles under the blows of globalization or such recent developments as humanitarian intervention and the fight against terrorism, the more states cling to what is left to them.

Second, globalization has not profoundly challenged the enduring national nature of citizenship. Economic life takes place on a global scale, but human identity remains national—hence the strong resistance to cultural homogenization. Over the centuries, increasingly centralized states have expanded their functions and tried to forge a sense of common identity for their subjects. But no central power in the world can do the same thing today, even in the European Union. There, a single currency and advanced economic coordination have not yet produced a unified economy or strong central institutions endowed with legal autonomy, nor have they resulted in a sense of postnational citizenship. The march from national identity to one that would be both national and European has only just begun. A world very partially unified by technology still has no collective consciousness or collective solidarity. What states are unwilling to do the world market cannot do all by itself, especially in engendering a sense of world citizenship.

Third, there is the relationship between globalization and violence. The traditional state of war, even if it is limited in scope, still persists. There are high risks of regional explosions in the Middle East and in East Asia, and these could seriously affect relations between the major powers. Because of this threat, and because modern arms are increasingly costly, the "anarchical society" of states lacks the resources to correct some of globalization's most flagrant flaws. These very costs, combined with the classic distrust among international actors who prefer to try to preserve their security alone or through traditional alliances, prevent a more satisfactory institutionalization of world politics—for example, an increase of the UN's powers. This step could happen if global society were provided with sufficient forces to prevent a conflict or restore peace—but it is not.

Globalization, far from spreading peace, thus seems to foster conflicts and resentments. The lowering of various barriers celebrated by Friedman, especially the spread of global media, makes it possible for the most deprived or oppressed to compare their fate with that of the free and well-off. These dispossessed then ask for help from others with common resentments, ethnic origin, or religious faith. Insofar as globalization enriches some and uproots many, those who are both poor and uprooted may seek revenge and self-esteem in terrorism.

GLOBALIZATION AND TERROR

TERRORISM is the poisoned fruit of several forces. It can be the weapon of the weak in a classic conflict among states or within a state, as in Kashmir or the Palestinian territories. But it can also be seen as a product of globalization. Transnational terrorism is made possible by the vast array of communication tools. Islamic terrorism, for example, is not only based on support for the Palestinian struggle and opposition to an invasive American presence. It is also fueled by a resistance to "unjust" economic globalization and to a Western culture deemed threatening to local religions and cultures.

If globalization often facilitates terrorist violence, the fight against this war without borders is potentially disastrous for both economic development and globalization. Antiterrorist measures restrict mobility and financial flows, while new terrorist attacks could lead the way for an antiglobalist reaction comparable to the chauvinistic paroxysms of the 1930s. Global terrorism is not the simple extension of war among states to nonstates. It is the subversion of traditional ways of war because it does not care about the sovereignty of either its enemies or the allies who shelter them. It provokes its victims to take measures that, in the name of legitimate defense, violate knowingly the sovereignty of those states accused of encouraging terror. (After all, it was not the Taliban's infamous domestic violations of human rights that led the United States into Afghanistan; it was the Taliban's support of Osama bin Laden.)

But all those trespasses against the sacred principles of sovereignty do not constitute progress toward global society, which has yet to agree on a common definition of terrorism or on a common policy against it. Indeed, the beneficiaries of the antiterrorist "war" have been the illiberal, poorer states that have lost so much of their sovereignty of late. Now the crackdown on terror allows them to tighten their controls on their own people, products, and money. They can give themselves new reasons to violate individual rights in the name of common defense against insecurity—and thus stop the slow, hesitant march toward international criminal justice.

Another main beneficiary will be the United States, the only actor capable of carrying the war against terrorism into all corners of the world. Despite its power, however, America cannot fully protect itself against future terrorist acts, nor can it fully overcome its ambivalence toward forms of interstate cooperation that might restrict U.S. freedom of action. Thus terrorism is a global phenomenon that ultimately reinforces the enemy—the state—at the same time as it tries to destroy it. The states that are its targets have no interest in applying the laws of war to their fight against terrorists; they have every interest in treating terrorists as outlaws and pariahs. The champions of globalization have sometimes glimpsed the "jungle" aspects of economic globalization, but few observers foresaw similar aspects in global terrorist and antiterrorist violence.

Finally, the unique position of the United States raises a serious question over the future of world affairs. In the realm of interstate problems, American behavior will determine whether the non-superpowers and weak states will continue to look at the United States as a friendly power (or at least a tolerable hegemon), or whether they are provoked by Washington's hubris into coalescing against American preponderance. America may be a hegemon, but combining rhetorical overkill and ill-defined designs is full of risks. Washington has yet to understand that nothing is more dangerous for a "hyperpower" than the temptation of unilateralism. It may well believe that the constraints of international agreements and organizations are not necessary, since U.S. values and power are all that is needed for world order. But in reality, those same international constraints provide far better opportunities for leadership than arrogant demonstrations of contempt for others' views, and they offer useful ways of restraining unilateralist behavior in other states. A hegemon concerned with prolonging its rule should be especially interested in using internationalist methods and institutions, for the gain in influence far exceeds the loss in freedom of action.

In the realm of global society, much will depend on whether the United States will overcome its frequent indifference to the costs that globalization imposes on poorer countries. For now, Washington is too reluctant to make resources available for economic development, and it remains hostile to agencies that monitor and regulate the global market. All too often, the right-leaning tendencies of the American political system push U.S. diplomacy toward an excessive reliance on America's greatest asset—military strength—as well as an excessive reliance on market capitalism and a "sovereigntism" that offends and alienates. That the mighty United States is so afraid of the world's imposing its "inferior" values on Americans is often a source of ridicule and indignation abroad.

ODD MAN OUT

FOR ALL THESE TENSIONS, it is still possible that the American war on terrorism will be contained by prudence, and that other governments will give priority to the many internal problems created by interstate rivalries and the flaws of globalization. But the world risks being squeezed between a new Scylla and Charybdis. The Charybdis is universal intervention, unilaterally decided by American leaders who are convinced that they have found a global mission provided by a colossal threat. Presentable as an epic contest between good and evil, this struggle offers the best way of rallying the population and overcoming domestic divisions. The Scylla is resignation to universal chaos in the form of new attacks by future bin Ladens, fresh humanitarian disasters, or regional wars that risk escalation. Only through wise judgment can the path between them be charted.

We can analyze the present, but we cannot predict the future. We live in a world where a society of uneven and often virtual states overlaps with a global society burdened by weak public institutions and underdeveloped civil society. A single power dominates, but its economy could become unmanageable or disrupted by future terrorist attacks. Thus to predict the future confidently would be highly incautious or naive. To be sure, the world has survived many crises, but it has done so at a very high price, even in times when WMD were not available.

Precisely because the future is neither decipherable nor determined, students of international relations face two missions. They must try to understand what goes on by taking an inventory of current goods and disentangling the threads of present networks. But the fear of confusing the empirical with the normative should not prevent them from writing as political philosophers at a time when many philosophers are extending their conceptions of just society to international relations. How can one make the global house more livable? The answer presupposes a political philosophy that would be both just and acceptable even to those whose values have other foundations. As the late philosopher Judith Shklar did, we can take as a point of departure and as a guiding thread the fate of the victims of violence, oppression, and misery; as a goal, we should seek material and moral emancipation. While taking into account the formidable constraints of the world as it is, it is possible to loosen them.

Victim or Criminal

The Experiences of a Human-Trafficking Survivor in the U.S. Immigration System

by Leticia M. Saucedo

In 2004, "Mae," a Chinese woman who was exploited by human traffickers, was detained by the U.S. federal government for passport fraud as she tried to enter the United States through an international airport in the Southwest. Mae was incarcerated for several months in a contract detention center run by the local police department. I joined forces with students at the Thomas and Mack Legal Clinic in the law school at the University of Nevada, Las Vegas, to represent Mae in her claims for asylum and release from detention. All of us witnessed the ways in which U.S. society increasingly equates the immigrant experience with criminality. The restrictive parameters and hostile attitudes of the immigration system encourage prosecution of immigrants rather than determination of asylee status. Mae's story illustrates these realities, particularly the experiences of many women who are coerced into human trafficking for purposes of involuntary labor and/or sexual servitude.

We learned Mae's story one hour at a time, over countless visits, due to visiting restrictions. Before Mae was released after fifteen months, she had to tell her story piece by piece to people she hardly knew, within the context of a legal system she didn't understand, under totally unpredictable conditions. Here is Mae's story.

MAE'S STORY

Mae was an eighteen-year-old Chinese woman from a rural, desolate part of China, where employment was scarce and salaries were meager. She appeared to be no more than fourteen years old when we first met. She had gone to school in China only until she was eleven. She spoke no English, and she knew very little about the United

Leticia M. Saucedo, "Victim or Criminal: The Experiences of a Human-Trafficking Survivor in the U.S. Immigration System," Interrupted Life: Experiences of Incarcerated Women in the United States, ed. Rickie Solinger et al., pp. 282-286. Copyright © 2009 by University of California Press. Reprinted with permission.

States or where she had landed in the country. In China, Mae's father had physically and emotionally abused her and her mother. Her father called Mae stupid and told her that she was not worth his financial support; he eventually sold his only child to an older man from the city. As this man's second wife, Mae explained, she was expected to be a concubine and also do housekeeping for the first wife. Mae resisted this fate and tried to escape. Her father and the would-be husband found her and forced her to return. Mae begged her mother to help her. Mae's mother turned to her own brother, Mae's uncle, for help. This man had sent his own daughter to the United States earlier.

Mae's uncle put her mother in contact with the "snakeheads," or traffickers, who had arranged his daughter's trip. Mae said that she did not know how much her mother paid the snakeheads as a down payment. When her mother arranged the trip, neither she nor Mae knew what her final destination would be. Mae's mother sent her daughter out of the country so that she could escape her fate of forced marriage, not knowing what other dangers Mae would face when she arrived at her destination. For Mae's mother, this was the only choice. For Mae, following her mother's directive to leave the country seemed like a better choice than becoming someone's house slave.

Mae traveled in fear of both the traffickers and the unknown every step of her trip. Following the instructions of her contacts, Mae went from Hong Kong to Mandalay to Tokyo and finally to the United States. She did not know where she was going until the last minute. At one point, the snakeheads took Mae's passport and gave her a passport belonging to a Singapore citizen, because Singaporeans do not require visas to enter the United States. They also gave her the phone number of her snakehead contact in the United States.

When Mae got to the airport in the United States, government officials looked at her passport and refused to let her enter. They arrested her and put her in jail. Mae called the snakehead's number, and the man who answered the phone told her she was a stupid girl for not getting rid of the passport before she got off the plane. He told her she would have to pay "a snakehead lawyer" over five thousand dollars to get out of jail, but of course Mae did not have such funds.

The court appointed a federal public defender to Mae's case. She was charged with a felony for attempting to enter the country with a false passport. Mae was detained for more than a year before she pled guilty to passport fraud. Mae had no choice but to plead guilty: if she didn't cooperate, she risked more time in jail or deportation.

Mae remained in detention after her guilty plea for another four months, this time awaiting an immigration removal hearing. The immigration clinic, having been contacted by the federal public defender's office, agreed to take Mae's case and defend her in immigration court. As Mae's immigration lawyers, my students and I helped Mae seek asylum and apply for a trafficking visa. We spent months meeting with her during visiting hours and preparing the documentation for her asylum and trafficking applications. Because Mae spoke no English when she arrived, she talked to us through an interpreter. After a few weeks, she made friends with some of the other female detainees, some of whom were themselves trafficking victims. They communicated in Chinese for the most part, but they also began to teach her English. One of them left her a Chinese-English dictionary before she moved to another detention facility, and Mae started to study it every day. She also took some English classes, but they were not offered very regularly. These few classes were the extent of the learning opportunities in the detention center, and Mae learned little from them.

The longer Mae was detained, the more the detention staff became accustomed to the shy, unassuming, hardworking young woman. They started allowing Mae to help prepare the dining room before meals and clean up after the meals, among other routine tasks, to help her fight the boredom of detention. Mae told us she communicated with staff and other detainees through sign language until she learned a few English phrases to get her through a day. She hated the food, and she lost weight.

After a few months, Mae became restless and depressed, and my students felt powerless to help her through this long period of uncertainty. They tried to do what they could within the legal system to obtain her release. They tried to obtain a bond for her, but the judge refused to grant it. Mae maintained sporadic correspondence with her mother in China and with her cousin and best friend in the United States. She also phoned them, although not often because the calling cards sold at the detention center were expensive. Through her correspondence with her cousin and best friend, she learned that, had she not been detained, she likely would be living like they were: housed in dormitory quarters with other women and girls from China who worked in Chinese restaurants throughout the country. As she explained to us, the girls were paid about two thousand dollars in cash every month but were obliged to return fifteen hundred dollars of their salary each month to the restaurant owners to pay off the snakehead fee.

Despite what she learned about the economic exploitation of these girls, Mae decided that if she were released and allowed to stay in the United States, she would take this work, because returning to China and the slavery of a forced marriage was not an option.

Finally, about fifteen months after she was arrested, Mae was able to tell her story in immigration court. The court let her go free and granted her asylum status in January 2006. She was granted asylum status in part because of her fear of further persecution for resisting a forced marriage and in part because the court recognized that she was trafficked into the United States. Mae immediately moved to New York to work in a restaurant that paid Mae's passage from Nevada to New York.

Mae's obligations to the snakeheads and the terms of repayment are unknown. Presumably, Mae continues to pay off an enormous debt to the traffickers despite her legal status, because, in the end, they know where her family lives in China. Even with legal status, Mae told us, she had to find a way to pay off the traffickers because she feared for her mother's safety.

REFLECTIONS ON MAE'S STORY: CRIMINALIZATION OF THE VICTIM

Mae's story and circumstances fit the classic experience of a human-trafficking victim in that she was caught before she was able to start her debt-peonage arrangement. Her story reveals the unwillingness of the immigration enforcement system to readily accept the realities of forced marriage, domestic violence, and other oppressive conditions that cause women to flee. More important, the system is devoted to defining each individual's immigration story as an instance of "economic necessity." This explanation eclipses the fact that even when economic circumstances are part of the reason for leaving home, many immigrants fall prey to exploitative, dangerous, and coercively powerful human-trafficking rings. This fate especially falls to women and girls from poor countries, because they lack economic self-sufficiency and are vulnerable to traffickers' promises to save them from desperate situations at home.

Mae was willing and able to provide prosecutors with details about her trip, her contacts with the snakeheads, their control over her travels, and the labor ring into which the snakeheads delivered her. But the sophisticated trafficking ring made sure that she did not possess sufficient details to give prosecutors ammunition for a successful trafficking conviction. FBI investigators could accept her story and open a federal—and possibly national and international—investigation, or reject her story and move forward with a much more limited prosecution investigation. Confronted with limited resources and staff, as well as the inability to mount a coordinated investigation with other offices facing similar cases, the FBI chose the less costly option. The result was a long negotiation and jail time for Mae. In the end, Mae pled guilty to carrying a false passport.

The U.S. attorney in charge of the case also had strong incentives to prosecute. She recognized that Mae might have a trafficking claim but did not consider the claim to cancel out her wrongdoing. In other words, the facts that Mae feared persecution in her home country and that an organized ring took advantage of her fear did not matter. She could still apply for asylum or other relief even though she had a conviction for passport fraud. The prosecution, a relatively simple one, kept the government's objectives in mind, sent a message, and the government hoped, prevented similar instances of illegal entry.

Mae and others in her predicament will continue to navigate life in the United States as perpetrators, with all of the consequences of being labeled a criminal in the United States. Thus, although Mae was granted asylum status, her adjustment to legal permanent residency (LPR) status will require her to disclose her conviction and may even bar her from adjustment, depending on the discretion of the adjudicating immigration officer. Under the statute, Mae is subject to deportation once she asks to change her status from asylee to LPR. Under the Immigration and Nationality Act, conviction of a crime of moral turpitude, such as fraud, is considered grounds for removal.

If Mae seeks adjustment, she will have to retell her story and risk (again) that an officer will not credit her story or her existing status as an asylee. She may not win a waiver of her conviction even though, if the system had worked appropriately, she would not have been charged once officials recognized that she was a potential asylum applicant.

The same result would occur had Mae been deemed a trafficking victim instead of an asylee. Mae could not overcome the presumption of her criminal status through any of the immigration routes available to her.

Throughout this ordeal, did Mae fully understand the nuances of a legal system that labels her a criminal? More likely, she understood that she dare not choose any course of action that could send her back to China. Although Mae never considered herself a criminal, and she is clearly more a victim than a lawbreaker, the legal system has given her a criminal identity. This label will have consequences for Mae as she assumes a range of identities in the United States: as worker, young woman, survivor, Chinese person, and, finally, immigrant. Ultimately, Mae's story reveals that the government is implementing a harsh, punitive enforcement strategy, mixing immigration law with criminal law, and that the legal system turns a blind eye to the legitimate attempts of trafficking survivors to enter this country with safety, dignity, and appropriate legal status.

Precious Commodity
The Trade in Human Lives

by Alice Hill and Ramona Carey

The trafficking of humans for labor and sex is often said to be one of the world's fastest growing criminal enterprises. Addressing the plague of modern-day slavery requires focusing more on the victims themselves.

n Mexico, 19-year-old "Anna" is standing by a bus stop in a small town when she meets a charming young man. After winning her trust, he smuggles her into the United States. Once there, he forces Anna to prostitute herself with migrant workers in a canyon outside San Diego.

In New York, an Indonesian woman in her fifties, "Nettie", wanders around an affluent neighborhood in rags. It appears as if someone has tried to cut off her ears. A worker in a donut shop invites her to come inside. After spotting Nettie's injuries, the worker calls the police. An investigation reveals that Nettie's employers had held her and another Indonesian woman captive, physically abused them, and forced them into domestic servitude.

In Mali, 12-year-old "Malik" begs in the streets for hours to earn money for his "teacher." The boy left his home in Niger after the alleged teacher promised his parents he

Alice Hill and Ramona Carey, "Precious Commodity: The Trade in Human Lives," Americas Quarterly, vol. 4, no. 2, pp. 63-68.

tourists in Thailand and abused cocoa workers in Cote D'Ivoire. Legal definitions of human trafficking differ, but unlike human smuggling, human trafficking, at least for adults, always involves force, coercion or fraud.

A GLOBAL SCOURGE

Human trafficking has a long history, with roots in the slave trade. However, it only received broad government and public recognition beginning in the 1990s. The U.S. Congress first passed anti-trafficking legislation in 2000 with the Trafficking Victims Protection Act (TVPA).[2] Similarly, the international community first collectively addressed human trafficking in 2000 with the United Nations Protocol to Prevent, Suppress, and Punish Trafficking in Persons, Especially Women and Children.[3] Since then, numerous countries have adopted their own anti-trafficking in persons legislation.

U.S. and international figures on human trafficking vary widely. The International Labor Organization (ILO) estimated in 2005 that 43 percent of 2.4 million trafficking victims were sold into sexual exploitation, 32 percent fell prey to forced labor servitude and the remaining 25 percent were caught up in both.[4] In contrast, the United Nations Office on Drugs and Crime (UNODC) estimated in 2009 that 79 percent of the victims of human trafficking were procured for sexual exploitation.[5]

Even in the U.S., the number of trafficking victims is unknown. In 2004, the State Department estimated that between 14,500 and 17,500 people were trafficked into the United States. But in the previous year, the State Department put the figure at between 18,000 and 20,000. The State Department's 2003 estimate was significantly lower than the Central Intelligence Agency's 1999 estimate, which claimed that the U.S. was the destination

would receive a good education abroad. Once in Mali, Malik was sent to the streets to beg alongside other Nigerien boys also deceived by false promises of schooling.[1]

Although their stories differ, each of these individuals has suffered the same fate. They are victims of human trafficking—a crime that targets countless men, women and children worldwide. Human trafficking often follows a predictable pattern: the victim is recruited or abducted in one country, transferred to another, and eventually exploited for sex or labor. Trafficking, however, need not be transnational—it may occur within a single country's borders. Victims include migrant farm workers held in unsanitary conditions, children forced into prostitution for

---

Alice Hill, *a retired judge for the Los Angeles Superior Court, is the Senior Counselor to the Secretary of the United States Department of Homeland Security. Ramona Carey, Presidential Management Fellow and Special Assistant to Alice Hill, contributed to this article.*

for between 45,000 and 50,000 trafficking victims. [6]

Had the numbers really plummeted? Reliable statistics are in fact hard to come by. Human trafficking is difficult to detect because victims are often reluctant to report trafficking. Many fear deportation by national authorities or retribution by the traffickers against themselves or their families back home. National policies that criminalize victims rather than protect them, the absence of witness protection programs, and lengthy judicial proceedings that result in victims reliving their traumatic experiences also encourage victims' silence.[7]

Some victims do not perceive that they are being trafficked and do not self-identify as victims. Some might accept exploitative conditions as a means to repay a debt to the trafficker, further complicating the work of law enforcement authorities who may not recognize the signs of trafficking. This results in unreported or misreported cases.

Even if a trafficking case goes to court, prosecutors may pursue related criminal charges rather than those under human trafficking statutes because such charges are easier to prove.[8] As a result, law enforcement statistics on human trafficking are likely to be incomplete.

LINKS TO ORGANIZED CRIME

Human trafficking is often said to be the world's fastest growing criminal enterprise[9] and the largest source of criminal profits after narcotics and weapons trafficking.[10] According to one study, over 90 percent of law enforcement agencies surveyed in the U.S. reported a connection between human trafficking and other criminal networks.[11]

In practice, the differences between "organized crime" and "crime that is organized" can be subtle. To a certain extent, all traffickers are organized. The key is the degree of organization, which can range from ad hoc collections of two or three individuals to sophisticated, robust networks that outlive discrete cases of trafficking.

The likelihood of a nexus between human trafficking and organized crime grows with the size of the trafficking operation. Large operations require sophisticated services such as document forgery, money transfer and advanced communications technology.[12] Organized crime syndicates involved in drug smuggling and other illicit trade possess these capabilities.

Given the high profits and relatively low risk of arrest or conviction associated with human trafficking, a relationship with organized crime syndicates seems likely. Moreover, in some cases the apparent unwillingness of authorities to prosecute traffickers and the fact that legal services for defendants are available very quickly suggest the involvement of well-organized criminal groups.[13]

An association between human and narcotics trafficking is apparent in varying degrees around the world. In Latin America, drug mules have been sold into sexual or domestic servitude upon arrival in the United States.[14]

CRIMINALIZING HUMAN TRAFFICKING

Criminal law regarding trafficking has undergone broad revision in Central America and the Dominican Republic in recent years. Panama and Nicaragua introduced new criminal codes in 2007; Costa Rica, El Salvador and Honduras partially reformed their codes; and the Dominican Republic and Guatemala classified trafficking in persons as a crime. These reforms were in part a response to new international human rights commitments as codified in the United Nations Convention against Transnational Crime (2000) and the accompanying Protocol to Prevent, Suppress, and Punish Trafficking in Persons, Especially Women and Children.

The tri-border area of Argentina, Brazil and Paraguay is rife with criminal activity associated with drugs, weapons, and—as reported in this journal in 2008—human trafficking.[15] (In 2005, the ILO estimated that approximately 250,000 of the 2.4 million people trafficked worldwide were in Latin America and the Caribbean).[16]

Working from the assumption that transnational criminal organizations regularly engage in multiple forms of illicit trafficking simultaneously,[17] some overlap between the trade in arms, drugs and humans seems inevitable. Global criminal actors from countries such as Russia, the former Soviet republics, Poland, Croatia, Serbia, Hungary, Albania, and Romania that are present in Latin America and maintain relations with Latin American criminal groups[18] could also be involved.

Academics may disagree on the extent of the involvement between human trafficking and global organized crime groups. Nevertheless, studies suggest that most trafficking is regional and tends to be conducted by people whose nationality is the same as that of the victim.[19] The International Organization for Migration's data show that in a majority of cases, contact with recruiters is based on personal relationships.

More and better data are needed to better understand the connection between human trafficking and organized crime or other forms of transnational crime. According to Laura Langberg, an anti-trafficking in persons specialist at the Organization of American States, "the Latin American and Caribbean regions are two of the most under-researched and under-funded regions in the world on trafficking in persons."[20] In the U.S. there is a growing recognition that domestic trafficking is a major problem.

HOW TO STOP THEM

Even as experts argue about what the statistics show, the current consensus on human trafficking is shifting to greater attention on the victims themselves. U.S. anti-trafficking policy, codified in the TVPA, gives prevention and protection equal priority with prosecution.

Educating the public, including potential employers and clients of trafficking victims, is considered an essential first step in combating the crime both here and abroad by U.S. authorities. The U.S. is supporting international campaigns aimed at alerting potential victims to the risks associated with emigrating illegally and "too-

Human Trafficking:
Sexual Exploitation.
Forced to Work
Against My Will.

Hidden in Plain Sight
Report It: 1-866-DHS-2-ICE

U.S. Immigration
and Customs
Enforcement

www.ice.gov

good-to-be-true" employment offers in other cities and countries. In February, 2010 the U.S. Customs and Border Protection of the Department of Homeland Security (DHS) launched *No Te Engañes*, ("Don't Be Fooled"), an anti-trafficking campaign involving television, radio and print media in Guatemala, El Salvador and Mexico. Domestically, in October 2009, DHS Immigration and Customs Enforcement (ICE) launched "Hidden in Plain Sight," an anti-trafficking campaign in 14 U.S. cities on billboards and in public transportation venues.

New approaches to combating human trafficking also prioritize the protection of victims from further exploitation. Public outreach campaigns aimed at enabling victims to seek help and become aware of their rights are combined with advanced training for law enforcement, health professionals and other community service providers to help them recognize the signs of human trafficking and to respond appropriately.

Victim protection also includes forms of immigration relief, including the granting of T-visas in the U.S., which allow eligible victims of trafficking to remain in the U.S. for up to four years, or longer in select circumstances. [21] T-visa holders who have been in the U.S. continuously for at least three years can apply for permanent residency.

Engaging victims more deliberately and effectively as a result of public outreach and training will help gather much-needed first-hand insight into how victims are approached and recruited. This will contribute to more meaningful statistics that will, in turn, help refine governments' ability to provide victim services.

Given the challenges of detecting human trafficking, comparatively few human traffickers are forced to an-

swer for their crimes. According to the State Department, there were only 5,212 prosecutions in 2008 for trafficking worldwide—and just 2,983 convictions.[22] In the U.S., federally funded human-trafficking task forces recorded only 1,229 incidents allegedly involving human trafficking between January 2007 and September 2008. More than 80 percent of those were related to the sex trade, suggesting that cases of labor trafficking were under-reported.[23]

As human trafficking is a transnational crime, it requires collaboration and partnership across borders to identify the patterns and stamp it out. The DHS and the Department of Justice (DOJ) are cooperating to increase the number of human trafficking prosecutions at home and abroad. DOJ supports 40 human trafficking task forces in the U.S. dedicated to identifying, investigating, prosecuting, and convicting trafficking cases.[24] DOJ also funds studies to identify obstacles to prosecuting traffickers and to recommend ways to overcome them.

Overseas, DHS agents conduct human-trafficking training for international law enforcement. That has already produced results. Thanks to anti-trafficking

legislation developed with U.S. help, Mexico filed its first prosecutions against human traffickers in 2009. DHS also conducts human trafficking training, outreach and technical assistance through ICE offices in Brazil, Colombia, Ecuador, Argentina, Guatemala, and Panama, among others. But as the worldwide economic crisis continues to exact a heavy toll, it is likely that the modern scourge of slavery will shadow the globe for years to come. AQ

FOR SOURCE CITATIONS SEE: **www.americasquarterly.org/hill**

ENDNOTES

1 U.S. Department of State. (2006, June). Trafficking in Persons Report, p. 9. Retrieved February 27, 2010, from http://www.state.gov/g/tip/rls/tiprpt/2006/index.htm. **2** U.S. Department of State. (2004, June). Trafficking in Persons Report, p. 23. Retrieved February 27, 2010, from http://www.state.gov/g/tip/rls/tiprpt/2004/index.htm. **3** One predecessor of the TVPA was the Mann Act of 1910 (18 U.S.C. § 2421 et seq.), which pro-hibited the transportation of individu-als in interstate or foreign commerce for the purpose of prostitution or other criminal sexual activity. **4** The protocol was part of the United Nations Convention against Transnational Organized Crime, adopted in 2000. The protocol was ratified in 2003. **5**International Labour Organization. (2005). Forced Labour Sta-tistics. Retrieved February 27, 2010, from http://www.ilo.org/declaration/info/factsheets/lang--en/docName--WCMS_DECL_FS_20_EN/index.htm **6** United Nations Office on Drugs and Crime. (2009, February). Global Report on Trafficking in Persons, p 6. Retrieved February 27, 2010, from http://www.unodc.org/unodc/en/human-trafficking global-report-on-trafficking-in-persons.html. **7** Gozdziak, E.M., & Collett, E.A. (2005). Research on Human Trafficking in North America: A Review of Literature. International Migration, 43, 99-128. **8** Langberg, L. (2005). A Review of Recent OAS Research on Human Trafficking in the Latin American and Caribbean Region. International Migration, 43, 129-139. **9** Laczko, F. (2002, November 1). Human Trafficking: The Need for Better Data. Retrieved Febru-ary 27, 2010, from Migration Information Source website: http://www.migrationinformation.org/Feature/print.cfm?ID=66. **10** Gozdziak, E.M., & Bump, M. N. (2008, March). Victims No Longer: Research on Child Survi-vors of Trafficking for Sexual and Labor Exploitation in the United States, p 12. Retrieved February 27, 2010, from the National Criminal Justice Reference Service website: http://www.ncjrs.gov/pdffiles1/nij/grants/221891.pdf. **11** U.S. Department of State. (2004, June). Trafficking in Persons Report, p. 6. Retrieved February 27, 2010, from http://www.state.gov/g/tip/rls/tiprpt/2004/index.htm. **12** Fahy, S., Farrell, A., & McDevitt J. (2008, December). Understanding and Improving Law En-forcement Responses to Human Trafficking: Final Report, p 2. Retrieved February 27, 2010, from the Na-tional Criminal Justice Reference Service website: http://www.ncjrs.gov/pdffiles1/nij/grants/222752.pdf. **13** Shelley, L. (2007). Human Trafficking as a Form of Transnational Crime. In M. Lee (Ed.), Hu-man Trafficking (pp. 116-137). Portland, OR: Willan. **14** Bruckert, C. & Parent, C. (2002, June). Trafficking in Human Beings and Organized Crime: A Literature Review. Retrieved February 27, 2010, from the Royal Canadian Mounted Policy website: http://www.rcmp-grc.gc.ca/pubs/index-eng.htm. **15** International Organization for Migration. (2009, May). Straddling the Border: Drug Mules and Human Trafficking. Global Eye, 5. Retrieved February 27, 2010, from http://www.iom.int/jahia/webdav/site/myjahiasite/shared/shared/mainsite/projects/showcase_pdf/global_eye_fifth_issue.pdf. **16** Vasquez, E. (2008). Duped and Sold: Human Trafficking in Paraguay. Americas Quarterly, Summer 2008, 99-101. **17** Ibid. **18** United Nations Office on Drugs and Crime. (2009, February). Global Report on Trafficking in Persons, p 7. Retrieved February 27, 2010, from http://www.unodc.org/unodc/en/human-trafficking/global-report-on-trafficking-in-persons.html. **19** Langberg, L. (2005). A Review of Recent OAS Research on Human Trafficking in the Latin American and Caribbean Region. International Migration, 43, 129-139. **20** U.S. Depart-ment of State. (2009, June). Trafficking in Persons Report, p 47. Retrieved February 27, 2010, from http://www.state.gov/g/tip/rls/tiprpt/2009/index.htm. **21** Department of Justice, Bureau of Justice Statistics. (2009, January). Characteristics of Suspected Human Trafficking Incidents, 2007-2008. Retrieved February 27, 2010, from http://bjs.ojp.usdoj.gov/index.cfm?ty=pbdetail&iid=550. **22** http://www.ojp.usdoj.gov/BJA/grant/httf.html

Required Readings Available Online

Freidman, Thomas. "It's a Flat World After All" *New York Times,* April 3 2005 [online], http://www.nytimes.com/2005/04/03/magazine/its-a-flat-world-after-all.html?_r=1

Ghemawat, Pankaj, 2012. "Actually the world isn't flat," TED Talk published on October 22, 2012, https://www.youtube.com/watch?v=KPNn880KWfU.

Additional Works Cited

Gallagher, Anne. 2013. "Trafficking, smuggling and human rights: tricks and treaties. Forced Migration Review 12, pp. 25-28.

Held, David and Anthony McGrew David Goldblatt and Jonathan Perraton. 1999. *Global Transformation: Politics, Economics and Culture.* Stanford University Press, 32-86.

Hirst, P and T. Grahame. 2001. *Globalization in Question: The International Economy and the Possibilities of Governance.* Trade Paperback.

Leeson, Peter T. and Andrea M. Dean. "The Democratic Domino Theory: An Empirical Investigation," *American Journal of Political Science* 53(3): 533-551.

Schiff, Maurice and Alan Winters. 2003. *Regional Integration and Development.* Washington, DC: World Bank.

II. MODULE TWO

International Organizations and Relations

In this chapter, we explore a variety of efforts to achieve greater international cooperation. One important international organization devoted to collective security was the League of Nations, established after World War I. The League had some significant successes. Most notably, it led to the creation of the Permanent Court of International Justice and the International Labor Organization. However, the League is also criticized for being unable to fulfill its primary purpose, preventing World War II.

When World War II ended, leaders came together to create the United Nations. The UN is the only international intergovernmental organization with nearly universal membership. As such, it occupies a special place in international studies. The United Nations was formed as a collective security organization by a coalition of the great powers that emerged from World War II. That configuration still shapes the UN and the work it is able to do today. The specialized agencies within the UN system make major contributions to solving problems of global scope and significance.

The United Nations is a good example of political globalization: nation-states coming together to give up some of their power in the interest of cooperation. Another example of political globalization and interdependence is the European Union. The European Union evolved out of the European Coal and Steel Community (ECSC), an organization that envisioned sharing strategic natural resources as one way to avoid future conflict. The ECSC also marked the end of punishing the losers of a conflict by making them pay for damages. The minds behind the creation of the European Union believed this practice led to more conflict. A series of treaties changed this initial union to create the European Union we know today. The European Union thus is the paradigmatic example of international cooperation and interdependence.

Over fifty years of integration have transformed the economic and political landscape of Europe and given unprecedented power to a new set of supranational institutions. But there are many remaining questions. From the beginning, there have been clashing visions of what Europe should become. As Staab has written, "Regardless of the outcome of this debate, the European Union represents a hugely influential vehicle for organizing Europe and constitutes a unique experiment of 'deep international cooperation.'" (2011: ix)

Readings

In "The United Nations in World Politics" **Karen Mingst** and **Margaret Karns** provide a balanced view of the international organization and place in some historical perspective. This excerpt from their book-length volume on the United Nations is primarily concerned with contrasting the vision and the reality of the United Nations. These authors are more optimistic about the United Nations than many you will read. They point to peacekeeping efforts and the support of self-determination for nations as among the early successes in advancing the organization's goals. They see the United Nation following de-colonization as playing an significant role with regard to a whole range of issues in which states are interdependent including human rights (the topic of chapter three) the environment (a topic in chapter four), and development (the topic of chapter five).

Mingst and Karns also provide an introduction to three of the main theories of international relations that shape scholars' thinking: realism, liberalism, and constructivism. Each perspective sheds light on aspects of international affairs. These theories are far from abstract: they inform policies and proscriptions about how to solve problems in the world today.

In addition to its significant successes, the UN faces some daunting challenges. As Mingst and Karns see the organization, the first challenge is that in spite of the need for global governance, the UN remains underfunded. Compounding matters is that the balance of power within the UN does not align with the balance of power in the world today. Another challenge is that the way in which states remain the primary actors in world politics sometimes "incapacitates" or undermines international efforts. A final major challenge has to do with what these authors see as something of a power vacuum, in spite of the continuing need for leadership.

In "International Regimes and Organizations," **David Galbraith** provides an excellent tour of the many actors in international politics, and the requirements for their cooperation. What you learned from Mingst and Karns about realism, liberalism, and constructivism will prove useful in understanding the argument about the reasons that states create and join international institutions provided here.

Finlayson reminds us that even amidst rapid globalization, nationalism remains a significant force in world politics. As a political ideology, nationalism offers not just a way of thinking about the world, but a way of being within it. Nationalism is itself a perspective on the international system.

John McCormick and **Jonathan Olsen** tell the story of the formation of the European Union in this excerpt from their book by the same title, *The European Union*. Pay particular attention to the five institutions of the European Union described on page 6-7 as this is key to any subsequent reading you do on the European Union. McCormick and Olsen emphasize that the European Union is still evolving and must be understood as "a work in progress" (page 7). This helps explain some of the dissatisfaction – and confusion – surrounding European Union institutions. McCormick and Olsen make a compelling argument that the European Union still warrants attention. One reason is economic. The United States does as much as one-fifth of its merchandise trade with the EU (page 9). Another reason is political in nature. The power of the European Union relative to the United States has grown, and this affects world politics as a whole.

The United Nations in World Politics

by Karen Mingst and Margaret Karns

It is hard to imagine a world without the United Nations. Despite many ups and downs over more than sixty-five years, the UN has not only endured but also played a key role in reshaping the world as we know it. It has embodied humankind's hopes for a better world through the prevention of conflict. It has promoted a culture of legality and rule of law. It has raised an awareness of the plight of the world's poor, and it has boosted development by providing **technical assistance**. It has promoted concern for human rights, including the status of women, the rights of the child, and the unique needs of indigenous peoples. It has formulated the concept of environmentally sustainable development. It has contributed immensely to making multilateral diplomacy the primary way in which international norms, public policies, and law are established. It has served as a catalyst for global policy networks and partnerships with other actors. It plays a central role in **global governance**. Along the way, the UN has earned several Nobel Peace Prizes, including the 2005 award to the International Atomic Energy Agency (IAEA) and its chief, Mohamed ElBaradei; the 2001 prize to the UN and Secretary-General Kofi Annan; the 1988 award to UN peacekeepers; and the 1969 honor to the International Labour Organization (ILO).

In the many areas of UN activity, we can point to the UN's accomplishments and also to its shortcomings and failures. More than sixty-five years after its creation, the UN continues to be the only **international organization (IO)** or, more correctly, **international intergovernmental organization (IGO)** of global scope and nearly universal membership that has an agenda encompassing the broadest range of governance issues. It is a complex system that serves as the central site for multilateral diplomacy, with the UN's General Assembly as center stage. Three weeks of general debate at the opening of each fall assembly session draw foreign ministers and heads of state from small and large states to take advantage of the opportunity to address the nations of the world and to engage in intensive diplomacy.

As an intergovernmental organization, however, the UN is the creation of its member states; it is they who decide what it is that they will allow this organization to do and what resources—financial and otherwise—they will provide. In this regard, the UN is very much a political organization, subject to the winds of world politics and the whims of member governments. To understand the UN today, it is useful to look back at some of the major changes in world politics and how they affected the UN.

THE UNITED NATIONS IN WORLD POLITICS: VISION AND REALITY

The establishment of the United Nations in the closing days of World War II was an affirmation of the desire of war-weary nations for an organization that could help them avoid future conflicts and promote international economic and social cooperation. As we discuss further in Chapter 2, the UN's Charter built on lessons learned from the failed League of Nations created at the end of World War I and earlier experiments with international unions, conference diplomacy, and dispute-settlement mechanisms. It represented an expression of hope for the possibilities of a new global security arrangement and for fostering the social and economic conditions necessary for peace to prevail.

The United Nations and Politics in the Cold War World

The World War II coalition of great powers (the United States, the Soviet Union, Great Britain, France, and China), whose unity had been key to the UN's founding, was nevertheless a victim of rising tensions almost before the first General Assembly session in 1946. Developments in Europe and Asia between 1946 and 1950 soon made it clear that the emerging Cold War would have fundamental effects on the UN. How could a **collective security** system operate when there was no unity among the great powers on whose cooperation it depended? Even the admission of new members was affected between 1950 and 1955 because each side vetoed applications from states that were allied with the other.

The Cold War made Security Council actions on threats to peace and security extremely problematic, with repeated sharp exchanges and frequent deadlock. Some conflicts, such as the French and American wars in Vietnam and the Soviet interventions in Czechoslovakia and Hungary, were never brought to the UN at all. The UN was able to respond to the North Korean invasion of South Korea in 1950 only because the Soviet Union was boycotting the Security Council at the time.

In order to deal with a number of regional conflicts, the UN developed something never mentioned in its charter, namely, **peacekeeping**; this has involved the prevention, containment, and moderation of hostilities between or within states through the use of lightly armed multinational forces of soldiers, police, and civilians.

Peacekeeping was a creative response to the breakdown of great-power unity and the spread of East-West tensions to regional conflicts. UN peacekeeping forces were used extensively in the Middle East and in conflicts arising out of the decolonization process during the Cold War period. Thirteen operations were deployed from 1948 to 1988. The innovation of peacekeeping illustrates what the Cold War did to the UN: "It had repealed the proposition that the organization should undertake to promote order by bringing the great powers into troubled situations. . . . Henceforward, the task of the United Nations was to be defined as that of keeping the great powers out of such situations."[1]

The Effects of the Nuclear Revolution. The UN Charter had just been signed when the use of two atomic bombs on Japan on August 6 and 10, 1945, began a scientific and technological revolution in warfare that would have a far-reaching impact on the post–World War II world. At the United Nations, the earliest and most obvious effect of nuclear weapons was to restore the issue of disarmament (and its relative, arms control) to the agenda. Disarmament as an approach to peace had been discredited during the interwar era. The UN almost from its inception in early 1946 became a forum for discussions and negotiations on **arms control and disarmament**. Hence, the nuclear threat not only transformed world politics but also made the UN the key place where statespersons sought to persuade each other that war had become excessively dangerous, that disarmament and arms control were imperative, and that they were devoted to peace and restraint.

The Role of the United Nations in Decolonization and the Emergence of New States. At the close of World War II, few would have predicted the end of colonial rule in Africa and Asia. Yet twenty-five years after the UN Charter was signed, most of the former colonies had achieved independence with relatively little threat to international peace and security. Membership in the UN more than doubled from 51 states in 1945 to 118 in 1965 and had tripled by 1980 (see Figure 1.1), the vast majority of these new members being newly independent states. The UN played a significant role in this remarkably peaceful transformation, much of which took place during the height of the Cold War. Twenty-six new states were later seated in the UN after the Cold War's end, mostly as a result of the dissolution of the Soviet Union and Yugoslavia.

The UN Charter endorsed the principle of **self-determination**. Already independent former colonies, such as India, Egypt, Indonesia, and the Latin American states, used the UN as a forum to advocate an end to colonialism and independence for territories ruled by Great Britain, France, the Netherlands,

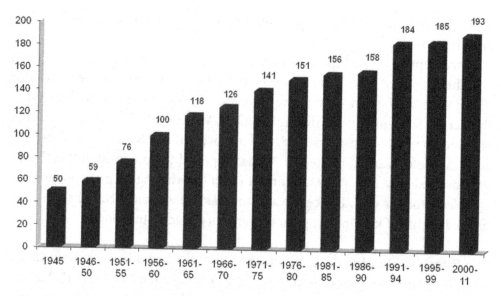

FIGURE 1.1. Growth in UN Membership, 1945–2011

SOURCE: Compiled from Robert E. Riggs and Jack C. Plano, *The United Nations: International Organization of World Politics*, 2nd ed. (Belmont, CA: Wadsworth, 1994), 45, and updated.

Belgium, Spain, and Portugal. Success added new votes to the growing anticolonial coalition.

By 1960 a majority of the UN's members favored decolonization. General Assembly Resolution 1514 that year condemned the continuation of colonial rule and preconditions for granting independence (such as a lack of preparation for self-rule) and called for annual reports on the progress toward independence for all remaining colonial territories. The UN provided an important forum for the **collective legitimation** of a change in international norms (that is, colonialism and imperialism were no longer acceptable patterns of state behavior, and colonial peoples had a right to self-determination). The international system was fully internationalized to include all sovereign, independent states that sought membership.

The consequences of decolonization and the expanded number of independent states were manifold. The less developed, often newly independent states of Africa, Asia, and Latin America formed a strong coalition within the UN known as the **Group of 77 (G-77)**; after 1960 this coalition commanded a majority of votes on a broad range of issues. Whereas the Cold War had shaped politics in the UN until 1960, the G-77, and what became known as "North-South issues," shaped much of the politics thereafter. The two sets of issues became entwined in complex ways, and political divisions changed. The Soviet Union and many Western European states often sided with the G-77, and the United States frequently found itself in a small minority.

Beginning in the 1960s, new issues proliferated on the UN's agenda, many at the urging of the G-77. For example, in 1967, Arvid Pardo, the representative from Malta, argued on behalf of newly independent states that the resources found on the deep seabed were the "common heritage of mankind," not the property of any specific nation. This would subsequently have an impact on emerging environmental issues as well as on the law of the sea. Of all the issues pushed by the G-77, however, none received more attention than the drive for economic and social development.

The North-South Conflict. By the late 1960s, UN agendas were dominated by issues of economic and social development and the relations between the developed countries of the industrial North and the less developed countries (LDCs) of the South. The ideological leaning of the G-77 in the 1960s and 1970s toward a heavy government role in economic development and redistribution of wealth shaped many UN programs and activities. In the 1970s the G-77 pushed for a **New International Economic Order (NIEO)**, marshaling support in the UN General Assembly for "A Declaration on the Establishment of a New International Economic Order" and "A Charter of Economic Rights and Duties of States." For most of the decade, the NIEO debates dominated and polarized the UN system, with the deep divide between North and South at times making agreement on both economic and security issues impossible to achieve.

The North-South conflict continues to be a central feature of world politics, and hence of the UN, although the rhetoric and issues of the NIEO sharply diminished in the late 1980s and 1990s. For example, the UN's treatment of environmental issues, which first began with the Stockholm Conference on the Human Environment in 1972, has been permeated by North-South differences. The 1997 Kyoto Conference on Climate Change heard echoes of the North-South conflict when developing countries insisted that industrial countries make the first reductions in carbon dioxide emissions. Those echoes still persisted at the 2009 Copenhagen conference on climate change. The G-77, however, is no longer as cohesive a group; its members' interests increasingly diverged in the 1980s when some states, especially in Southeast Asia, achieved rapid economic growth and as many developing countries shifted from statist-oriented economic policies to neoliberal ones, calling for open markets and privatization. Chapter 5 discusses these shifts further as well as the increased emphasis on poverty alleviation that accompanied the **Millennium Development ment Goals (MDGs)** approved in 2000.

World Politics Since the Cold War's End

The Cold War's end in 1990 meant not only new cooperation among the five permanent members of the Security Council but also a resurgence of nationalism, civil wars, and ethnic conflicts; the new phenomenon of failed states; and a related series of humanitarian crises. The consequence was greater demands than ever before on the United Nations to deal with threats to peace and security as well as environmental and developmental issues, democratization, population growth, humanitarian crises, and other problems. UN peacekeepers were called on to rebuild Cambodia; create peace in Bosnia; organize and monitor postconflict elections in Nicaragua, Namibia, and many other places; monitor human rights violations in El Salvador; and oversee humanitarian relief in Bosnia, Somalia, Rwanda, Kosovo, the Democratic Republic of the Congo (DRC), East Timor, and Afghanistan. Beginning with Iraq's invasion of Kuwait in 1990, the UN's enforcement powers were used more in the post–Cold War era than at any previous time.

With the spread of **democratization** to all regions of the globe from Latin America, Eastern Europe, and states created from the former Soviet Union to Africa and Asia, many authoritarian governments in the late 1980s and 1990s were forced to open their political processes to competing political parties, adopt more stringent human rights standards, and hold free elections. Since 1990 the UN has been in heavy demand to provide observers for elections in countries around the world. UN-sanctioned intervention in Haiti in 1993 marked the first time the UN took action to restore a democratically elected government. In Namibia, Kosovo, Bosnia, and East Timor, the UN was called upon to assist with organizing the elements of newly independent states, including the provision of transitional administrations, writing of constitutions, training of police and judges, and organization of elections.

By 1995, however, the early post–Cold War optimism about the United Nations had faded. The peacekeepers in Somalia, Bosnia, and Rwanda found little peace to be kept, although their presence did alleviate much human suffering. Despite almost continuous meetings of the UN Security Council and numerous resolutions, the UN's members lacked the political will to provide the military, logistical, and financial resources needed to deal adequately with these and other complex situations. In addition, the UN faced a deep financial crisis in the late 1990s caused by the increased cost of peacekeeping and other activities and the failure of many members, including the United States, to pay their assessed contributions. The organization clearly needed significant reforms to meet the increased demands and address weaknesses in its structures and operations, but member states failed to use either the occasion of the UN's fiftieth anniversary in 1995 or the UN's sixtieth anniversary in 2005 to approve many of the necessary changes. The UN did not stand still, however. Some changes could be made without member states' approval; other reforms were approved at the 2005 World Summit. And, in its responses to many complex conflicts, humanitarian crises, new threats to peace posed by nuclear weapons proliferation and terrorism, as well as persistent global poverty, the UN demonstrated that it was still central to many aspects of global governance, as discussed in subsequent chapters.

Well before the Cold War's end, the UN played an important role on a nexus of **interdependence** issues by convening global conferences and summits on topics ranging from the environment, food, housing, the law of the sea, disarmament, women, and water to human rights, population and development, and social development. These conferences have articulated new international norms; expanded international law; set agendas for governments, as well as for the UN itself, through programs of action; and promoted linkages among the growing communities of **nongovernmental organizations (NGOs)** active on different issues, the UN, and member states' governments.

Still, the UN has never played a central role in international economic relations. Although economic topics have appeared on the agendas of the General Assembly and the United Nations Economic and Social Council (ECOSOC), the major decisionmaking has always taken place in institutions that have never really been part of the UN system: the World Bank, the International Monetary Fund (IMF), the World Trade Organization (WTO), and the **Group of 7 (G-7)**, as well as in Washington, Tokyo, London, and the headquarters of major corporations and banks. The UN has, however, been active from its earliest years in efforts to promote economic and social development, introducing the ideas of development aid in the 1950s, sustainable development in the 1980s, and human development in the 1990s. Many of the global conferences contributed other ideas and reinforced understanding of the way development overlaps with the status of women, population, food, and other problems. UN Secretary-General Kofi Annan used the occasion of the new millennium to convene a Millennium Summit in 2000. In suggesting the special gathering, the secretary-general hoped "to harness the symbolic power of the millennium to the real and urgent needs of people everywhere."[2] His special report, *We the Peoples*, provided his views of the state of the world, the major global challenges, and the need for structural reform of the UN itself. The three days of meetings drew the largest gathering of world leaders ever: There were 147 heads of state or government and representatives from forty-four other countries.

The Millennium Declaration adopted at the close of the extraordinary summit reflected the high degree of consensus on two priorities: peace and development. Different leaders had stressed different aspects of the issues, ranging from globalization and nuclear weapons to fairer economic systems, ethnic tolerance, and human immunodeficiency syndrome (HIV/AIDS). They had disagreed about how to restructure the UN, but not about the importance of the world organization; they concurred with lofty language about values and principles and also committed themselves to the series of specific objectives known as the MDGs that include halving the number of people living on less than one dollar a day by the year 2015 and reversing the spread of HIV/AIDS, malaria, and other major diseases. The declaration outlined special measures to meet the needs of Africa, and it intensified efforts to reform the Security Council, to strengthen ECOSOC and the International Court of Justice (ICJ), to make the General Assembly a more effective deliberative and policymaking body, and to ensure that the UN has the resources to carry out its mandates. The MDGs and their implementation are discussed further in Chapters 5 and 7.

Rising globalization has been a major feature of world politics since the Cold War's end. **Globalization** is the process of increasing worldwide integration of politics, economics, social relations, and culture that often appears to undermine state sovereignty. In the 1990s this process of increased connectivity greatly accelerated, especially in the area of economic activities across state borders with the rapid growth in flows of finance, goods and services (trade), and investment, as well as diffusion of technology. Many regard globalization as desirable because it has fueled greater prosperity and higher standards of living in many parts of the world. Others, however, point to the growing inequality among and within nations and the ways in which globalization creates both winners and losers, such as those whose jobs in developed countries are lost to workers in developing countries who are paid lower wages. There is also the dark side of globalization that has facilitated the growth of trafficking in drugs, persons, and other criminal enterprises.

The UN itself and various **specialized agencies** within the UN system have struggled to address globalization issues. Although the International Labour Organization, World Health Organization (WHO), and World Intellectual Property Organization (WIPO) are very much involved in globalization-related issues of labor, health, and intellectual property rights, the fact that the targets of antiglobalization protesters have been the World Bank, IMF, G-7, and WTO underscores the UN's marginal role in international economic relations. Yet globalization has fueled the growth of NGOs. Subsequent chapters illustrate how the UN and NGOs, which represent what some have called global civil society, are working out new partnerships that will make each more responsive to globalization issues.

The emergence of the United States as the world's sole superpower has been a related aspect of post–Cold War world politics, the era of globalization, and the early twenty-first century. The economic and military capabilities of the United States have far exceeded those of any other state, and, with the collapse of the Soviet Union, the United States had no serious rival. Many worried that this development would result in the UN's marginalization, particularly if, or when, the United States chose to act unilaterally. This view was borne out when the United States invaded Iraq in 2003 in defiance of international opposition. An alternative view was that the UN could become a puppet of the sole superpower, dependent upon its goodwill for funding and subservient in authorizing US actions. Yet in the late 1990s and first decade of the twenty-first century, we have seen groups of states and of NGOs willing to push ahead with policy initiatives even when the United States has opposed them, examples being the International Criminal Court, the Convention on Landmines, the Kyoto Protocol on Climate Change, and its successor. Although its support has fluctuated, in fact, the United States has always been important to the United Nations, as discussed further in Chapter 3.

Now, with the rapid rise of China, India, South Africa, Brazil and other emerging powers as well as the reassertiveness of Russia (a group collectively known as the **BRICS**), world politics is again shifting, and the years ahead will likely see significant changes in how these shifts play out within the UN. Already in international economic relations, the G-7 has been effectively replaced by the **Group of 20 (G-20)**, and the emerging powers have pushed for changes in their voting shares within the World Bank and IMF. The reform of UN Security Council membership will gain new attention and urgency with these power shifts.

To understand the links between world politics and the United Nations, it is also important to examine the major international relations theories to see how they explain global changes and the roles of IGOs such as the UN.

CONTENDING INTERNATIONAL RELATIONS THEORIES

For much of the post–World War II era, **realist theory**, or **realism**, provided the dominant explanation for international politics. Realists see states as the most important actors in the international system. They view states as unitary actors that define their national interests in terms of maximizing power and security. States' **sovereignty** means that they coexist in an anarchic international system and, therefore, must rely primarily on themselves to manage their own insecurity through balance of power, alliances, and deterrence. International rules (law) and norms, as well as international organizations, do not carry much weight with realists because they lack enforcement power. In realists' view, IGOs and NGOs are marginal actors. IGOs, in particular, do not enjoy autonomy or capability for independent action on the world stage. Rather, they reflect the interests of their members, especially the most powerful ones. In this view, the UN is constrained by its members' willingness to work through it in dealing with specific problems, to comply with and support its actions, to provide peacekeeping contingents (military or civilian), and to pay for its regular operations and special programs. In realist theory, cooperation among states is not impossible, but states have little incentive to enter into international arrangements, and they are always free to exit from them.[3]

For many international relations scholars, however, realist theory is an inadequate theoretical framework for analyzing world politics, and especially the rapid changes since the Cold War's end as well as the expanded practice of **multilateralism** and the activities of the UN and other IGOs. One major alternative is **liberalism**.[4]

Liberals regard states as important actors, but they place importance on a variety of other actors in the international system, including IGOs, NGOs, **multinational corporations (MNCs)**, and even individuals. States, in their view, are pluralistic, not unitary, actors. Moral and ethical principles, power relations, and bargaining among different domestic and transnational groups and changing international conditions shape states' interests and actions. There is no single definition of national interest; rather, states vary in their goals, and their interests change. Liberal theorists characterize the international system as an interdependent one in which there is both cooperation and conflict and where actors' mutual interests tend to increase over time. States' power matters, but it is exercised within a framework of international rules and institutions that help to make cooperation possible.

Neoliberal institutionalists have provided a somewhat different explanation for why cooperation occurs. For classical liberals, cooperation emerges from establishing and reforming institutions that permit cooperative interactions and prohibit coercive actions. For neoliberal institutionalists, cooperation emerges when actors have continuous interactions with each other. Institutions help prevent cheating; they reduce transaction and opportunity costs for those who seek gains from cooperation within them. Institutions are essential; they build upon common interests. They help to shape state's interests and state preferences. IGOs such as the United Nations make a difference in world politics by altering state preferences and establishing rules that constrain states. They are not merely pawns of the dominant powers but actually modify state behavior by creating habits of cooperation and serving as arenas for negotiation and policy coordination.

For some liberal theorists, the growth of multilateralism, IGOs, and international law is indicative of a nascent international society in which actors consent to common rules and institutions and recognize common interests as well as a common identity or sense of "we-ness." Within this emerging society, international institutions are changing the way states and other actors interact with each other. Many scholars argue that the growing role of nongovernmental actors represents an emerging global civil society.[5]

A third and relatively recent approach to international relations is **constructivism**, which has become important for studying various aspects of global governance, particularly the role of norms and institutions. Constructivism has several variants, and questions have arisen about whether it is a theory of politics. Yet it offers a valuable way of studying how shared beliefs, rules, organizations, and cultural practices shape the behavior of states and other actors as well as their identities and interests. Among the key norms affecting state behavior in constructivists' view is multilateralism. Several studies have examined the impact of norms and principled beliefs on international outcomes such as the evolution of the international human rights **regime**, bans on certain types of weapons, and humanitarian intervention in which the UN and other IGOs have played a role. They have found that international organizations can be not only "teachers" but also "creators" of norms; as such, they can socialize states into accepting certain political goals and values.[6]

Constructivists tend to see IGOs as actors that can have independent effects on international relations and as arenas in which discussions, persuasion, education, and argument take place that influence government leaders', businesspeople's, and NGO activists' understandings of their interests and of the world in which they live. The consequences are not always positive, however, because IGOs can also stimulate conflicts, their actions may not necessarily be in the interests of their member states, and IGO bureaucracies such as the UN Secretariat may develop agendas of their own, be dysfunctional, lack accountability, tolerate inefficient practices, and compete for turf, budgets, and staff.[7]

Realism, liberalism, and constructivism, then, are different "lenses" through which scholars view world politics and the United Nations.

DILEMMAS THE UN FACES IN THE 21ST CENTURY

No matter which theory one finds most valuable, understanding the role of the UN in the twenty-first century requires the exploration of three dilemmas.

Dilemma 1: Needs for Governance Versus the UN's Weaknesses

The United Nations has faced increasing demands that it provide peacekeeping and peacebuilding operations, initiate international regulation to halt environmental degradation and alleviate poverty and inequality in the world, promote greater human economic and social well-being, provide humanitarian relief to victims of natural disasters and violence, and protect human rights for various groups. These are demands for global governance—not world government—demands for rules, norms, and organizational structures to manage transboundary and interdependence problems that states acting alone cannot solve, such as terrorism, crime, drugs, environmental degradation, pandemics, and human rights violations.[8]

These governance demands test the capacity and the willingness of states to commit themselves to international cooperation and the capacity of the UN and other international organizations to function effectively. Can they meet these new demands without simply adding more programs? How can the initiatives be funded? Can the UN be more effective in coordinating the related activities of various institutions, states, and NGOs? Can it improve its own management and personnel practices? Can it adapt to deal with the changing nature of conflicts and persistent poverty and inequality? The most important issues concerning the global economy are discussed and decided outside the UN system. The UN Charter's provisions are designed for interstate conflicts, yet most post–Cold War conflicts have been intrastate civil wars. The UN's membership has grown from 50 to 193 states. The Security Council was structured to reflect power realities in 1945, not the twenty-first century.

Clearly, the UN needs to reform to increase its capacity to meet new demands, to mobilize resources, to reflect the changing distribution of power and authority in the twenty-first century, and to strengthen its links with nonstate actors. One of the UN's strengths to date has been its flexibility in response to new issues and a membership more than three times the size of the original membership. Its weaknesses are the rigidity of its central structures, its slowness to accommodate nonstate actors and the changing realities of geopolitics, and the continuing inability of member states to agree about major reforms. It has also been weakened by states' failure to meet their commitments for funding and their reluctance to empower the UN Secretariat too much. Yet the current demands for global governance require the commitment of states and enhanced institutional capacity in the UN; they therefore also require that states give up more of their sovereignty. This leads to the second dilemma.

Dilemma 2: Sovereignty Versus Challenges to Sovereignty

The longstanding principles of state sovereignty and nonintervention in states' domestic affairs are affirmed in the UN Charter, yet sovereignty has eroded on many fronts and is continually challenged in this era of globalization by issues and problems that cross states' borders and that states cannot solve alone. Historically, sovereignty empowered each state to govern all matters within its territorial jurisdiction. **Nonintervention** is the related principle that obliges other states and international organizations not to intervene in matters within the internal or domestic jurisdiction of a sovereign state. Global telecommunications, including the Internet, and economic interdependencies such as global financial markets, international human rights norms, international election monitoring, and environmental regulation are among the many developments that infringe on states' sovereignty and traditional areas of domestic jurisdiction. The growing activities of IGOs and NGOs have eroded the centrality of states as the primary actors in world politics. For example, Amnesty International (AI) and the International Commission of Jurists have been key actors in promoting human rights, sometimes exerting more influence than states themselves. Multinational corporations with operations in several countries and industry groups such as oil, steel, textiles, automobiles, and shipping are important players in trade and climate change negotiations, some having more resources than some states. Partnerships between the UN and private sector, including multinational corporations, have become increasingly important for a variety of governance challenges. The Global Compact initiated by UN Secretary-General Kofi Annan in 1999 was a step in this direction.

How is sovereignty challenged by these developments? Global telecommunications and particularly the Internet as well as heightened economic interdependence have diminished the control that governments can exercise over the information their citizens receive, the value of their money, financial transactions, and the health of their countries' economies. NGOs can influence legislators and government officials both from within countries and from outside through transnational networks and access to the media.

International norms and rules, such as those on trade, the seas, intellectual property rights, ozone-depleting chlorofluorocarbons (CFCs), and women's rights, have been established through UN-sponsored negotiations. They set standards for states and relevant industries as well as for consumers and citizens. When states themselves accept commitments to uphold these standards (by signing and ratifying international treaties and conventions), they are simultaneously exercising their sovereignty (the commitment they make) and accepting a diminution of that sovereignty (the agreement to international standards that will then be open to international monitoring). Climate change poses particularly daunting challenges for both global governance and state sovereignty.

Although multilateral institutions in theory take actions that constitute intervention in states' domestic affairs only with their consent, there is now a growing body of precedent for **humanitarian intervention**, which has emerged as a new norm of **responsibility to protect (R2P)** to justify international actions to alleviate human suffering during violent conflicts without the consent of the "host" country. It was first invoked to provide food relief and reestablish civil order in Somalia in 1993–1994, then to justify the bombing of Yugoslavia and Kosovo by the North Atlantic Treaty Organization (NATO) in 1999, and to call for international action against genocide in the Darfur region of Sudan in 2005–2006. The

2005 World Summit endorsed the R2P norm, but many states, particularly developing countries, feared its consequences for the norms of nonintervention and sovereignty. The case of Libya in 2011 is discussed in Chapter 4.

Despite these apparent limitations on states' sovereignty, the reality remains that "the capacity to mobilize the resources necessary to tackle global problems also remains vested in states, therefore effectively incapacitating many international institutions."[9] That includes the United Nations. Thus, the dilemma associated with state sovereignty links also to the third dilemma: the need for leadership.

Dilemma 3: The Need for Leadership

World politics in the twenty-first century was marked initially by the dominance of the United States as the sole superpower and a diffusion of power among many other states, the European Union (EU), and a wide variety of nonstate actors that exercise influence in different ways. As noted above, however, even before the end of the first decade, it was apparent that the rise of emerging nations such as Brazil, India, and China as well as constraints on the United States were leading to shifting patterns of power and leadership. Yet traditional measures of power in international politics do not necessarily dictate who will provide leadership or be influential within the UN.

Multilateral institutions such as the UN create opportunities for small and middle powers as well as for NGOs, groups of states, and IGOs' executive heads to exercise initiative and leadership. UN secretaries-general, in fact, have often been important figures in the international arena depending on their personality and willingness to take initiatives such as mediating conflicts or proposing responses to international problems that may or may not prove acceptable to member states. Both Boutros Boutros-Ghali and Kofi Annan are noted, for example, for their leadership both within and outside the UN. Prominent individuals, such as former Australian prime minister Gareth Evans and Mohamed Sahnoun of Algeria, who chaired the independent International Commission on Intervention and State Sovereignty that in 2001 proposed the new norm of responsibility to protect as an obligation of states, can exercise leadership through technical expertise and diplomatic skill. Middle powers such as Australia, Canada, Brazil, and India have been influential in international trade negotiations on agricultural issues, as they have long been in peacekeeping and development. Canada provided leadership for the effort in the late 1990s to ban antipersonnel land mines, while Norway led a similar effort on cluster munitions that culminated in a treaty in 2008. Brazil, Japan, and India led the effort in 2005 to secure Security Council reform.

NGOs can also provide leadership along with states, UN secretaries-general, and other prominent individuals. The success of both the land-mine and cluster-munitions efforts owed much to the leadership of coalitions of NGOs. The Inter-governmental Panel on Climate Change (IPCC) has been a lead actor in international efforts since the late 1980s to analyze data on climate and to promote efforts to address the problem.

Still, states matter, and leadership from major powers with resources and influence matters. Hence, the dilemma. With the demise of the Soviet Union in 1991, the United States became the sole remaining superpower—the only state with intervention capabilities and interests in many parts of the globe. US economic, military, technological, and other resources still vastly exceed those of all other countries, notwithstanding China's rapid economic growth and emergence as a major economic power. The US gross domestic product is more than two and a half times that of China, whose GDP surpassed Japan's in 2010, and the American military expenditure is almost half that of the entire world. Power disparity such as this may still make the United States "bound to lead," but the style of leadership required in a world marked by multilateralism is not one of unilateral action but one geared to building coalitions and consensus and achieving active consultation and cooperation.

Furthermore, dominance tends to inspire resistance. A dominant power can rely on its sheer weight to play hardball and get its way—up to a point. The prolonged insurgency and failures in Iraq following US military intervention in 2003 demonstrated the limits of hard power. Leadership (and inspiring follower-ship) depends on soft power's inspiration and cultivation. In the late 1990s, US opposition to the creation of the International Criminal Court, the convention banning antipersonnel land mines, the Comprehensive Test Ban Treaty, and the Kyoto Protocol on Climate Change signaled a "go-it-alone" pattern that continued in the early years of the twenty-first century with the Bush administration's opposition to international treaties and invasion of Iraq.[10] This made many countries less willing to accept US dominance.[11] It also fueled anti-Americanism in many parts of the world.[12] Consequently, the United States lost a good deal of its soft power and ability to lead. President Obama has rectified some of that and been more inclined to forge international consensus, limiting US interventions, mindful also of the constraints of the US budget deficit and military commitments. In any case, the history of US engagement with the UN is one of "mixed messages" and considerable variation. As discussed further in Chapter 3, Congress blocked full payment of US dues to the UN from the mid-1980s until 2000, and with the huge budget deficit, as well as Republican majority in the House of Representatives following the 2010 midterm elections, US payments to the UN are targeted for cuts again.

In a world of emerging powers, the likelihood that the United States can lead, even when it chooses to, is inevitably diminished. Yet those rising powers may not be willing or able to assume leadership either.

CONCLUSION

Subsequent chapters explore these dilemmas in the context of different areas of UN activity. Chapter 2 outlines the historical foundations of the United Nations and describes the various structures, politics, and processes within it as well as efforts at reform. Chapter 3 considers the major actors in the UN system, including NGOs, coalitions and blocs, small states and middle powers, and the United States and other major powers, as well as the UN secretary-general and the Secretariat. Chapter 4 deals with the UN's role in peace and security issues, including peacekeeping, enforcement, peacebuilding, humanitarian intervention, counterterrorism, and nuclear proliferation, with case studies of Somalia, Bosnia, the Democratic Republic of the Congo, and Darfur. In Chapter 5, which covers the role of the UN system in promoting development, we explore case studies of women and development and the MDGs and poverty alleviation. Chapter 6 analyzes the role of the UN in the evolution of international human rights norms with case studies of the anti-apartheid movement, the women's rights agenda, human trafficking, and the issues of genocide, crimes against humanity, and war crimes. Chapter 7 on **human security** deals with environmental degradation and health issues, with case studies of ozone and climate change and HIV/AIDS. It also includes a case study of statebuilding for human security in Haiti. Chapter 8 explores the questions of what the UN has done best, where it has fallen short, and whether and how it can make a difference in the world of the twenty-first century.

To aid readers in pursuing further research on the subject matter in the book, we have provided lists by topic area of sources for additional research at the end of the book along with Internet sites. The notes with each chapter are also an excellent place to start for learning more.

Notes

1. Inis L. Claude Jr., *The Changing United Nations* (New York: Random House, 1965), 32.

2. Christopher S. Wren, "Annan Says All Nations Must Cooperate," *New York Times*, September 6, 2000.

3. See, for example, Hans Morgenthau, *Politics Among Nations*, 4th ed. (New York: Alfred A. Knopf, 1967); and John J. Mearsheimer, "The False Promise of International Institutions," *International Security* 13, no. 3 (1994–1995): 5–49.

4. See, for example, Michael W. Doyle, "Liberalism and World Politics," *American Political Science Review* 80, no. 4 (December 1986): 1151–1169; Hedley Bull, *The Anarchical Society: A Study of Order in World Politics* (New York: Columbia University Press, 1977); Robert O. Keohane and Joseph S. Nye, *Power and Interdependence*, 3rd ed. (New York: Longman, 2001); and Robert O. Keohane and Lisa L. Martin, "The Promise of Institutionalist Theory," *International Security* 20, no. 1 (1995): 39–51.

5. See, for example, Ronnie Lipschutz, "Reconstructing World Politics: The Emergence of Global Civil Society," *Millennium: Journal of International Studies* 21, no. 3 (1992): 398–399; and Craig Warkentin, *Reshaping World Politics: NGOs, the Internet, and Global Civil Society* (Lanham, MD: Rowman and Littlefield, 2001).

6. See, for example, John Gerard Ruggie, "Multilateralism: The Anatomy of an Institution," in *Multilateralism Matters: The Theory and Praxis of an Institutional Form*, ed. John Gerard Ruggie (New York: Columbia University Press, 1993), 3–47; Martha Finnemore, *National Interests in International Society* (Ithaca: Cornell University Press, 1996); and Martha Finnemore and Kathryn Sikkink, "Taking Stock: The Constructivist Research Program in International Relations and Comparative Politics," *Annual Review of Political Science* 4 (2001): 391–416.

7. Michael Barnett and Martha Finnemore, *Rules for the World: International Organizations in Global Politics* (Ithaca: Cornell University Press, 2004).

8. Margaret P. Karns and Karen A. Mingst, *International Organizations: The Politics and Processes of Global Governance*, 2nd ed. (Boulder: Lynne Rienner, 2009).

9. Thomas G. Weiss and Ramesh Thakur, *Global Governance and the UN: An Unfinished Journey* (Bloomington: Indiana University Press, 2010).

10. Stewart Patrick and Shepard Forman, eds., *Multilateralism and U.S. Foreign Policy: Ambivalent Engagement* (Boulder: Lynne Rienner, 2002).

11. David M. Malone and Yuen Foong Khong, eds., *Unilateralism and U.S. Foreign Policy: International Perspectives* (Boulder: Lynne Rienner, 2003).

12. Joseph S. Nye Jr., *Bound to Lead: The Changing Nature of American Power* (New York: Basic Books, 1990); Joseph S. Nye, *The Paradox of American Power: Why the World's Only Superpower Can't Go It Alone* (Oxford: Oxford University Press, 2002).

International Regimes and Organizations

by David Galbreath

International relations encompasses the study of conflict and cooperation and international institutions are one of the most important mechanisms through which conflict and cooperation occur. Indeed, many would argue that international institutions have become important actors in international relations in their own right, transcending the sum of their parts. One only needs to look around today to see international institutions at work. For example, the United Nations (UN) is present throughout the world, from Afghanistan to Zambia, providing peacekeeping, food aid, water projects, health services and protection of children's rights, to name only a few tasks. International institutions help govern our life. The World Trade Organization (WTO) and Organization for Economic Cooperation and Development (OECD) help govern our trade and economic cooperation. Institutions like the European Union (EU) and Mercusur in Latin America help bring regions together. The North Atlantic Treaty Organization (NATO) and the African Union (AU) provide for regional security. Institutions like the Council of Europe and Organization for Security and Cooperation in Europe (OSCE) promote democracy and human rights. Most of these institutions in fact have multiple functions that are strategic, political, economic and cultural. These inter-governmental organizations often rely heavily on the work of international non-governmental organizations or INGOs such as the International Red Cross (IRC), Médecins Sans Frontières (Doctors without Borders), Amnesty International and Oxfam. Together, all of these institutions create a web of cooperation and collaboration that forms the foundation of international relations.

This chapter aims to explain the evolution and development of international institutions and to chart their contemporary relevance in international relations. Why do states find it necessary to cooperate? Where did the idea of international institutions originate? When was the first international organization created? What do international institutions do? Why do we have so many international institutions in the world today? What impact do international organizations have on international relations in general, and on individuals specifically? Such questions allow the reader to engage critically with the concept of international organizations and will inform the majority of this chapter.

COOPERATION AND INSTITUTIONS

Any examination of international institutions should begin with a discussion defining cooperation and institutions. Individually, it is clear what both of these terms mean but their relationship in terms of international relations is significantly more complex. Cooperation 'requires that the actions of separate individuals or institutions – which are not in pre-existent harmony – be brought into conformity with one another through a process of policy coordination' (Keohane 1984: 51). In other words, cooperation requires each party of the relationship to change their behaviour in relation to the behaviour of other parties. Importantly, it also distinguishes co-operation from harmony. States may cooperate to prevail in military and political conflict. Rich states may cooperate to keep themselves rich and poor states poor. 'International cooperation does *not necessarily* depend on altruism, idealism, personal honour, common purposes, internalised norms, or a shared belief in a set of values embedded in a culture' (Keohane 1988: 380, emphasis added). However, many states do cooperate because they share interests, ideals, norms, values and belief systems. A cooperative relationship demands that there be some level of trust between two or more parties. Not only are international institutions predicated on these shared understandings, but international institutions also offer an arena through which parties can witness the behaviour of other states.

Nevertheless, cooperation can occur outside of international institutions with a large proportion of cooperation between states occurring through bi-lateral relationships that are not dictated by institutions. However it remains that international institutions facilitate the greatest amount of cooperation. We can define international institutions as 'international social institutions characterized by behavioural patterns based on international norms and rules, which prescribe behavioural roles in recurring situations that lead to a convergence of reciprocal expectations' (Rittberger and Zangl 2006: 6). We can also identify two types of international institutions: international inter-governmental organizations and international regimes. The first set of international institutions is ordinarily what we refer to when discussing international organizations such as the UN, EU and OSCE. These institutions have a range of issue-areas that they address. On the other hand, Stephen Krasner has defined regimes as 'principles, norms, rules and decision-making procedures around which actor expectations converge in a given issue-area' (Krasner 1982: 185). In other words, international regimes are issue-specific. Overall, international regimes aim to coordinate communication about a specific issue, such as trade, whaling, air quality, and nuclear proliferation. International organizations differ from international regimes because they can engage in 'goal-directed activities' such as raising and spending money, policy-making, and making flexible choices (Keohane 1988: 384, fn. 2). In both cases international institutions provide for formalized cooperation in international relations and form a specific and complex area of study for students of international relations.

Why does cooperation occur in international relations? In politics, people come together to cooperate towards common and collective goals – common goals being goals that all can share and collective goals being those that can only be achieved if parties work together. At the domestic level political communities work in cooperation to provide common public services such as roads, telecommunications, disaster relief, and education. The average member of the population does not work specifically in any of these areas but instead pays the state (through taxation) to carry these services out on their behalf. The state and its institutions work together to meet the common needs of the population.

As the world becomes metaphorically smaller, states and their citizens are forming international institutions. Just as citizens act together within a state for common and collective goals, states come together in international institutions for common goals such as in 1815 with the creation of the Rhine River Commission. Today, the Rhine runs through Switzerland, Liechtenstein, Austria, Germany, France and the Netherlands. Historically, the Rhine was an important trade route for Western Europe so that during the 1815 Congress of Vienna states came together for the common goal of ensuring freedom of navigation on the river. Eventually, the commission developed into a regulatory and policing body and as early as the 1860s the commission developed provisions for regulating hazardous materials and water pollution. The Rhine River Commission (also known as the Central Commission for Navigation on the Rhine or CCNR) is important because affected states could come together to agree common rules and regulations for navigation along the Rhine. The commission is also important for being the first international organization and it still exists to this day.

Like citizens of a state, member states of an international institution are constrained by their membership. Before considering why states act together to form international institutions, it is important to first understand some underlying assumptions about international relations. The first assumption is that states desire ultimate sovereignty and control over their own geographical area, and, secondly, that states strive to maximize their sovereignty. These assumptions present us with something of a conundrum: if states desire to maximize their sovereignty, why would they agree to become members of an organization that by its very existence will constrain their sovereignty? The simple answer is that states are willing to sacrifice a bit of sovereignty to gain common and collective goals. For example, acquiring clean air is a common and collective good. Having clean air is common because everyone can use it, and collective because having clear air requires cooperation between all parties who would seek to benefit by having it. In other words, it only takes one bad polluter to make the air bad for the rest of us and therefore we must work together to avoid the collective bad of air pollution.

International institutions are ordinarily suited to address common and collective goals towards dealing with borderless problems such as water pollution, acid rain, malaria, HIV-AIDS, nuclear reactor disasters, terrorism, organized crime and the global economy. Furthermore, these problems require a huge amount of resources simply to address, much less to eliminate. The majority of states do not have the resources to combat such problems and consequently seek out other similar states to pool their resources akin to traditional military alliances where states act in unison to defeat, attack or prevent another state or group of states from acting contrary to their interests. The development of international institutions such as NATO and the OSCE is a contemporary development of traditional alliance politics.

BOX 9.3 THE COOPERATION DILEMMA

International institutions occur when states wish to maximize sovereignty but are willing to sacrifice in order to gain common and collective goods, as they realize that these goods are beyond their own individual capacities and that they need to pool resources

The development of international institutions can be surmised in two debates. The first debate concerns the importance of international institutions in the international system and whether international organizations are actors in their own right or simply a subject of their constituent parts (member states). The realist agenda argues that states are the key actors in international relations and international institutions represent the interests of their member states, especially those which have the most power. Realists argue that states are unlikely to invest in formal institutions to the extent that they cede power to that organization. Anarchy impedes international cooperation and thus reduces the importance of international institutions in international relations. The liberal agenda argues that international institutions can be important actors in international relations because states have a rational and strategic interest in investing in long-term cooperation and international institutions. Liberals argue that cooperation and interdependence produce grounds for stable, trusting relationships between states. Once created and imbued with powers, international institutions then affect their constituent member states. While both realists and liberals accept the anarchical state of the international system, there are core differences in their interpretation of cooperation.

BOX 9.4 REALIST *VERSUS* LIBERAL ASSUMPTIONS

- *Realist*: States are key actors; institutions represent interests; states do not wish to cede power
- *Liberal*: Institutions can be important actors; states have rational and strategic interests in long-term cooperation and interdependence; institutions can affect state behaviour

The second debate covers the reasons why states create and join international institutions. There are two theoretical sides to this debate: rationalism and constructivism. Rationalism assumes that actors will seek the strategy (or strategies) that benefits themselves. In the study of international institutions, the rationalist approach argues that cooperation can be mutually beneficial and that states come together in international institutions to reduce the transaction costs of such cooperation. International institutions also reduce the uncertainty of cooperation by providing information and stabilizing expectations. The rationalists argue that international institutions develop where there are mutual expectations of benefits from cooperation. Where the costs of cooperation are too great (e.g. too many restrictions, favourable conditions for others), it is unlikely that international institutions will emerge. Alternatively, constructivism argues that actors' decisions are determined by their own values and perceptions of the world around them. The constructivist (also referred to as reflective) approach concentrates on the importance of social interactions and international institutions. Constructivists argue that actors are not only acting in their own rational self-interest, but are also acting as a response to shared values and norms (e.g. economic, political culture). This approach does not look for a constellation of shared interests but rather a constellation of shared norms to explain the development of international institutions. Thus, while states may have a shared interest in a given issue-area, an international institution only forms once states have a shared understanding of the problem. The recent debates over carbon emission are a good illustration of the difficulties of cooperation in general and institutions specifically. All of the major greenhouse gas-producing countries accept that carbon emission is a problem leading to environmental damage. Nevertheless, global cooperation is extremely underdeveloped, even within an established organization like the EU.

The post-Cold War international system has witnessed a renewed interest in international institutions. Specifically, the second debate has been largely played out in terms of regional integration, primarily focusing on the development of the EU. Andrew Moravcsik (1997) emphasizes the role of interests and preferences in the development of the EU, while others such as Jeffrey Checkel (2001), Karin Fierke and Antje Wiener (1999) focus on the importance of norms and values in further integration and

BOX 9.5 RATIONALISM AND CONSTRUCTIVISM

- *Rationalism*: States will benefit themselves; cooperation is beneficial; cooperation reduces transaction costs and uncertainty
- *Constructivism*: Actors respond to shared values and norms

enlargement. However, these two approaches are not poles apart. Many authors, these included, have recognized interests and norms as connected (Schimmelfennig 2001). Rationalists have begun to look at the importance of social communication while constructivists have begun to focus on decision-making. As we look at specific international institutions more closely, we will see that both interests and norms are important in our study since they characterize the very institutions that form the basis of the study.

INTERNATIONAL INSTITUTIONS AND THEIR FUNCTIONS

International cooperation has been evident throughout history but international institutions only emerged in the early nineteenth century. The impetus for the first international institution was the European Napoleonic Wars of 1804–1815 and the defeat of Napoleon Bonaparte at Waterloo in March 1815, after which the victorious powers came together to organize a post-conflict Europe known as the Congress of Vienna (from September 1814 to June 1815). Borders were re-drawn, political leaders were removed or created, and colonies were confirmed or forfeited. While this was not so much a Congress as a place for informal discussions between powers, it was a concerted effort to seek cooperation and consensus across a great number of actors. The Congress of Vienna led to much longer lasting institutionalized forms of cooperation, including the previously discussed Rhine River Commission. The Congress also resulted in a condemnation of slavery, confirming the move towards the end of the trans-Atlantic slave trade.

By the early part of the twentieth century Europe was once again at war. The First World War (1914–18) had many causes, one of which was the breakdown of an informal, non-institutionalized arrangement between the great powers in Europe, orchestrated by Germany's Otto van Bismarck. Following the end of the war the victorious powers in Europe came together in the Paris Peace Conference (January 1918 to January 1919) to dictate the terms of peace. The conference established the League of Nations in January 1919 as an attempt to prevent another great war. Prior to the creation of the League, there had been two peace conferences in The Hague in 1899 and 1907 which are largely considered to be the forerunners to an institutionalized attempt at peace (Scott 1973). The League had its first meeting in 1920 in London but was moved to Geneva later that year. The organization was devoted to conflict prevention through disarmament and diplomatic negotiation.

The structure of the League consisted of a Secretariat, a Council, and an Assembly; a structure that has maintained itself repeatedly in the formation of international institutions. The Secretariat worked as a civil service or bureaucracy and the Council had the authority to deal with any problem challenging international peace. Similar to the UN Security Council, the Council of the League of Nations initially had four permanent members – the United Kingdom, Italy, France and Japan – although it was originally intended to also have the United States as a fifth member. The Council also had a series of non-permanent members as determined by the Assembly. The Assembly met once a year, every September, to discuss the non-permanent membership of the Council and to discuss and decide on mechanisms to deal with any problems in the international community. Over time, the Assembly created seven other bodies – including the International Labour Organization (ILO), the Permanent Court of International Justice, and the World Health Organization (WHO) – all of which would eventually become part of the League's successor organization, the United Nations.

BOX 9.6 INSTITUTIONS OF THE LEAGUE OF NATIONS AND THE UN

League of Nations

- *Secretariat*: Led by Secretary General
- *Council*: Initially four permanent seats (France, Italy, Japan, United Kingdom)
- *Assembly*: Representatives of all member states (42 founding members)

United Nations

- *Secretariat*: Led by Secretary General
- *Security Council*: Five permanent seats (China, France, Russian Federation, UK, USA) and ten non-permanent members
- *General Assembly*: Representatives of all member-states (192 member-states at time of writing)
- *Economic and Social Council*: 54 seats allocated by region and voted for by the General Assembly
- *International Court of Justice*: 15 judges voted for by the General Assembly and Security Council
- *Trusteeship Council (suspended in 1994)*: Five permanent members of the Security Council

The League of Nations is most remembered for its failure to prevent the Second World War. However, the League of Nations had a beneficial influence on many areas of potential conflict that has largely gone unnoticed except by scholars of international institutions. Several cases are worth mentioning. After the First World War, Austria and Hungary were committed by the Treaty of Versailles (passed by the first act of the League of Nations in 1920) to pay substantial reparations to the victors of the war, the financial stress of which was forcing both states into bankruptcy. However, the League stepped into the crisis by arranging financial loans and thus preventing economic meltdown. Secondly, the League intervened in the dispute between the newly established states of Yugoslavia and Albania. After the war, Yugoslav troops still held Albanian territory but the League was instrumental in organizing a withdrawal of Yugoslav troops by 1921. (Ironically, however, the United Nations would find itself in the same region approximately eighty years later for very similar reasons.) Finally, the League resolved a conflict between the new states of Turkey and the UK-mandated Iraq regarding the city of Mosul. Formerly a part of the Ottoman Empire, Mosul was claimed by both the empire's successor state, Turkey, and by the British to become part of the new Iraq. The League sided with the British and Iraqis claiming protection of the Kurdish autonomy and by 1926 all parties agreed to the settlement. (However, the Kurdish struggle for a Kurdish state in Turkey and northern Iraq still haunts the region to this day.) In these events and many more, the League of Nations illustrated an ability to mediate between opposing forces and utilized observer missions, peacekeepers and diplomatic bargaining to encourage compliance – the same mechanisms used by many contemporary international institutions and especially the United Nations.

Although aimed at conflict prevention, the League of Nations could not stop the rise of a belligerent Germany, Italy and Japan. The failure of the League to act in the case of Japan's invasion of Chinese Manchuria in 1933 or the German invasion of Poland and Czechoslovakia in 1939 spelled the end of the organization. The organization also suffered as a result of the West's general disinterest in the League. The United States Senate never ratified the Treaty of Versailles (which would have brought the United States into the League) and the UK and France demonstrated a continued preference to work outside the confines of the organization. Eventually the onset of the Second World War ended all interest and faith in the League of Nations, although it officially continued to exist until 1946. Where the Napoleonic Wars and the First World War begot the Congress of Vienna and League of Nations respectively, the Second World War produced the United Nations, which in its turn would face even greater challenges to international peace and security.

Nearing the end of the Second World War the soon-to-be allied victors met at the Dumbarton Oaks Conference in Washington, DC, to establish a new international institution. From April to June 1945, fifty states met in San Francisco at the United Nations International Conference to discuss the Dumbarton Oaks recommendations, the result of which was the establishment of the United Nations and the creation of the UN Charter. The charter sets out four core aims: prevention of inter-state conflict, ensuring human rights, establishing international law and encouraging development. Such aims are similar to those of the League of Nations but the UN was empowered by its charter to be a much stronger actor and has consequently been able to be far more active than the League of Nations.

In many ways the structure of the UN mirrored that of the League: a secretariat, a council and an assembly, as well as a plethora of other councils and commissions. Importantly, the core institutions of the UN were located in New York. The United Nations is composed of six principal organs: the Secretariat, the General Assembly, the Security Council, the Economic and Social Council, the International Court of Justice and the Trusteeship Council. The Secretariat is the bureaucratic heart of the UN with almost 9,000 employees from 170 member states and headed by Secretary-General Ban Ki-Moon since 2007. The Secretary-General is not only the director of the UN Secretariat and the UN in general but is also chair of the UN Security Council. The General Assembly has representatives from each of the 192 member states and has the authority to pass resolutions affecting UN policies. There are also several bodies established under the General Assembly, including the Human Rights Council (see Mertus 2005). The

Security Council is the most visible organ in the United Nations for two reasons (Luck 2006). First, international politics is often played out in the Security Council, as seen in the lead-up to the 2003 US-led invasion of Iraq. Second, the Security Council is the only body that can give the UN the mandate to intervene in a military dispute and to permit UN peacekeepers.

The Economic and Social Council (ECOSOC) looks at the international aspects of economic and social issues. The council has 42 seats voted for by the General Assembly and allocated by geographic region. Through this forum, ECOSOC is able to make policy recommendations to other parts of the UN. ECOSOC coordinates several high-profile, autonomous specialized agencies, including the WHO, the UN Educational, Scientific and Cultural Organization (UNESCO) and the ILO. The International Court of Justice (not to be confused with the International Criminal Court) has 15 judges that need to be approved by both the General Assembly and the Security Council. The ICJ's role is to settle any legal disputes brought to it by member states and to issue legal advisory opinions when requested by other UN agencies. The first case brought to the ICJ was the *Corfu Channel Case (United Kingdom v. Albania)* submitted on 22 May 1947. At the time of writing, there have been 136 cases brought to the ICJ's attention. Finally, the UN Trusteeship Council was established to oversee decolonization and the establishment of state institutions. Following the independence of Palau (southern Pacific Ocean) in 1994, the Trusteeship voted to suspend operations. The Trusteeship Council can be recalled by a majority vote in the Security Council or General Assembly, or by its five permanent members (China, France, Russian Federation, UK and USA).

BOX 9.7 EXPANDED FUNCTIONS OF THE UN

- Avoidance of war
- Promotion of order and stability
- Maintaining international peace and security
- Functional cooperation
- Disarmament
- Socio-economic improvements
- Establishment of international law
- Encouraging human rights
- Encouraging development

The UN also has a huge network of other agencies and commissions, such as the International Monetary Fund (IMF), the World Bank, and the Universal Postal Union. These other agencies and commissions are collectively referred to as the UN System. Overall, there was a significant expansion of responsibilities and infrastructure from the League of Nations to the United Nations. The UN is the largest international institution in the world and has the ability to intervene in armed conflict, enforce resolutions through political, economic or military means, and even to dissolve states and validate new ones.

The Cold War played a major role in shaping the development of the UN – on one hand, the permanent seats on the Security Council helped keep the Cold War from becoming a hot war, on the other hand, the permanent seats allowed five nations to have a veto over UN actions rendering the UN less effective and less responsive in many cases. The UN is ever changing, although some would argue that it is not changing fast enough. Reform in the UN is difficult because many member states have an interest in maintaining the current structure, specifically the structure of the Security Council. While many parts of the UN are evolving, the Security Council remains rooted in the same structure as was established in 1945, much to the frustration of those who seek to see a more contemporary and representative Security Council.

Regional institutions

There are many global international institutions, but many would argue that regional institutions are of equal and arguably more immediate relevance to individual lives. As Box 9.8 illustrates, every geographic region in the world has established a regional institution, although there continue to be many states that remain outside regional institutions. The box also shows that Europe is particularly heavily laden with regional institutions, in many cases with overlapping functions. Other regions, such as Asia and Africa, have fewer and weaker regional institutions. This section looks at prominent regional organizations and considers why some regions are better organized than others.

Since the Second World War Europe has seen a significant growth in the number of institutions as well as a proliferation of their functions. The EU is Europe's most visible regional institution and it has the widest remit in terms of functions. The road to the EU began with the establishment of the European Coal and Steel Community (ECSC)

BOX 9.8 PROMINENT REGIONAL INSTITUTIONS

Region	Organization
Africa	African Union (formerly OAU)
	Southern African Development Community
Asia	Association of Southeast Asian Nations
Europe	Council of Europe
	European Union
	North Atlantic Treaty Organization*
	Organization for Security and Cooperation in Europe (OSCE) (formerly CSCE)
	Western European Union
North America	North American Free Trade Agreement
	Organization of American States
South America	Andean Community
	Mercosur
	Union of South American Nations

Note: *Trans-Atlantic regional institutions

in 1951, The founding members of this were West Germany, France, Italy, Belgium, the Netherlands and Luxemburg. On the basis of the ECSC, the same countries came together in the European Economic Community (later to be renamed the European Community in 1992) and the European Atomic Energy Community (EURATOM) in 1957 (Treaties of Rome). For a generation there were four major institutions in the Communities – the Council of Ministers, the Commission, the Assembly (Parliament) and the European Court of Justice. There are now five with the addition of the Court of Auditors. In 1992, the Treaty of Maastricht was signed, creating the European Union which then came into effect in November 1993.

The EU that we have today is unlike any other international institution, having assumed the role of governance with involvement in most areas of public policy, from consumer safety to foreign policy. Importantly, however, the EU remains closely linked to its member states, particularly France and Germany. The current pillar system, created in 1992, established a procedure for decision-making in different issue-areas and represents the breadth of issues dealt with by the EU. The first pillar corresponds to the original purposes of the European Economic Community: the movement of people, money and trade. The second pillar deals with Common Foreign and Security Policy (CFSP) and European Security and Defence Policy (ESDP). The third pillar deals with regional police issues, such as organized crime, corruption and terrorism.

BOX 9.9 THE EUROPEAN UNION

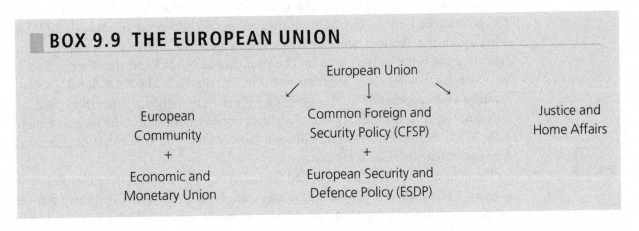

The EU is an ever evolving and developing organization and has undergone a variety of major changes since its inception. Firstly, the EU is in the process of negotiating a European Constitution that would increase the state-like status of the EU but which has so far failed to galvanize the necessary support from the member states. Current negotiations to revive the Constitutional Treaty primarily focus on issues related to proposed changes which would see the pillar structure replaced by increased decision-making power for the member states at the EU capital. Secondly, the EU expanded to include 12 new members in 2004 and 2007 and consequently experienced a significant change in political culture.

Predecessor organizations to the EU primarily focused on improving finance and trade. The emergence of policy issues such as human rights, democracy and social protection on the EU agenda is a relatively recent occurrence. However, the Council of Europe – founded in 1950 by Belgium, Denmark, France, Ireland, Italy, Luxembourg, the Netherlands, Norway, Sweden and the UK and not to be confused with the EU's

European Council – was created in 1950 to address such issues. Where the European Communities were aimed at rebuilding Europe, the Council of Europe was aimed at ensuring that war and genocide did not recur based on the principles of the European Convention for Human Rights. The Council has a Parliamentary Assembly (drawn from national parliaments), a Committee of Ministers who represent each state, a Commissioner for Human Rights and the European Court of Human Rights (not to be confused with the EU's European Court of Justice). Following the end of the Cold War the Council of Europe also expanded to take in more states to the East, including the Russian Federation in 1996. Although the EU has become an increasingly substantial actor with these issues, the Council of Europe still remains an important voice for human rights and democracy.

The final two prominent European institutions are NATO and the OSCE. NATO's founding in 1949 was in response to perceived Soviet plans to expand into Western Europe (see Lindley-French 2006) and saw many Western European states (with the notable exceptions of Ireland and Spain), the US and Canada come together in a collective defence organization in response to the Soviet threat. Following the formation of NATO, the Soviet Union and its allies came together in the so-called Warsaw Pact to form a counter-collective defence organization. NATO's stronghold on defence politics was maintained throughout the duration of the Cold War but was later complemented by the creation of the Conference on Security and Cooperation in Europe, or CSCE, during the period of détente (Galbreath 2007) in 1961 when the Western allies and the Soviets were on diplomatic speaking terms following the brink of nuclear war. The countries of NATO and the Warsaw Pact as well as neutral states came together to formulate the Helsinki Final Act to increase stability and cooperation in Europe. The Final Act is divided into three areas of cooperation: political-military, economic and environmental, and the human dimension. While the period of détente did not last for long, the CSCE has continued to function albeit with limited impact.

The end of the Cold War changed both NATO and the CSCE although not in ways that many observers would have expected. NATO remains a collective defence organization but now operates out-of-area as in the cases of Afghanistan and, to a limited extent, in the Darfur region of Sudan. The CSCE changed from the Conference to the Organization in 1994 the same time as it developed a secretariat, council, and assembly. In addition, the now OSCE developed mechanisms of conflict prevention such as the Conflict Prevention Centre and the High Commissioner on National Minorities. Both NATO and the OSCE would expand to the East, with the former including several former Soviet republics (the Baltic States) and the latter encompassing the entire former Soviet region.

An examination of the EU, Council of Europe, NATO and the OSCE reveals two specific points. The first is that Europe, unlike any other region, has become highly institutionalized. The second point is that the increasing enlargement and integration of the EU is encroaching more and more on the development and enlargement of alternative organizations. Already another European institution, the Western European Union, has been subsumed by the EU. The EU now has security and defence mechanisms and focuses intensely on issues such as human rights and democracy as well as the original issues of finance and trade. Additionally, all EU member states maintain membership of one or more additional institutions. For instance, the UK is a member (or participating state in the case of the OSCE) of all four institutions and consequently questions are increasingly being asked concerning how such significant functional and membership overlaps can be maintained in Europe.

No other region maintains the complex institutional fabric of Europe, but nevertheless, every region has institutions. North America is partially integrated into the European institutions, with US and Canadian membership of NATO and the OSCE, and is additionally a member of the North American Free Trade Agreement (NAFTA). NAFTA was created in 1994 by the governments of Canada, the US and Mexico following a 1988 free-trade agreement between the US and Canada (see Duina 2006). NAFTA aims to reduce trade barriers (whilst protecting intellectual copyright) between the three states, but does not reflect the structure of several of the other institutions that we have seen so far in this chapter. Instead, it is a multilateral treaty governed jointly by the three states. What makes NAFTA more than a trade agreement and, rather, a regional institution worth examining here is the subsidiary bodies of the North American Agreement on Environmental Cooperation (NAAEC) and the North American Agreement on Labour Cooperation (NAALC). Negotiators of the original NAFTA articulated two potential problems with its creation – firstly, that environmentally destructive companies would simply leave Canada and the US and move to Mexico and, secondly, that labour standards would suffer – and consequently the NAAEC and the NAALC were created. Both these organs have councils of ministers as well as tri-national secretariats to support them. Other forms of cooperation exist in North America but do so outside the confines of a regional institution, perhaps as a result of the limited number of potential member states (as opposed to Europe).

South American and Asian regional cooperation has been similar to the North American experience. Both regions have developed major economic institutions: Mercosur (Southern Common Market) and ASEAN respectively. Mercosur, which maintains a Committee of Permanent Representatives in Montevideo, Uraguay, was born out of the economic relations between Argentina and Brazil in the 1980s (see Manzetti 1993; Carranza 2003). In 1991, Argentina, Brazil, Paraguay and Uruguay came together to negotiate a common market, resulting in the Treaty of Asunción that was later developed into a regional institution by the 1994 Treaty of Ouro Preto. Mercosur suffered from the general economic slump in South America and was hit especially hard by the Argentine economic collapse of 2001. However, Mercosur enlarged to include Venezuela in 2006 and is now negotiating to join with the Andean Community (another trade bloc) to form the Union of South American Nations.

ASEAN was founded as an anti-communist organization by Indonesia, Malaysia, the Philippines, Singapore and Thailand in 1967 and has since expanded and evolved to include six more countries including Vietnam, Cambodia, Laos, Myanmar, the Philippines and Singapore. East Timor currently has candidate-state status in the organization. ASEAN has expanded from its anti-communist roots and now focuses on being a larger economic and security community, such as the EU and the early CSCE respectively (Narine 1998). ASEAN also works to expand the cultural exchange between member states in a function similar to the Council of Europe. The largest problem facing ASEAN is Myanmar's (formerly Burma's) membership which has prevented ASEAN/EU trade talks. Unlike the OSCE, ASEAN does not factor domestic politics into its negotiations.

Africa's relationship with regional institutions is less visible. A pan-African institution has gone through several phases from the Organization of African States to the Organization of African Unity and today's African Union is a descendant of these past institutions (Magliveras and Naldi 2002). The African Union was established in 2002, following a campaign to resurrect an African regional organization by the Libyan government. At the time of writing, every African state – except Morocco – is a member of the African Union. The African Union largely adopted principal organs akin to those of the EU when the Constitutive Act of the African Union (2001) established an executive council, a commission, a body of permanent representatives and an assembly. Any comparisons to the EU, however, should consider that the African Union still very much remains an inter-governmental institution, unlike its European counterpart. The African Union's biggest challenge to date has been the ongoing military crisis in the Darfur region in Sudan. Begrudgingly, the Sudanese government has allowed African Union peacekeepers into the Darfur region, but only in low numbers and the African Union has not had the resources to bring peace to the Darfur region, much less limit the violence. Additionally, African Union peacekeepers have been frequent targets of the violence. The Darfur crisis not withstanding, the African Union has made great strides towards creating cooperation in the region.

CONCLUSION

International relations have increasingly become organized around international institutions, as is evident with the global presence of the UN and the regional presence of the EU, ASEAN and the African Union. In some cases, member states have bequeathed their institutions with functions that challenge the primacy of the state but this phenomenon largely seems limited to Europe. In other regional institutions, member states still maintain considerable control over their own politics. Nevertheless, by the very act of entering into an international institution, member states have agreed to be bound by certain constraints as a result of common rules and procedures, even when these rules and procedures appear to be a redundant function. Most importantly, international institutions are about serving states, and also about serving the citizens of those member states. International institutions have come to affect us in our everyday life, from the food we eat and the products we buy, to the cars we drive and rights we have.

REFERENCES AND FURTHER READING

Carranza, M. E. (2003) 'Can Mercosur Survive? Domestic and International Constraints on Mercosur', *Latin American Politics and Society* 45: 67–103.

Checkel, J. T. (2001) 'Why Comply? Social Learning and European identity change', *International Organization* 55: 553–88.

Duina, F. (2006) 'Varieties of Regional Integration: The EU, NAFTA and Mercosur', *Journal of European Integration* 28: 247–75.

Fierke, K., and Wiener, A. (1999) 'Constructing Institutional Interests: EU and NATO Enlargement', *Journal of European Public Policy* 6: 721–42.

Galbreath, D. J. (2007) *The Organization for Security and Cooperation in Europe*. London: Routledge.

Gordenker, L. (2005) *The UN Secretary-General and Secretariat*. London: Routledge.

Grieco, J. M. (1988) 'Anarchy and the Limits of Cooperation: A Realist Critique of the Newest Liberal Institutionalism', *International Organization* 42: 485–507.

Keohane, R. O. (1984) *After Hegemony: Cooperation and Discord in the World Political Economy*. Princeton, NJ: Princeton University Press.

Keohane, R. O. (1988) 'International Institutions: Two Approaches', *International Studies Quarterly* 32: 379–96.

Keohane, R. O. and Nye, J. S. (1974) 'Transgovernmental Relations and International Organizations', *World Politics* 27: 39–62.

Krasner, S. D. (1982) 'Structural Causes and Regime Consequences: Regimes as Intervening Variables', *International Organization* 36: 1–21.

Lindley-French, J. (2006) *The North Atlantic Treaty Organization: The Enduring Alliance*. London: Routledge.

Luck, E. C. (2006) *The UN Security Council: Practice & Promise*. London: Routledge.

Magliveras, K. D. and Naldi, G. J. (2002) 'The African Union: A New Dawn for Africa?', *International and Comparative Law Quarterly* 51: 415–425.

Manzetti, L. (1993) 'The Political Economy of Mercosur', *Journal of Interamerican Studies and World Affairs* 35: 101–41.

Mertus, J. (2005) *United Nations and Human Rights*. London: Routledge.

Moravcsik, A. (1997) 'Taking Preferences Seriously: A Liberal Theory of International Politics', *International Organization* 51: 513–53.

Narine, S. (1998) 'ASEAN and the Management of Regional Security', *Pacific Affairs* 71: 195–214.

Peterson, M. J. (2005) *The United Nations General Assembly*. London: Routledge.

Rittberger, V. and Zangl, B. (2006) *International Organization: Polity, Politics and Policies*. Basingstoke: Palgrave.

Ruchay, D. (1995) 'Living with water: Rhine River basin management', *Water Science and Technology* 31: 27–32.

Schimmelfennig, F. (2001) 'The Community Trap: Liberal Norms, Rhetorical Action, and the Eastern Enlargement of the European Union', *International Organization* 55: 47–80.

Scott, G. (1973) *The Rise and Fall of the League of Nations*. London: Hutchinson.

Stein, A. A. (1990) *Why Nations Cooperate: Circumstances and Choice in International Relations*. Ithaca, New York: Cornell University Press.

Introduction

by John McCormick and Jonathan Olsen

We cannot aim at anything less than the union of Europe as a whole, and we look forward with confidence to the day when that union will be achieved.

—Winston Churchill, The Hague Congress, May 1948

That such an unnecessary and irrational project as building a European superstate was ever embarked on will seem in future years to be perhaps the greatest folly of the modern era.

—Margaret Thatcher, Statecraft: Strategies for a Changing World, 2003

The European Union is the world's wealthiest capitalist marketplace, the world's biggest trading power, and—along with the United States—one of the two most influential political actors in the world. Its emergence has changed the character and definition of Europe, helped bring to the region the longest uninterrupted spell of general peace in its recorded history, and altered the balance of global power by helping Europeans reassert themselves on the world stage. By building a single market and developing common policies in a wide range of different areas, Europeans have come to relate to each other differently and have set aside many of their traditional differences in the interests of cooperation. The EU has brought fundamental changes to the way Europe functions, the way it is seen by others, and the way others—most notably the United States—work with Europe.

And yet the European project has raised many doubts and attracted many critics, even more so in the wake of a severe debt crisis that is testing the staying power of the euro, the EU's common currency. Some question the wisdom of European states transferring authority to a joint system of governance that is often criticized for its elitism and its lack of accountability and transparency. Others debate whether the EU works as efficientl as it might and whether it has outgrown itself. It is often faulted for its inability to reach common agreement on critical foreign and security policy issues and to match its economic and political power with military power.

Skeptics have routinely drawn attention to the EU's economic difficulti (such as sluggish economic growth and pockets of high unemployment), to its mixed record on dealing with ethnic and religious diversity, and to worries about demographic trends as birthrates decline and Europeans become older. For journalists and academics it has become almost de rigueur to talk and write of the crises in European governance, to point with alarm and foreboding at the latest example of a failure by European leaders to agree, and to question the long-term viability of the EU. Indeed, in the light of recent economic problems, some have even begun to doubt whether the European project will survive or whether the EU can truly be considered a world powerhouse.

In a recent editorial in the *New York Times*, Timothy Garton Ash argued that to include the EU with the United States and China in a "global Big Three" would be to invite laughter from elites in Beijing, Washington, or other world capitals. For Garton Ash, the crisis in the eurozone had demonstrated that the "five great drivers of European unification"—the legacy of "never again" left behind by World War II; the Soviet threat; the determination of Germany, as Europe's economic powerhouse, to sacrifice its own interests for those of "Europe"; the desire of Eastern European countries to belong to a common Europe; and the assumption that the EU would mean a continuous rise in living standards—have been exhausted. If the EU is really going to play the role it sees itself as playing, Garton Ash concludes, then it will have to pursue a course of more thoroughgoing integration, with a common identity and more comprehensive and muscular policies, from the social and economic spheres to—most especially—foreign affairs.[1]

Meanwhile, many Europeans are puzzled and uncertain about how the EU functions and what difference it makes to their lives. Americans are even more puzzled; many are—or at least have been, until recently—only vaguely aware of its existence and do not yet fully understand what difference it has made to Europe or to transatlantic relations. American political leaders are more attuned to its implications, as are corporate and financial leaders who have had to learn to deal as much with a twenty-eight-member regional grouping as with each of the individual states in the EU; even American tourists have noticed a difference as they use the euro in place of many different national currencies. But doubts remain about the bigger picture and about what difference the EU has made. To complicate matters, there is no agreement on just how we should define and understand the EU. It is not a European superstate, and suggestions that it might one day become a United States of Europe are greeted with a volatile mixture of enthusiasm and hostility.

The origins of the EU, and the motives behind European integration, are relatively clear. Frustrated and appalled by war and conflict, many Europeans argued over the centuries in favor of setting aside national differences in the collective interest. The first serious thoughts about a peaceful and voluntary union came after the horrors of World War I, but the concept matured following the devastation of World War II, when the most serious Europeanists spoke of replacing national governments with a European federation. They dreamed of integrating European economies and removing controls on the movement of people, money, goods, and services; they were driven by the desire to promote peace and to build a single European market that could compete with the United States.

The first tangible step came in April 1951 with the signing of the Treaty of Paris, which created the European Coal and Steel Community (ECSC), set up at least in part to prove a point about the feasibility and benefits of regional integration. Progress in the 1950s and 1960s was modest, but then the European Economic Community (EEC) was launched, membership began to expand, the goals of integration became more ambitious, and we now have today's European Union: an entity that has its own institutions and body of laws, twenty-eight member states and more than 500 million residents, a common currency used by more than half its members, and increasing agreement on a wide range of common policy areas. The Cold War–era political and economic divisions between Western and Eastern Europe have almost disappeared, and it is now less realistic to think of European states in isolation than as partners in an ever-changing European

Map 0.1 The European Union

Union. The fudge-word *integration* is used more often than *unification* to describe what has been happening, but those who champion the EU suggest that political union of some kind is almost inevitable. It may not be a United States of Europe, and it may turn out to be a loose association in which more power rests with the member states, but they find it hard to imagine a future in which European political union is not a reality.

Like it or not, the EU cannot be ignored, and the need to better understand how it works and what difference it makes becomes more evident by the day. Hence this book, written mainly for students in courses on European politics in the United States and Canada. In three parts it introduces the EU, goes through the steps in its development, explains how it works, and provides an overview of its policy activities.

Part 1 (chapters 1–4) provides context by first surveying the most important theories and concepts of regional integration and then showing how and why the EU has evolved. Giving the background on the earliest ideas about European unification sets the scene for the creation of the ECSC, whose founding members were France, West Germany, Italy, Belgium, the Netherlands, and Luxembourg. This was followed in 1957 by the signing of the two Treaties of Rome, which created the EEC and the European Atomic Energy Community (Euratom). With the same six members as the ECSC, the EEC set out to build an integrated multinational economy among its members, to achieve a customs union, to encourage free trade, and to harmonize standards, laws, and prices among its members. It witnessed greater productivity, channeled new investment into industry and agriculture, and became more competitive in the world market.

By the late 1960s, the EEC had all the trappings of a new level of European government, based mainly in Brussels, the capital of Belgium. Analysts refused to describe it as a full-blown political system, but it had its own executive and bureaucracy (the European Commission), its own protolegislature (the European Parliament), its own judiciary (the Court of Justice), and its own legal system. Over time, the word *Economic* was dropped from the name, giving way to the European Community (EC). Its successes drew new members, starting with Britain, Denmark, and Ireland in 1973, and moving on to Greece, Portugal, and Spain in the 1980s, East Germany joining via German unification, and Austria, Finland, and Sweden joining in the 1990s. The most recent round of enlargement came in 2004–07 with the addition of twelve mainly Eastern European member states, including Hungary, Poland, and the three former Soviet Baltic states, and Croatia became the EU's newest member in 2013. The character and reach of integration have been changed along the way with revisions to the founding treaties:

- In 1987 the Single European Act (SEA) led to the elimination of almost all remaining barriers to the movement of people, money, goods, and services among the twelve member states.
- In 1993 the Maastricht Treaty on European Union committed the EC to the creation of a single currency, a common citizenship, and a common foreign and security policy, and gave new powers over law and policy to the EC institutions. It also made the EC part of a broader new entity called the European Union.

- In 1998 and 2003 the treaties of Amsterdam and Nice built on these changes, fine-tuned the powers of the institutions, and helped prepare the EU for new members from Eastern Europe.
- An attempt was made in 2002–04 to provide focus and permanence by replacing the accumulated treaties with a European constitution. But the finished product was lengthy, detailed, and controversial, and it had to be ratified by every EU member state before it could come into force. When French and Dutch voters turned it down in 2005, there was another brief "crisis" before European leaders reached agreement in 2007 to draw up a new treaty based on much of the content of the failed constitution.
- The resulting Treaty of Lisbon fundamentally reformed several of the EU's institutions and attempted to give more coherence to the Union's policies, even while avoiding the language and trappings of a constitution that had been unpopular with many EU citizens.

The European Union today is the largest economic bloc in the world, accounting for one-fourth of global gross domestic product (GDP) and about 20 percent of global trade. It has replaced many of its national currencies with a new single currency, the euro, which has taken its place alongside the U.S. dollar and the Japanese yen as one of the world's primary currencies (its recent problems notwithstanding). There is now virtually unlimited free movement of people, money, goods, and services among most of its member states. The EU has its own flag (a circle of twelve gold stars on a blue background) and its own anthem (the "Ode to Joy" from Beethoven's Ninth Symphony); national passports have been replaced with a uniform EU passport, and in many ways Brussels has become the new capital of Europe.

Part 2 (chapters 5–10) looks at the European institutions, explaining how they work and how they relate to each other. Their powers and authority have grown steadily since the 1950s, although their work is often misunderstood by Europeans, and analysts continue to disagree over their character and significance. There are five main institutions:

- *The European Commission.* Based in Brussels, this is the executive and administrative branch of the EU, responsible for developing new EU laws and policies and for overseeing their implementation.
- *The Council of the EU.* Also based in Brussels, this is the major decision-making body of the EU, made up of government ministers

from each of the member states. Working with the European Parliament, the Council makes the votes that turn Commission proposals into European law.

- *The European Parliament.* Divided among Strasbourg, Luxembourg, and Brussels, the members of the European Parliament are directly elected to five-year terms by the voters of the member states. Although it cannot introduce proposals for new laws, Parliament can discuss Commission proposals, and it has equal powers with the Council of Ministers over adoption.
- *The European Court of Justice.* Based in Luxembourg, the Court interprets national and EU law and helps build a common body of law that is uniformly applied throughout the member states. It bases its decisions on the treaties, which in some respects function as a constitution of the EU.
- *The European Council.* This is less an institution than a forum, consisting of the political leaders of the member states. They meet at least four times per year to make broad decisions on policy, the details of which are worked out by the Commission and the Council of the EU.

Part 3 (chapters 11–16) focuses on the policies pursued by the European Union, looking at what integration has meant for the member states and for Europeans themselves. Covering economic, monetary, agricultural, cohesion, environmental, social, foreign, and security policies, this section examines the EU policy-making process, identifies the key influences on that process, and looks at its consequences and implications. The final chapter focuses on relations between the EU and the United States, which have blown hot and cold over the years.

Because European integration continues to be a work in progress, with a final destination that remains unclear, the relative balance of power among national governments and EU institutions is still evolving. That balance will continue to change as more countries join the EU and as integration reaches further into the lives of Europeans. All of this raises the key question: Why should Americans care about the EU? More specifically: What does it matter on this side of the Atlantic, and what effect will these changes have on our lives?

The most immediate implications are economic. Through most of the Cold War, the U.S. had it relatively good: it was the world's biggest national economy and national exporter, it had the world's strongest and

Table 0.1 The EU in Figures

	Area (Thousand Square Miles)	Population (Millions)	Gross Domestic Product ($ Billion)	Per Capita Gross National Income ($)
Germany	137	82.3	3,571	43,980
France	212	62.8	2,773	42,420
United Kingdom	94	62.0	2,432	37,780
Italy	116	60.5	2,195	35,330
Spain	195	46.0	1,491	30,990
Netherlands	16	16.6	836	49,730
Sweden	174	9.4	538	53,230
Poland	121	38.3	514	12,480
Belgium	12	10.7	512	46,160
Austria	32	8.4	418	48,300
Denmark	17	5.5	333	60,390
Greece	51	11.4	299	25,030
Finland	130	5.4	266	48,420
Portugal	36	10.7	238	21,250
Ireland	27	4.5	217	38,580
Czech Republic	30	10.5	215	18,520
Romania	92	21.5	180	7,910
Hungary	36	10.0	140	12,730
Slovakia	19	5.5	96	16,070
Croatia	21	4.4	64	13,850
Luxembourg	1	0.5	59	78,130
Bulgaria	43	7.5	54	6,550
Slovenia	8	2.0	50	23,610
Lithuania	25	3.3	43	12,280
Latvia	25	2.3	28	12,350
Cyprus	4	1.1	25	29,450
Estonia	17	1.3	22	15,200
Malta	0.1	0.4	9	18,620
TOTAL	1,691	504.8	17,616	33,982
United States	3,718	310.4	15,094	48,450
China	3,705	1,341.0	7,298	4,930
Japan	146	126.5	5,867	45,180
Brazil	3,286	195.0	2,477	10,720
Russia	6,593	143.0	1,858	10,400
India	1,269	1,225.0	1,848	1,410
Canada	3,852	34.0	1,736	45,560
World	57,309	6,894.6	69,971	9,488

Source: Population figures for 2010 from the UN Population Division, http://www.un.org/esa /population. Economic figures for 2011 from the World Bank, 2012, http://data.worldbank.org. Eurozone states indicated in boldface.

most respected currency, its corporations dominated the international marketplace and sold their products and services all over the world, and it led the world in the development of new technology. But much has changed in recent decades with the rise of competition first from Japan, then from Europe, and increasingly from China and India. The U.S. still has the world's biggest national economy, but the combined European market is nearly 20 percent bigger, and its population is nearly two-thirds bigger. European corporations are becoming bigger, more numerous, and more competitive; and the EU long ago displaced the U.S. as the world's biggest exporter and importer. And as one of the world's economic powers, naturally the EU's economic problems also have global economic significance.

All of this also applies to the bilateral relationship between the U.S. and EU. The U.S. does about one-fifth of its merchandise trade with the EU, which is the source of about two-thirds of all the foreign direct investment in the United States and Canada, most of it coming from Britain, the Netherlands, and Germany. Subsidiaries of European companies employ several million Americans—more than the affiliate of all other countries combined—and account for about 15 percent of all manufacturing jobs in the United States and Canada. U.S. corporations, meanwhile, have made their biggest overseas investments in the EU. We often see and hear worried analyses in North America about the rise of China, but while the volume of Chinese imports to the U.S. is certainly catching up with that from the EU, Europe is still by far the most important economic partner of the United States.

The rise of the EU also has important political implications for North America. During the Cold War the most critical political relationship in the world was that between the United States and the Soviet Union—much else that happened in the world was determined by the attempts of the two adversaries to outwit and outmaneuver one another. With the collapse of the USSR and the end of the Cold War, it became usual to see the United States described as the world's last remaining superpower, and even perhaps as a hyperpower. But while the United States is unmatched in the size, reach, and firepower of its military, globalization has helped make political and economic relationships more important than investments in the ability to wage war. The U.S. spends almost as much on defense every year as the rest of the world combined, but this has not guaranteed its security, and in the view of many critics has actually made both the U.S. and the world less safe.

Meanwhile, the political influence of the EU has grown. Its economic might cannot be ignored, its policy positions are often less controversial than many of those taken by the United States (particularly toward the Middle East), and while the U.S. is associated (not always fairly) with hard power (coercion, threats, and the use of military force), the EU is associated with soft power (diplomacy, economic opportunity, and negotiation). The contrast is clear in the records of the U.S. and the EU on the promotion of democracy. Recent American leaders have made much of the importance of spreading democracy, but they have invested more time and money in using military means to achieve their objectives. Meanwhile, the promise of access to the European marketplace or even—for the select few—of membership in the European Union has arguably had a greater effect on promoting lasting democratic change and economic development, at least for Europe's closest neighbors. It was reasoning such as this that was behind the award to the European Union in 2012 of the Nobel Prize for Peace.

Just in the past few years, the relative roles of the United States and the European Union in the international system have been transformed. During the Cold War, Western Europe relied on the United States for security guarantees and economic investment. The two partners gave the impression that they saw eye to eye and made many public statements of solidarity. But behind the scenes there were tensions and crises as they disagreed over policy and over how to deal with the Soviet threat. Since the end of the Cold War, the disagreements have spilled into the open. The two are now economic competitors, Europeans are less willing to accede to U.S. policy leadership, and the two have become increasingly aware of what divides them. They differ not just over the use of military power but on how to deal with many international problems (including terrorism, climate change, nuclear proliferation, and the ArabIsraeli problem) and on a wide range of social values and norms. The result has been the emergence of two models of government, two sets of opinions about how the world works, and two sets of possible responses to pressing international concerns.

For all these reasons, we cannot ignore the European Union, nor can we understand the world today without understanding how the EU has altered the balance of global power. Not everyone is convinced that European integration is a good idea or that the EU has been able to fully capitalize on its assets and resources, but—like it or not—the changes it has wrought cannot be undone. The pace of global political and economic change is accelerating, and the results of the European experiment have fundamentally changed the way in which the world functions and the place of the United States in the international system.

Notes

1. Timothy Garton Ash, "Can Europe Survive the Rise of the Rest?," *New York Times*, September 2, 2012, B5.

Nationalism

by Alan Finlayson

You are a nationalist. You may or may not have a strong sense of belonging to a particular country but you are still a nationalist. You may like to think of yourself as a twenty-first-century citizen of the world. Perhaps you use the internet to chat with people from the United States or the Ukraine, speak several languages and feel more attached to Manchester, Glasgow, Cardiff or Belfast than to England, Scotland, Wales or Ireland. But you are a nationalist alongside those who openly claim to prefer 'our' ways to 'theirs' and relish the opportunity to wave a national flag and sing an anthem.

At a time of much discussed 'globalisation', when nationally based governments seem to have less power than a century ago, culture is increasingly dominated by largely American 'global' media and many people travel freely across borders, the world is still largely nationalist. The independent and largely homogeneous nation with its own state is still the primary shape of the otherwise varied political structures under which most of us live. Our cultural habits and attitudes may increasingly be fluid but arguments about them still take place within and between nations. Perhaps most obviously, though still significantly, we think of the world largely in terms of nations and national peoples. Our 'mental map' of the world generally divides it into sovereign states and classifies people, albeit loosely, according to their nationality.

Nationalism is not just something that happens 'over there' in places you only ever hear about on the evening news. It is not just something that involves warfare and atrocity. Nationalism has shaped, and continues to shape, many aspects of the political make-up of our continent and country. For these reasons, because of all these facts, you and I are nationalists.

But, despite this fundamental significance and ubiquity, the phenomenon of nationalism presents something of a challenge to theorists and analysts of political ideology. It does not offer a clear, systematic body of doctrine that can be transplanted and reapplied wholesale from one context to another. By its very nature, the claims of nationalist ideology vary according to the location in which they are found. They are concerned with the singular nature of an individual nation. An ideology such as socialism has been thought about, reflected upon, revised and developed by theorists in many different historical, cultural and geographical contexts, each seeking to draw on an initial body of theory and to apply or develop it in accordance with their particular circumstances. But nationalism, which has also been thought about and practised in many different places, is not so clearly based around core themes and propositions as something such as socialism. It does not immediately lend itself to the kind of excavation of ideas and their historical development and deployment that one may undertake with regard to other political ideologies. Indeed, nationalism, until relatively recently, has been somewhat neglected by political theorists (at least explicitly) and has more often been investigated by historians and sociologists, who tend to understand it as a form of social or political movement or a general idea rather than a political ideology.

This chapter will examine nationalism in a way that leads us into wider questions about the nature of ideology and the ways in which it may be conceptualised. We will begin by looking further at some of the things analysts have said about nationalism as an ideology and the different interpretations they have advanced. Then we will consider some of the ways in which nationalism has been understood as the product of a particular kind of historical period or epoch. The third section will consider more broadly the relationship between ideologies and social movements and look at the way ideologies such as conservatism or socialism often combine with nationalism to produce powerful and successful political movements. It will also look at some recent developments in political theory which have posited it as a viable way of providing solidarity or community within a polity. By way of conclusion we will consider the question of whether or not nationalism is likely to recede in the face of so-called globalisation.

Nationalism as ideology

As you will have seen in earlier chapters of this book, looking at ideologies such as socialism, conservatism or liberalism, it is not difficult to pull out the main tenets of such philosophies; to establish how they understand human nature, the role they believe the state should take, their moral values and so forth. There may be much dispute as to how these things are understood within an ideology, maybe even a large degree of confusion, but nevertheless they form points of reference, co-ordinates perhaps, within which are shaped the kinds of debates that occur within that ideology, the points of principle over which adherents may squabble. They will also shape and clarify points of disagreement with other ideological configurations. But one would be hard put to find within those writings considered purely nationalist the clear expression of a configuration that could be said to belong purely to nationalist ideology. On the whole, nationalists the world over don't hold colloquia or congresses, form think-tanks or create international confederations dedicated to sharing, refining and spreading the doctrine of nationalism. Certainly leaders of nations may get together and discuss tactics if they believe they share some common problems or foes (such as the meetings of African or European nations). But they don't do so in order to discuss the finer points of nationalist reasoning.

However, some have undertaken to interpret nationalism as a more or less fixed constellation of political ideas. According to Elie Kedourie:

> Nationalism is a doctrine invented in Europe at the beginning of the nineteenth century . . . the doctrine holds that humanity is naturally divided into nations, that nations are known by certain characteristics which can be ascertained, and that the only legitimate type of government is national self-government.

> (Kedourie, 1960: 12)

This is helpful as a starting point. If we were to try and reduce nationalism to a straightforward doctrine we would have to include something like the claim to national self-determination and the view that nations are a natural unit of social and political organisation. But this sort of view suggests that a kind of 'universal' claim lurks within nationalist thinking. That is to say, a claim that can, and should, be applied to all peoples and that is equally valid for everyone. Certainly there is a part of nationalist ideology that often implies and sometimes explicitly advances such a claim. But it is not really what nationalist politicians or ideologues, with some notable exceptions, are primarily concerned with. The nationalist is concerned with his or her own nation more than with anyone else's. It may make political sense to link a claim about the rights of a people in one place to the rights of people in another. Those experiencing subjugation by a colonial power would be entirely sensible to forge connections with those also under such unwelcome rule, and to use similar motivating arguments and assumptions. But such strategic alliance is not the same as constructing a theory intended to have a general relevance to diverse peoples.

Nevertheless, something like the doctrine described by Kedourie could be said to have shaped the way we think about international politics. Organisations such as the United Nations and the frameworks of international law base themselves, in large part, on just such an assumption. International relations are often conducted as if nations can be treated as individual agents, the basic units of world politics. It is the breakdown of this kind of arrangement, the increased salience of supra-national and sub-national organisations, and of direct region-to-region relations, that has led some to speak of a 'post-nationalist' world order. But peoples in search of some kind of freedom, or simply looking for someone to blame for what they regard as their poor political or economic condition, still seek national self-determination, the right to form their own state based on the integrity of their putative nation and to be free from the interference of others. Furthermore, nationalist ideology, as Kedourie points out, holds nations to be identifiable by specific characteristics. Certainly it is part of our everyday common sense or mental shorthand to speak of 'the French' or 'the Germans' or 'the Russians' as meaningful entities with national characteristics of which we are all, supposedly, aware.

But it is not clear that the general view that the political world consists of nations with obvious characteristics is an ideology in the same sense as other 'isms'. For one thing the ideologies of conservatism or liberalism are quite likely to share such a belief and even those socialists keen to emphasise the importance of an international structure of class oppression can happily support struggles for national independence, as may environmentalists, who likewise take a global perspective on things.

Because of this Michael Freeden has argued that nationalism should be thought of as a 'thin' ideology. It is not entirely substantial in itself but it can function so as to maintain 'host' ideologies. For Freeden, ideologies 'enable meaningful political worlds to be constructed' (1996: 749). They produce identifiable sets of meaning or 'conceptual configurations'. Nationalism doesn't provide a unique constellation of such concepts, nor does it provide a broad range of answers to political questions. It often holds to a 'restricted core' and a 'narrower range' of political concepts but is also often just a component of other ideologies, something that complements them in some way.

Freeden attempts to isolate a core of concepts or claims that may always be found within nationalism: that nations are central to human relationships and a particular nation is particularly important; that this should result in a proper state for each nation (or at least some kind of institutional guarantee of its continuance) for example. He also argues that nationalism is always marked by strong emotionalism and attachment to the ways in which history can be seen as a story about the continuous existence or persistence of a people, and to a particular territory – the place where that history has been, and should continue to be, played out (1996: 751–4).

But the way in which these components are organised and configured may vary across cases. As Freeden shows, 'each core concept of nationalism . . . logically contains a number of possible meanings . . . [and they may be] attached to as many adjacent and peripheral concepts as there are interpretations of nationalism'. Furthermore 'the core concepts of nationalism cannot rival the possibilities available to mainstream ideologies such as conservatism, liberalism or socialism – all of which have core conceptual structures which permit a far fuller range of responses to socio-political issues' (1996: 752).

We seem to face a paradox. On the one hand we have an ideology that is so weak and thin that it offers little in the way of a comprehensive political or social philosophy. Yet it is able to inspire the most emotional of commitments and seems to shape our very consciousness of how the international order functions. It is a particular doctrine that forms the primary animating force of certain political movements *and* it is a more general framework that helps make sense of the world for many different social and political actors at both an international and everyday level. It is quite possible for politics (as well as you and me) to be shaped by the latter even if we have little regard for the former. Whatever it is, nationalism is not a body of thought easily assimilated into a taxonomy of ideologies. Perhaps then we should be wary of thinking of nationalism as an ideology at all.

Benedict Anderson opens his renowned and important study of nationalism by declaring that it is less like ideologies such as liberalism or fascism than like 'kinship or religion'. He goes on to suggest that we should define the nation as 'an imagined political community – imagined as both inherently limited and sovereign' (Anderson, 1992: 5). It is imagined because its members cannot possibly know or even hear of all their fellows 'yet in the minds of each lives the image of their communion' (1992: 6). It is limited because all nations consider themselves to have boundaries beyond which are other nations (perhaps against which the nation is defined) and sovereign because they demand to occupy the centre of political arrangements, to stand in the place where once we would have found divinely ordained monarchs. In short, the modern world imagines itself to be made up of nations and makes them the centre of its political arrangements. Rather than a single coherent, doctrinal ideology, nationalism is perhaps a kind of governing principle for the organisation of modern sociality.

In defining nationalism against ideology Anderson may seem to be making it into a subjective phenomenon, something that exists just when a bunch of people think it does. The analysis of nationalism is haunted by this tension between objective and subjective definitions. As the historian Hugh Seton-Watson has declared, in a tone that sounds somewhat exasperated: 'All that I can find to say is that a nation exists when a significant number of people in a community consider themselves to form a nation, or behave as if they formed one' (1977: 5). This is the basis of a widespread division in the field. Some seek to emphasise the objective features of the phenomenon of nationalism – the social facts considered necessary for its emergence. These may include a shared language, fixed territory, certain historical conditions and so forth. Others emphasise more 'subjective' aspects such as belief, commitment, will and imagination. The classic example of this latter approach is probably that of Ernest Renan, who, at the end of the nineteenth century, asked the question 'Qu'est-ce qu'une nation?' 'What is a nation?' and answered that 'a nation is a spiritual principle', constituted by 'possession in common of a rich legacy of remembrances' and by 'the desire to live together, the will to continue to value the heritage which all hold in common'. For Renan a nation is founded on a 'tangible deed' of consent which he famously called 'a daily plebiscite' (Renan, 1990). A plebiscite is a referendum, a popular vote. Renan is suggesting not that we really do vote to accept our nationality but that there can be nations and nationalism only because the people of a given nation continually accept it. It is something to which we affirm our allegiance in our everyday actions.

Probably the best contemporary exponent of such an approach is Walker Connor. For Connor the essence of a nation is 'a psychological bond that joins a people and differentiates it, in the subconscious conviction of its members, from all other people in a most vital way'. 'What ultimately matters,' argues Connor, 'is not *what is* but *what people believe is* . . . a nation is a matter of attitude and not of fact' (1994: 93). In other words being a nation does not necessarily mean that a people are all of the same genetic stock or share exactly the same history but it does mean that they act as if, or believe, that they do.

It is not the case that those who emphasise the subjective aspect of nations are abandoning the possibility of an objective analysis, even less that they are endorsing all the claims of nationalism. Rather, one of the things that nationalism is is the subjective attachment to certain ways of experiencing the world. We might say that nationalism is itself a kind of social theory – a kind of theory about how the world works, of what gives us a place in it, how we should think of our relations with other people and of how it should be politically organised. And in this sense we might argue that nationalism is definitively an ideology. But it is peculiar among ideologies in that its subjective and emotional aspects are foregrounded. Other ideologies certainly inspire emotional attachment and even a partisan sense of belonging. But they tend to suppress these in place of forms of rational argument, claim and counter-claim. At the level of formal argument nationalist ideologues are more than capable of attempting to be calmly rational in their argument. But they also acknowledge that sentiment and emotion are important bases of political life while the supporters of nationalism are most often likely to make their fervour both known and noticeable. As Freeden points out: 'All ideologies . . . carry emotional attachments to particular conceptual configurations, both because fundamental human values excite emotional as well as rational support, and because ideologies constitute mobilising ideational systems to change or defend political practices' (1996: 754). For this reason nationalism perhaps has much to teach us about ideology. Where others suppress their emotional rhetoric when they advance philosophical arguments, nationalism makes a virtue of them. And where other ideologies may be portrayed as aloof from the world, offering a distanced but rational comment and guide, nationalism makes a virtue of being supposedly embedded in our sense of what we are.

Perhaps this is one of the key things that ideologies do – provide us with a sense of who we are and then make us feel proud of it. Ideologies are not just ways of thinking about the world but ways of being within it. They give us a sense of what is going on, organise our perceptions of certain things and orient us in certain directions. This is a broader sense of ideology than is perhaps usual and it does suggest that we all, in a sense, 'live' in ideology. But it is also a way of thinking about ideology that can help us make sense of nationalism.

However, we need not neglect the attempt to understand the kinds of objective conditions that make it more or less likely (or even make it possible) that people will develop a nationalist sensibility. We know that ideologies such as socialism and liberalism have their roots in certain social conditions, that they emerge at reasonably clear moments in history, although this is not always seen as part of the way in which we should make sense of these ideologies. But, with nationalism, questions as to its origin are the main ones that have been investigated.

When was nationalism?

There is a common assumption that outbursts of nationalist fervour are indicative of a kind of latent tribalism, a primordial or atavistic trait of human nature, something that has been with us for ever. While there may be a case to say that some sort of group loyalty has always been intrinsic to human social organisation it is much less clear that nationalism, as we know it, is such a perennial feature. For many historians it appears to be a specifically modern phenomenon, emerging out of the social transformations of seventeenth and eighteenth-century Europe. For example, Seton-Watson declares that 'the doctrine of nationalism dates from the age of the French Revolution' (1977: 27).

Greenfeld suggests, and with some good reasons, that the 'original modern idea of the nation emerged in sixteenth-century England, which was the first nation in the world' (1992: 14). For Greenfeld, what makes the concept of the nation new in sixteenth-century England is its use as synonymous with 'the people'. Thought of as a nation, the idea of 'a people' loses the negative connotations of terms such as 'rabble' or 'mob'. It also removes the implication that a people is a group which is not part of the ruling elite, nobility or monarchy. Instead the people-as-one-nation become a kind of elite. Because they are part of the nation they share in something that elevates them, that makes them, in some sense, chosen (see Greenfeld, 1992: 7):

> The assertion of the nationality of the English polity went hand in hand with the insistence on the people's right of participation in the political process and government through Parliament. In fact in this case 'nation', England's being a nation, actually meant such participation. The representation of the English people as a nation symbolically elevated it to the position of an elite which had the right and was expected to govern itself, and equated nationhood with political citizenship.
>
> (Greenfeld, 1992: 30)

Nationalism then, was fundamentally related to the idea of popular sovereignty or democracy.

However, despite the clear ways in which concepts of nationhood acquire a specific and 'new' meaning in the modern period there is no uniform scholarly opinion on just how new it is or on how much emphasis we should give to the novelty and pure 'modernity' of nationhood and nationalism. In fact there is considerable argument about its emergence into history and the status to be attached to its possible precursors.

The key to such debates is the claim that nationalism has to be understood as rooted in social and economic transformations and not just political or intellectual ones. Many claim that nationalism is the result of 'modernisation'. This is nothing to do with the policies of the Blair government, although these are often declared to be connected with 'modernisation'. Nor is it to do with being particularly contemporary. When social scientists talk of modernisation or modernity they mean the shift from simple and traditional forms of social organisation to industrialised societies based around the complex interaction of the economy, large-scale state bureaucracies and mass communication systems that bring larger and larger groups of people into contact with each other. As such, modernisation is not a moment in history but a process. It is also something that may take place at different times in different places. Indeed, some places on our planet have not become fully modernised (perhaps they have been prevented) while others, it has been claimed, are now postmodern.

So how might nationalism be connected with this process of modernisation? In essence the argument is that under the conditions of upheaval and dislocation wrought by modernisation the reproduction of everyday social life and culture cannot be 'taken for granted'. The ways in which people are used to doing things, their habits, their traditions, their prejudices, are all thrown off kilter. This could lead to a total breakdown in society. But nationalism serves to reintegrate populations into this new social context.

Ernest Gellner (1983), for example, traces the sources of nationalism to the transformation from predominantly agricultural to industrial society, a transformation that significantly alters the relationship between culture and politics. He characterises agrarian societies as predominantly local in their orientation, hierarchical in structure and, crucially, semi-literate. That is to say, they were fairly closed and rigid forms of social organisation with limited variation between people in any particular social unit. Literacy is a skill monopolised by religious clerics and the ruling class exists in rigid separation from the peasantry. People are limited in their social as well as geographical mobility. They cannot move up or down the social ladder.

Industrialisation alters all this. People move through society and get mixed up much more. Industrial society, unlike agrarian society, is open-ended and always developing, demanding flexibility. For Gellner, nationalism 'is rooted in a certain kind of division of labour, one which is complex and persistently, cumulatively changing' (1983: 24). This necessitates a change in the place of culture in social organisation. No longer confined to single craft-based or agricultural occupations, but rather moving about and having to fulfil numerous different tasks, people require a basic training in literacy and numeracy. This makes their mobility possible:

> in industrial society notwithstanding its larger number of specialisms, the distance between specialisms is far less great. Their mysteries are far closer to mutual intelligibility, their manuals have idioms which overlap to a much greater extent and re-training though sometimes difficult is not generally an awesome task.

> (1983: 26–7)

The generation of a widely shared 'high' culture becomes necessary, since, without some basic homogeneity between people, society cannot function. Only widespread educational systems can accomplish this and they in turn require a state large enough to organise them. Thus culture and the state become linked. If cultures are to survive they need to have their own 'political roof', their own state. This, for Gellner, is the origin of nationalism. Its genesis as a cultural principle of social organisation lies in this transformation of social structure.

This is what scholars call the 'modernisation thesis' of nationalism. While Gellner is an exemplar of this approach he is not alone in arguing for it. Many social scientists and political theorists have adopted something like a modernisation-based approach, though their precise rendition of it may vary. For many Marxist theorists, for example, capitalist modernisation generates nations because, for example, it standardises languages (in order to increase the size of available markets and so to make obtaining profit easier) and it uses nationalism as a way of providing legitimacy for an oppressive state, obscuring what should be the international consciousness of the working class (see Nimni, 1994).

But there are a number of criticisms that may be made of the modernisation thesis. Not the least is that such theories are often taken to imply that the era of nationalism has passed. This may have looked like the case at one stage but it certainly doesn't look like that now that nationalist and ethnic conflicts have become such a part of Central and Eastern European politics. But modernisation theorists might claim that this is in fact symptomatic of a form of new modernisation happening as a result of the collapse of Soviet domination.

It is not always clear though, whether nationalism is to be understood as a result of modernisation or as a necessary condition. Does it make it possible for societies to industrialise or is it something that industrialisation produces? The modernisation thesis is a very general theory of nationalism that needs supplementing with more detailed analysis of any particular example. Even if it is entirely correct it may not tell us very much about how nationalism works as a political ideology. Things are always more complicated than epochal descriptions of social change allow.

But perhaps the most serious challenge to the modernisation thesis is the argument that historically nationalism has not emerged alongside industrialisation. The historian Marc Bloch has argued that national consciousness is apparent in France and Germany as far back as 1100 – long before 'modernisation'. By contrast Eugen Weber (1979) has demonstrated that some people living in rural France did not consider themselves French as late as the end of World War I. They lived in isolation from the rest of the country, spoke distinct regional vernaculars and generally had little to do with urbanised 'modern' France. As Connor concludes, it is hard to date the precise emergence of a nation, since an elite may be attached to national consciousness long before there is any record of what the mass of people thought. A nation is formed through a long process and there is no single point when it turns into a nation (see Connor, 1994: 210–26; also Williams, 1991).

Anthony Smith stresses the necessity for modern nationalism of a prior 'ethnic core'. Although notions such as self-determination may be recent, nations have roots going much further back. We must be careful, Smith urges, not to confuse *state* formation with *nation* formation. Accepting that national*ism* as an ideology may be said to emerge in the eighteenth century, Smith stresses the significance of historic *ethnies* (French for 'ethnic communities') in making later nationalisms possible. They form the basis of deeply held nationalist sentiments. Historical factors such as prolonged warfare with other ethnic groups produce a strong bond of ethnicity and a sense of belonging to an immemorial community. Smith is not arguing that nations are formed out of actual ties of kinship: '*Ethnies* are constituted, not by lines of physical descent, but by the sense of continuity, shared memory and collective destiny' (Smith, 1986). This leads him to stress, in a way that the modernisation theorists tend not to, the importance of myths, collective memories, persistent traditions and shared symbols in the constitution of ethnic identifications. These can in turn provide the resources for modern nationalists to shape nationalisms: 'if nationalism is modern and shapes nations . . . then this is only half the story. Specific nations are also the product of older, often pre-modern ethnic ties and ethno-histories' (1998: 195). *Ethnies* compete with other modes of organisation for the basis of people's identity and sense of history, space and place (for example, social class, city, etc.) and are often very successful. The sheer number of such ethnic groups, their obvious presence and the plethora of material evidence from the past up to the present attest to the validity behind Smith's argument. Clearly, for example, though there is much truth in the claim that ethno-religious identification in Northern Ireland persists because of the instrumental manipulation of political elites, it is also obvious that history has bequeathed to that region the basis of such identities, which, although they are not unchanged over time, are something that is really there (see Whyte, 1990).

This is a good corrective to the more cavalier modernisation theories that can be too general in their search for laws of development rather than ways of looking at the importance of contexts that are not simply incidental. As Smith (1998) makes clear, it is not impossible to combine a modernisation thesis with the recognition of historicity. It does not mean we have to abandon questions as to the extent to which a shared ethnic memory is something that is reinvented or reworked. Nationalist intellectuals and activists may expend a great deal of effort recovering (perhaps inventing) traditions, folk tales, languages, songs and so forth (see Hobsbawm and Ranger, 1992). But it is not possible for them to invent absolutely new ethnic identities where there was no prior basis at all. Perhaps this is true of all ideologies – none can take root where there is no fertile ground in the first place or, rather, when ideologies do take root they do so in specific contexts and they will be altered by, and adapt to, those contexts. All ideologies are the result of the long historical effort of human beings to try and make sense of, and have an impact upon, the natural and social world in which they find themselves. Each of us has to do this but we can only ever do it against the backdrop of the history that has brought us to where we are and the ideologies which those before us have constructed.

Political movements, political ideologies and nationalism

We have seen how, in the sixteenth and seventeenth centuries, nationalism, or at least nationality, was closely linked with democratic sentiments – with the idea that 'the people' should have some say in their own government. In order to 'think' democracy people also needed to think of themselves as already united and connected with each other. Imagining themselves to be part of an ancient nation with ancient rights helped them do this. Thus the ideologies of democracy and nationalism were, for a time, inseparable and mutually supporting. Indeed, nationalism rarely travels alone. It always works with other ideologies, other kinds of political ideal, and these may be of the left as much as of the right. This raises the difficult question of whether nationalism is taking the leading or supporting role in its own political dramas. As Freeden asks, 'are democracy and community glosses on nationhood, or are nationhood and nationalism more generally, a gloss on ideologies in which democracy and community play a crucial part?' (1998: 759).

Elements of nationalism can contribute to other ideologies, giving them a much needed context and legitimacy. As Breuilly shows, nationalism 'arises out of the need to make sense of complex social and political arrangements' (1982: 343). Since the modern state developed by basing its claims to legitimacy on the sovereignty of the people, rather than of the monarch, the problem arose of which people exactly were sovereign, and 'Once the claim to sovereignty was made on behalf of a particular territorially defined unit of humanity it was natural to relate the claim to the particular attributes of that unit' (1982: 343). In other words, to justify political arrangements by finding them to be in accordance with the nature or spirit of the people, the national community. Thus, while nationalism may always need a 'host' ideology, it is also possible that other ideologies find a useful 'host' in nationalism – that they can enhance their persuasiveness by being associated with a supposed national character or sentiment. In fact this could be a way in which an ideology can make itself appear 'natural'. This is not to suggest that nationalism is always consciously employed by unscrupulous and manipulative politicians as a strategy for maintaining power. It may just be that politicians or ideologues, in trying to make sense of the world and to sustain their own arguments, find themselves seeing things in national terms. Just think of the extent to which British politicians routinely refer to the good of the nation or the national interest; the way they portray themselves as being more in tune with the national spirit than their opponents. This may not be nationalism in the sense of a singular and clear doctrine but it is nationalism in the sense that it draws on implicit assumptions about the naturalness of nations and uses them to articulate a political case (see Billig, 1995). In this way the claims of, say, conservatism (which often advocates an organic notion of some sort of unified community to which we owe allegiance) may combine with nationalism (which of course also advances a notion of a naturally unified community). But socialism too can combine with nationalism, particularly in the case of populist anti-colonial nationalisms, where both ideologies share a notion of the people as the source of all that is legitimate and true. We might also make mention of ecologism, which, given that it seeks in part to protect the landscape, is quite capable of being used by nationalism and of using nationalism and national sentiment as justification for opposition to certain kinds of social change.

There is also a relationship between feminism and nationalism. Feminism, like nationalism, often functions within the context of a relationship to an ideology such as liberalism or socialism. But the claims of feminism are sometimes related to those of nationalism, especially in the context of national liberation struggles, in which women (especially in non-Western contexts) often play a crucial part. We might also think of the use of aspects of gender and gendered symbolisation within nationalism which have been astutely analysed by feminist scholars. Nations are often imagined in mythic form as female figures. We speak of

Britannia and paint her as a woman. In France, Joan of Arc is a key female national icon and France itself is imagined as female. But this often means that the land or the country is being figured as a nurturing, mother figure whose sons must always be ready to defend her. Her daughters can consequently be instructed to continue the work of reproducing the nation both biologically and culturally. In fact a whole range of gendered and sexualised imagery almost always goes along with nationalism (e.g. Yuval-Davis, 1997; Walby, 1996; Mosse, 1985) and appeals to nationhood may be one way in which a certain form of anti-feminism is constructed.

What we are seeing here is the way in which ideologies combine and recombine with each other and with other political ideas in the attempt to forge a political belief system that seems both coherent and natural. Ideologies are not just about constructing doctrinal positions. They are also about establishing the legitimacy of one's own political claims and the illegitimacy of one's opponents'. One of the best ways of doing this is to suggest that your own views are not an ideology – they are normal and obvious – while everybody else's views are foolish philosophy. Conservatism very often makes this sort of claim. But nationalism and nationality can lend this naturalness to a range of ideologies because nationality seems a part of the everyday, natural world. Even if we consciously reject our nationality and claim to be global cosmopolitans it is still clear to us what it is we are rejecting, just as it will be clear to many other people what nationality it is we think of ourselves as trying to get away from.

So far, in looking at the interaction of political movements and ideologies with nationalism, we have not thought about liberalism. Since liberalism claims to champion the individual, to protect her or his liberty from the impositions of collectivist ideologies and always to promote tolerance, we might well presume that nationalism and liberalism are antagonistic ideologies. Certainly, nationalism generally has not been much admired by liberal political theorists. Isaiah Berlin, for example, while he understood the potency of the romanticist ideal of the organic community, criticised nationalism precisely because of the way in which it privileges the interests of the supposedly organic community over those of smaller groups or individuals. It can thus be despotic and oppressive (Berlin, 1979: 333–55). But Berlin makes the common distinction between national*ism*, the ideology, and nationality or 'mere national consciousness – the sense of belonging to a nation' (1979: 346). And it is nationality and liberalism that have often combined.

As we have noted, nationalism makes it possible to imagine a kind of community between people that has been important in sustaining claims about rights and legal equalities and useful in making government seem legitimate. Liberalism has long known this. J. S. Mill, the archetypal liberal thinker, noted that free government was virtually impossible in multinational states. It was, he thought, necessary for a governed people to feel some connection and solidarity with each other. Increasingly, contemporary liberal political theorists and ideologists are beginning to see ways in which a sense of nationality may be important for them. In part this has been stimulated by the criticisms of what is known as communitarianism. Communitarian thinkers have argued that liberalism is insufficiently attentive to the need of individuals to be part of a wider substantive community. They argue that values such as tolerance, justice, fairness and so forth take on meaning for people only within the context of an embedded, shared culture within which they can feel themselves a part of something (see Mulhall and Swift, 1992). As a result of this debate (and also perhaps because of actual problems of solidarity and civic commitment in many liberal democratic polities) some theorists have begun to think about the importance of the 'principle of nationality' to life in a good polity.

One thing that some liberals have done to effect this connection is make a distinction between good and bad nationalisms. This builds on a distinction that other scholars have established between what have been termed 'civic' and 'ethnic' conceptions of the nation (see Geertz, 1963; Plamenatz, 1976; Ignatieff, 1993) For the former the nation is primarily a 'political' unit with some sort of civic tie between a set people. This fosters duties, rights, responsibilities and obligations. By contrast 'ethnic' nationalisms are understood as interpreting the nation as bonded through some kind of blood tie or through a powerful shared historical or cultural consciousness. Through this distinction liberals try to distance themselves from the more aggressive aspects of nationalism. This distinction can be found, in varying forms, throughout writings on nationalism. Sometimes it is mapped on to a distinction between Eastern and Western nationalisms, where the latter are civic and democratic, the former cultural and authoritarian (see Kohn, 1944; Plamenatz, 1976). Other times the division is labelled 'civic–territorial' and 'ethnic–genealogical' (Smith, 1991) or 'individualistic–libertarian' and 'collectivist–authoritarian' (Greenfeld, 1992).

David Miller (1995) rejects such an easy distinction but instead defends what he calls 'a principle of nationality'. He argues that it need not be irrationally indefensible to claim that national identity is a part of one's identity. Nations are ethical communities (though this need not mean that we owe no ethical obligations to those beyond our nation or no special ethical obligations to a smaller unit such as our family). This in turn means that there should be some right to self-determination, though not necessarily to a sovereign state. For Miller this last claim is important, for it is in part the autonomous and self-determining nature of nations that makes their meaningful ethical status possible.

Miller's position is in part motivated by a sort of realism. He just thinks it unlikely that people will suddenly decide that their sense of nationality was a big fiction and so give up on it. Better then to think within nationality and see how it may fit with liberal, civic, principles. In any case many political philosophers already assume something like a national community, a body of people with a sense of shared history, continuity and so forth, when they begin to theorise about the nature of justice or rights and so forth. It is possible, Miller avers, to develop a sense of nationality that contributes to, rather than detracts from, a shared commitment to the civic principles of the liberal state. But this has implications for issues such as multiculturalism. Ethnic or cultural minorities within a liberal state have a right to expect that the state will make some effort to accommodate them but they too must accept their responsibility to be loyal to the national state. For Miller a politics of nationality is opposed to a narrow 'politics of identity'. A civic national identity does not impose itself upon other identities. Rather, it is a kind of framework for a common identity within which other identities may make legitimate claims.

Miller's arguments have come in for criticism on the grounds that they tend to lead to support for the *status quo* and thus downplay the extent to which the grievances of a minority may be severe and rooted in the unjust nature of present political arrangements. It has also been argued that Miller does not fully appreciate the interrelationship of civic and ethnic conceptions of nationalism, the fact that they provide each other with support (see O'Leary, 1996; Smith, 1998).

We can perhaps see that, whatever our initial feelings about nationalism, it is a kind of fundamental political ideology. This is not necessarily because that is how it has to be or can only be. It may simply derive from the ways in which people in the past have developed ideas and practices that helped explain to them why they should feel about each other in certain ways, how we should answer certain sorts of difficult political question. It is also, of course, the result of certain past political victories and disputes. It may be objected that in making this claim I am conflating those general sentiments of nationality with full-blown nationalism. But unless we recognise that the sentiment of nationality in the West comes from (and has been historically sustained and propagated by) what were once nationalisms – full-blown movements for national unity or liberation – we cannot understand the nature of nationalism as an ideology. It is not just or only a doctrine comprised of certain core claims. It is a set of general ideas that contribute to a larger 'world view' and which may be drawn on by a range of political actors and thinkers in different ways, at different times and in different contexts.

Conclusion

In this chapter we have looked at nationalism in a slightly unusual way. Rather than treat it as an isolated political doctrine we have considered the interaction of nationalism with other ideologies and touched on what this may tell us about the nature of ideology. Instead of reviewing studies of virulent and violent ethnic nationalisms we have been concentrating on the place of nationalism in our general political thinking and particularly in our ideas about democracy. This is not to ignore the instances of nationalist or ethnic conflict. Rather it is to stress that we need to take nationalism seriously as a political force and that means thinking about how it is part of 'us' and not just part of 'them', over there, somewhere, engaging in what we think of as unthinkable. Nationalism was a

European invention and it was Europe that exported it across the globe (see Chatterjee, 1986).

As one would expect of an ideology, nationalism offers answers to the big questions of social and political life. It makes a claim as to the basis of human sociality and relationships. It gives reasons for why we should (or shouldn't) feel obliged to others. It advances a case for what makes the best form of legitimate government and suggests something about citizens' relationship to the state. But it does not necessarily always say much more. When it comes to advancing a case about the distribution of wealth, for example, or about the way in which an economy should be run, nationalism alone is pretty useless. It may imply a kind of equality between all fellows but it may also advocate a hierarchical and authoritarian form of government in the interests of that national equality. Nationalism always needs to be in connection with wider social philosophies. This may be indicative of, as Freeden claims, how thin nationalist ideology is. It may also show how simplistic it is. But this may also be evidence of the fact that nationalism is, in a sense, a more fundamental ideology than others. It is successful to the point where we do not really notice many of the essentially nationalist assumptions we all make.

But for how much longer can nationalism function in this way? What happens to it in the face of globalisation? We are seeing something like the erosion of nation states or at least the growing separation of the national part from the state part. Supra-national political institutions such as the European Union are taking power away from single nations. Increasingly, non-governmental organisations such as worldwide pressure groups, multinational corporations and so forth move between and above national sovereignty. And there is also cultural globalisation. It is unlikely that the people within a single nation will partake in the same forms of cultural experience all the time or that they will even share in their own national culture. They may buy food from all over the planet, eating Chinese one day, Italian the next. They very probably travel to other countries and may even have jobs that necessitate them speaking to or visiting other nations very regularly.

People in the United Kingdom may well watch nothing but American or Hong Kong action movies on their televisions or DVD players manufactured in Taiwan. This may be a very important influence on the future directions of national sentiment. Human collectivities have always grasped their sense of being a collective through forms of artistic dramatisation and expression and the (often ritualised) public act of observing and maybe participating in them. The ancient Greeks, and especially the Athenians who lived in what many regard as the first democracy, regularly held festivals and competitions for everything from sport and athletics to drama and poetry. These were occasions when the collective, the 'imagined community' in Anderson's phrase, could experience itself as such and have its being reaffirmed. When it came to the dramatic festivals, the dramas themselves touched on and explored the question of what it was to be an Athenian citizen and held up ways in which the community might like (or might not like) to think of itself (see Goldhill, 1986). In our own time we still engage in such collective rituals though their place in our lives, and the extent to which they can be contained within singular collectivities, have certainly changed.

Scholars of nationalism have often pointed to the importance of communication systems in enabling people to develop a sense of shared culture and belonging. Anderson argues that the emergence of nationalism was closely related to the spread of trade in printed matter. In order to create viable markets this trade assembled varied dialects into more homogeneous languages, creating a bridge between elite clerical Latin and diverse popular vernaculars. For Anderson, it was this convergence between capitalism and the technology of printing that made it possible to begin imagining the national community. But, as Deutsch shows, communication entails not only language but also 'systems of writing, painting, calculating etc. . . . information stored in the living memories, associations, habits, and preferences . . . material facilities for the storage of information such as libraries, statues, signposts and the like' (1966: 96). The predominantly national basis of media institutions has made them of tremendous importance in the maintenance of national communities. Television has been understood by its own practitioners and professionals as a means of integrating millions of domestic family units into the rhythms and experiences of a national imaginary (Ang, 1996: 5). The media, far from simply reflecting national experiences, create them by their presence as recorders of events. Be it the coronation of a monarch, the swearing in of a president or the creation of a 'national' tragedy (such as the sudden death of a princess in a car crash or a football team in a penalty shoot-out) media events 'integrate societies in a collective heartbeat and evoke a renewal of loyalty to the society and its legitimate authority' (Dayan and Katz, 1992: 9). The mass media have, in a way, replaced the ancient festivals, and it is these forms of instantaneous electronic media that offer the rituals of collective life. But the media are increasingly internationalised and fragmented. It is now less and less likely that people will all simultaneously watch the same event at the same time, despite wide access to such media.

This sort of cultural 'globalisation' may already be having an impact on the way we experience nationality. But what we are seeing is not the development of an overarching cosmopolitan or 'world' identity. Rather we are seeing the proliferation of 'new' or resurgent nationalisms. In the United Kingdom, for example, devolution in Scotland and Wales is actually reinforcing certain kinds of nationalism or national sentiment. On the continent of Europe smaller regions such as the Basque country in Spain continue to fight their cause. Other regions, some spurred on by their capacity to address the European level of government directly, are growing in confidence and may begin demanding more power. In the United Kingdom this is represented by those calling for assemblies in the north of England. In Italy one can look at the (fluctuating) support for the separatist Northern League, motivated by resentment and prejudice towards the south of the country. Alternatively, we may look at the attempts by some supranational organisations to try and generate a supranational identity. The

European Union has tried to develop common cultural and media policies and seeks to fund, for example, film projects which it hopes may add to a sense of shared culture and identity across the countries of Europe. In a sense this reproduces the activities of the nation state, as understood by someone such as Gellner, in developing a shared 'high culture' across a territory. But we should also remember the persistence of nationalism and nation states. Even when people do travel widely and consume many forms of culture they are capable of reining them in to their national perspective. It does not follow that these things automatically erode a sense of nationality. Indeed, the growth of communication technologies makes it possible for peoples to maintain their sense of cultural identity and specificity regardless of territorial factors. Those in an ethnic diaspora can continue to keep up with news and culture from their home country and with their fellow nationals. They may even be an important force in maintaining separatist movements (see Seaton, 1999: 258). For this reason, cultural globalisation is as much a force for sustaining ethnic and national groups as a cause of the decomposition of nations from both above and below.

What we are also seeing, thanks in large part to computer technologies allowing the fast movement of information from one place to another, is the growth of global networks of political organisation. As political problems and issues begin to take on a global scale (as with environmental crises, for example, or the management of the capitalist economy) those involved begin to organise globally. So it is that we have seen the global co-ordination of oppositional campaigns to match the globalisation of economic power. Some argue that we need to develop a form of global civil society capable of responding to such phenomena (see Archibulgi *et al.*, 1998). Undoubtedly there are trends towards a reconfiguration of international political, economic and cultural space but whether or not things are moving inexorably upwards in scale remains to be seen.

In assessing the likely prospects of nationalism we should perhaps try to remember what it has been for. Nationalism is an ideology the central function of which is to provide an incontestable answer to the question of why we should think of ourselves as living together in certain ways rather than separately and of providing one part of a way in which we might do so. This, surely, is the fundamental question of any political theory. Indeed, it is perhaps the most fundamental aspect of all political ideologies, even if it is so fundamental that we hardly ever actually see it and think about it. But what is our relationship to each other? Why should I want to have anything to do with you? How is it even possible that I can have anything to do with you? On what basis can I trust you or enter into any sort of collaboration with you? Without an answer to these questions there can be no society. Political theory has provided answers to these questions in ways that are different from nationalism. In world history there have been other solutions to them too. Because nationalism answers these questions in ways that are often exclusivist, hostile to some people in order to favour others, some have sought to establish better and more open ways of answering these fundamental political questions while others have tried to 'co-opt' nationalism to their cause. Perhaps in the future we will develop yet more answers. If our world is to become more successful in managing interdependence between the varied peoples of the globe it will need to think of ways of understanding that interconnection that do not just rely on homogeneity, exclusivity and territorial boundaries. But, because no other ideology has yet succeeded in providing, on its own, an answer of sufficient emotional force, of institutionalising it and making it last, we are all, still, nationalists.

Further reading

The issues raised here are very much alive in a number of respects. For this reason students might be advised to look at the growing literature on globalisation and international governance. Aspects of this debate are considered in the essays that make up *Re-imagining Political Community* edited by Daniele Archibulgi, David Held and Martin Kohler (1998). Andrew Linklater's *The Transformation of Political Community* (1998) also looks at these issues.

On nationalism itself a good overview by a master of the field is Anthony D. Smith's *Nationalism and Modernism* (1998). This looks at all the theories considered here, as well as others. A useful reader with short extracts from many of the major writers on this topic is also edited by Smith along with John Hutchinson: *Nationalism: A Reader* (1994). The debate stimulated by David Miller's endorsement of the 'principle of nationality' is well represented by the special issue of the journal *Nations and Nationalism*. See Brendan O'Leary (ed.), 'Symposium on David Miller's *On Nationality*' (1996).

References

Anderson, Benedict (1992) *Imagined Communities*, 2nd edn, London: Verso.

Ang, Ien (1996) *Living Room Wars: Rethinking Media Audiences for a Postmodern World*, London: Routledge.

Archibulgi, Daniele, Held, David and Kohler, Martin, eds (1998) *Re-imagining Political Community: Studies in Cosmopolitan Democracy*, Cambridge: Polity Press.

Berlin, Isaiah [1979] (1997) 'Nationalism: past neglect and present power' in *Against the Current: Essays in the History of Ideas*, London: Hogarth Press.

Billig, Michael (1995) *Banal Nationalism*, London: Sage.

Breuilly, John (1982) *Nationalism*, Manchester: Manchester University Press.

Chatterjee, Partha (1986) *Nationalist Thought and the Colonial World*, London: Zed Books.

Connor, Walker (1994) *Ethnonationalism: The Quest for Understanding*, Princeton NJ: Princeton University Press.

Dayan, Daniel and Katz, Elihu (1992) *Media Events: The Live Broadcasting of History*, Cambridge MA: Harvard University Press.

Deutsch, Karl (1966) *Nationalism and Social Communication*, Cambridge MA: MIT Press.

Freeden, Michael (1996) *Ideologies and Political Theory*, Oxford: Oxford University Press.

Geertz, Clifford (1963) 'The integrative revolution: primordial sentiments and civil politics in the new states' in C. Geertz (ed.) *Old Societies and New States: The Quest for Modernity in Asia and Africa*, New York: Free Press.

Gellner, Ernest (1983) *Nations and Nationalism*, Oxford: Blackwell.

Goldhill, Simon (1986) *Reading Greek Tragedy*, Cambridge: Cambridge University Press.

Greenfeld, Liah (1992) *Nationalism: Five Roads to Modernity*, Cambridge MA: Harvard University Press.

Hobsbawm, Eric and Ranger, Terence (1992) *The Invention of Tradition*, Cambridge: Cambridge University Press.

Ignatieff, Michael (1993) *Blood and Belonging: Journeys into the new Nationalism*, London: Chatto & Windus.

Kedourie, Elie (1960) *Nationalism*, London: Hutchinson.

Kohn, Hans (1944) *The Idea of Nationalism: A Study of its Ideas and Background*, New York: Macmillan.

Linklater, Andrew (1998) *The Transformation of Political Community: Ethical Foundations of the post-Westphalian Era*, Cambridge: Polity Press.

Mill, John Stuart (1861) *On Representative Government*, Oxford: Oxford University Press, 1995.

Miller, David (1995) *On Nationality*, Oxford: Clarendon Press.

Mosse, George (1985) *Nationalism and Sexuality: Middle Class Norms and Sexual Morality in Modern Europe*, Madison WI: University of Wisconsin Press.

Mulhall, Stephen and Swift, Adam (1992) *Liberals and Communitarians*, Oxford: Blackwell.

Nimni, Ephraim (1994) *Marxism and Nationalism: Theoretical Origins of a Political Crisis*, London: Pluto Press.

O'Leary, Brendan, ed. (1996) 'Symposium on David Miller's *On Nationality*', *Nations and Nationalism*, 2 (3).

Plamenatz, John (1976) 'Two types of nationalism' in Eugene Kamenka (ed.) *Nationalism: The Nature and Evolution of an Idea*, London: Edward Arnold.

Renan, Ernest (1990) 'Qu'est-ce qu'une nation?' in Homi Bhaba (ed.) *Nation and Narration*, London: Routledge.

Seaton, Jean (1999) 'Why do we think the Serbs do it? The new "ethnic" wars and the media', *Political Quarterly*, 70 (3), pp. 254–70.

Seton-Watson, Hugh (1977) *Nations and States: An Enquiry into the Origins of Nations and the Politics of Nationalism*, London: Methuen.

Smith, Anthony (1986) 'The myth of the "modern nation" and the myths of nations', *Ethnic and Racial Studies*, 11, pp. 1–26.

Smith, Anthony D. (1991) *National Identity*, London: Penguin.

Smith, Anthony (1998) *Nationalism and Modernism*, London: Routledge.

Smith, Anthony and Hutchinson, John, eds (1994) *Nationalism: A Reader*, Oxford: Oxford University Press.

Walby, Sylvia (1996) 'Woman and nation' in G. Balakrishan (ed.) *Mapping the Nation*, London: Verso, pp. 235–45.

Weber, Eugene (1979) *Peasants into Frenchmen: The Modernisation of Rural France, 1870–1914*, London: Chatto & Windus.

Whyte, John (1990) *Interpreting Northern Ireland*, Oxford: Clarendon.

Williams, Glyn A. (1991) *When was Wales?* Harmondsworth: Penguin.

Yuval-Davis, Nira (1997) *Gender and Nation*, London: Sage.

Required Readings Available Online

"Human Security in Theory and Practice: An Overview of the Human Security Concept and the United Nations Trust Fund for Human Security." New York, NY: United Nations Trust Fund for Human Security, Human Security Unit. http://www.un.org/humansecurity/sites/www.un.org.humansecurity/files/human_security_in_theory_and_practice_english.pdf

Additional Works Cited

Paris, Roland. 2001. "Human Security – Paradigm Shift or Hot Air?" International Security 26(2): 87-102.

Dorn, Walter. "Human Security: An Overview" Paper prepared for the Pearson Peacekeeping Centre. http://walterdorn.net/23-human-security-an-overview. Accessed October 9, 2016.

III. MODULE THREE:

Human Rights and Humanitarianism

In the last module, we explored how the international state system is predicated on the notion of territorial sovereignty. This is a system in which each state is responsible for the safety and welfare of its citizens. States, however, often fall short of this task. When states become weak, corrupt, or fail, they have tremendous power to harm their own citizens. The concept of human rights, and a set of practices related humanitarianism have been developed to protect individual rights.

Human rights are the rights we have by virtue of being human. The concept of human rights recognizes the inherent dignity of every person, regardless national origin or any other characteristic, whether it be race, religion, gender, sexual preference, or ethnicity. With the exception of the right to self-determination, all of the rights in the Universal Declaration of Human Rights (described below) and the two Covenants that followed are individual rights.[7] In many ways then, human rights represent a way of asserting the moral primacy of the individual. This is part of what distinguishes our era of globalization from others. Accordingly, the individual is at the center of the conceptual and legal framework of human rights - one of the most impressive developments of the twentieth, and now twenty-first centuries.

Readings

Universal Declaration of Human Rights (UDHR), The United Nations Charter called for a Commission to be set up to draft a statement of human rights. Eleanor Roosevelt chaired the Commission that collectively authored the document. Every member nation of the United Nations would later have an opportunity to comment and contribute. The Universal Declaration has been ratified by every country in the world and has acquired significance as a guide for recognizing the inherent dignity of every human being. While the UDHR is a remarkable achievement, it is not an enforceable treaty. Therefore, its accomplishments are constrained by many factors.

In "Reflections on Intervention," **Annan** points out that the casualties in wars today are overwhelmingly civilians. When countries are unable to protect their citizens, the international community faces a difficult set of decisions with regard to whether or not to intervene. This leads Annan to explore the meaning of intervention. As Annan explains, Article 2.7 of the United Nations Charter forbids nations from intervening in matters that are within the jurisdiction of a state. While this notion of sovereignty remains a foundation of the state system, it should not be understood as precluding intervention. After all, the primary goal of the United Nations is preserving international peace and security. Chapter VII of the United Nations Charter therefore permits nation-states to intervene when international peace and security are at issue.

This speech by Annan is not a scholarly argument in favor of intervention or against it. Rather, his is primarily a moral appeal for each organization and person to do what they can to

---

[7] http://www.un.org/en/universal-declaration-human-rights/

correct injustices wherever they may be found, or at the very least speak out against them. Annan is in favor of the view that well-reasoned humanitarian intervention is not a form of imperialism, as some have charged, but a moral imperative.

In "Third World Perspectives on Humanitarian Intervention" Muhammed **Ayoob** takes a very different view than Kofi Annan (this volume). This is in part because one is a statesman making a speech (Annan) while the other is a scholar (Ayoob). This author explores question of when and when not to intervene from the perspective of the countries in which intervention most often takes place, rather than the United Nations. Countries in the developing world have observed humanitarian intervention tends to lead not just to the resolution of a crisis, but to more intervention. In fact, some form of what Ayoob calls "international administration" often follows. When it comes to intervention, then, the potential cost in terms of an erosion of sovereignty must be weighed against the benefits of having assistance.

Another concern, and one that has contributed to pessimism, is the selectivity, and potential bias that has been exercised by more wealthy and powerful states in the choice about whether to intervene or not. As described in module two, the unrepresentative nature of the Security Council and the ever-present possibility of a veto makes the Security Council a clumsy and imperfect mechanism for deciding when and how to intervene. Countries in the developing world are skeptical that it is always their best interests that are at the heart of an intervention.

Attitudes toward intervention vary from one region to the next, and within regions. In other words, it is wise to avoid treating the global South as homogenous. States in Asia and Latin America countries presume that humanitarian intervention is likely to occur when and where human rights are violated (p. 105). African states, by contrast, understand state failure to be the primary cause for crises that call for international intervention (p 105). Where the selectivity and the double standards that plague humanitarian intervention are most troublesome is the Middle East (p. 110).

Bajoria, Jayshree. 2013. In "The Dilemma of Humanitarian Intervention." Bajoria gives a basic overview of what is at stake in humanitarian intervention. She provides a "tour" of the major international agreements that are intended to govern decisions about whether or not to intervene, including the "Responsibility to Protect." She calls particular attention to the way that humanitarian intervention has, in the past, been used as a means to accomplish regime change (n.p.).

In "The Veil Controversy," **Mark Allen Peterson** explains different kinds of head coverings worn by Muslim women around the world, and the criticisms leveled against them by "anti-veiling" advocates. The wearing of the head scarf has undoubtedly become a politically charged issue. Peterson provides a compelling argument that the wearing of a headscarf (he sometimes reverts to calling it a veil) lacks a universal meaning. The meaning varies not only across societies, but among women within societies. This serves an reminder of the dangers of overgeneralization, and the necessity of investigating the real meaning - both those that are projected onto the head covering and those that are constructed by the people who choose to cover their heads.

Human Rights in World Politics

by Rhoda E. Howard and Jack Donnelly

The International Human Rights Covenants[1] note that human rights "derive from the inherent dignity of the human person." But while the struggle to assure a life of dignity is probably as old as human society itself, reliance on human rights as a mechanism to realize that dignity is a relatively recent development.

Human rights are, by definition, the rights one has simply because one is a human being. This simple and relatively uncontroversial definition, though, is more complicated than it may appear on the surface. It identifies human rights as *rights*, in the strict and strong sense of that term, and it establishes that they are held simply by virtue of being human. . . .

WHAT RIGHTS DO WE HAVE?

The definition of human or natural rights as the rights of each person simply as a human being specifies their character; they are rights. The definition also specifies their source: (human) nature. . . .

What is it in human nature that gives rise to human rights? There are two basic answers to this question. On the one hand, many people argue that human rights arise from human needs, from the naturally given requisites for physical and mental health and well-being. On the other hand, many argue that human rights reflect the minimum requirements for human dignity or *moral* personality. These latter arguments derive from essentially philosophical theories of human "nature," dignity, or moral personality.

From *International Handbook of Human Rights*, edited by Jack Donnelly and Rhoda E. Howard, pp. 79–106. Copyright © 1987 by Jack Donnelly and Rhoda E. Howard. Reproduced with permission of Greenwood Publishing Group, Inc., Westport, CT. Portions of the text have been omitted.

Rhoda E. Howard and Jack Donnelly, Selections from: "Introduction," International Handbook of Human Rights, pp. 1, 4-15, 18-21, 23-27.

Needs theories of human rights run into the problem of empirical confirmations; the simple fact is that there is sound scientific evidence only for a very narrow list of human needs. But if we use "needs" in a broader, in part nonscientific, sense, then the two theories overlap. We can thus say that people have human rights to those things "needed" for a life of dignity, for the full development of their moral personality. The "nature" that gives rise to human rights is thus *moral* nature.

This moral nature is, in part, a social creation. Human nature, in the relevant sense, is an amalgam consisting both of psycho-biological facts (constraints and possibilities) and of the social structures and experiences that are no less a part of the essential nature of men and women. Human beings are not isolated individuals, but rather individuals who are essentially social creatures, in part even social creations. Therefore, a theory of human rights must recognize both the essential universality of human nature and the no less essential particularity arising from cultural and socioeconomic traditions and institutions.

Human rights are, by their nature, universal; it is not coincidental that we have a *Universal* Declaration of Human Rights, for human rights are the rights of all men and women. Therefore, in its basic outlines a list of human rights must apply at least more or less "across the board." But the nature of human beings is also shaped by the particular societies in which they live. Thus the universality of human rights must be qualified in at least two important ways.

First, the forms in which universal rights are institutionalized are subject to some legitimate cultural and political variation. For example, what counts as popular participation in government may vary, within a certain range, from society to society. Both multiparty and single-party regimes may reflect legitimate notions of political participation. Although the ruling party cannot be removed from power, in some one-party states individual representatives can be changed and electoral pressure may result in significant policy changes.

Second, and no less important, the universality (in principle) of human rights is qualified by the obvious fact that any particular list, no matter how broad its cross-cultural and international acceptance, reflects the necessarily contingent understandings of a particular era. For example, in the seventeenth and eighteenth centuries, the rights of man were indeed the rights of men, not women, and social and economic rights (other than the right to private property) were unheard of. Thus we must expect a gradual evolution of even a consensual list of human rights, as collective understandings of the essential elements of human dignity, the conditions of moral personality, evolve in response to changing ideas and material circumstances.

In other words, human rights are by their essential nature universal in form. They are, by definition, the rights held by each (and every) person simply as a human being. But any universal list of human rights is subject to a variety of justifiable implementations.

In our time, the Universal Declaration of Human Rights (1948) is a minimum list that is nearly universally accepted, although additional rights have been added (e.g., self-determination) and further new rights (e.g., the right to nondiscrimination on the grounds of sexual orientation or the right to peace) may be added in the future. We are in no position to offer a philosophical defense of the list of rights in the Universal Declaration. To do so would require an account of the source of human rights—human nature—that would certainly exceed the space available to us. Nonetheless, the Universal Declaration is nearly universally accepted by states. For practical political purposes we can treat it as authoritative. . . .

INTERNATIONAL HUMAN RIGHTS INSTITUTIONS

The international context of national practices deserves some attention. There are, as we have already noted, international human rights standards that are widely accepted—in principle at least—by states. Thus the discussion and evaluation of national practices take place within an overarching set of international standards to which virtually all states have explicitly committed themselves. Whatever the force of claims of national sovereignty, with its attendant legal immunity from international action, the evaluation of national human rights practices from the perspective of the international standards of the Universal Declaration thus is certainly appropriate, even if one is uncomfortable with the moral claim sketched above that such universalistic scrutiny is demanded by the very idea of human rights.

In the literature on international relations it has recently become fashionable to talk of "international regimes," that is, norms and decision-making procedures accepted by states in a given issue area. National human rights practices do take place within the broader context of an international human rights regime centered on the United Nations.

We have already sketched the principal norms of this regime—the list of rights in the Universal Declaration. These norms/rights are further elaborated in two major treaties, the International Covenant on Economic, Social and Cultural Rights and the International Covenant on Civil and Political Rights, which were opened for signature and ratification in 1966 and came into force in 1976. Almost all of the countries studied in this volume have ratified (become a party to) both the Covenant on Civil and Political Rights and the Covenant on Economic, Social and Cultural Rights. . . . Even the countries that are not parties to the Covenants often accept the principles of the Universal Declaration. In addition, there are a variety of single-issue treaties that have been formulated under UN auspices on topics such as racial discrimination, the rights of women, and torture. These later Covenants and Conventions go into much greater detail than the Universal Declaration and include a few important changes. For example, the Covenants prominently include a right to national self-determination, which is absent in the Universal Declaration, but do not include a right to private property. Nevertheless, for the most part they can be seen simply as elaborations on the Universal Declaration, which remains the central normative document in the international human rights regime.

What is the legal and political force of these norms? The Universal Declaration of Human Rights was proclaimed in 1948 by the United Nations General Assembly. As such, it has no force of law. Resolutions of the General Assembly, even solemn declarations, are merely recommendations to states; the General Assembly has no international legislative powers. Over the years, however, the Universal Declaration has come to be something more than a mere recommendation.

There are two principal sources of international law, namely, treaty and custom. Although today we tend to think first of treaty, historically custom is at least as important. A rule or principle attains the force of customary international law when it can meet two tests. First, the principle or rule must reflect the general practice of the overwhelming majority of states. Second, what lawyers call *opinio juris*, the sense of obligation, must be taken into account. Is the customary practice seen by states as an obligation, rather than a mere convenience or courtesy? Today it is a common view of international lawyers that the Universal Declaration has attained something of the status of customary international law, so that the rights it contains are in some important sense binding on states.

Furthermore, the International Human Rights Covenants are treaties and as such do have the force of international law, but only for the parties to the treaties, that is, those states that have (voluntarily) ratified or acceded to the treaties. The same is true of the single-issue treaties that round out the regime's norms. It is perhaps possible that the norms of the Covenants are coming to acquire the force of customary international law even for states that are not parties. But in either case, the fundamental weakness of international law is underscored: Virtually all international legal obligations are voluntarily accepted.

This is obviously the case for treaties: states are free to become parties or not entirely as they choose. It is no less true, though, of custom, where the tests of state practice and *opinio juris* likewise assure that international legal obligation is only voluntarily acquired. In fact, a state that explicitly rejects a practice during the process of custom formation is exempt even from customary international legal obligations. For example, Saudi Arabia's objection to the provisions on the equal rights of women during the drafting of the Universal Declaration might be held to exempt it from such a norm, even if the norm is accepted internationally as customarily binding. Such considerations are particularly important when we ask what force there is to international law and what mechanisms exist to implement and enforce the rights specified in the Universal Declaration and the Covenants.

Acceptance of an obligation by states does not carry with it acceptance of any method of international enforcement. Quite the contrary. Unless there is an explicit enforcement mechanism attached to the obligation, its enforcement rests simply on the good faith of the parties. The Universal Declaration contains no enforcement mechanisms of any sort. Even if we accept it as having the force of international law, its implementation is left entirely in the hands of individual states. The Covenants do have some implementation machinery, but the machinery's practical weakness is perhaps its most striking feature. . . .

The one other major locus of activity in the international human rights regime is the UN Commission on Human Rights. In addition to being the body that played the principal role in the formulation of the Universal Declaration, the Covenants and most of the major single-issue human rights treaties, it has some weak implementation powers. Its public discussion of human rights situations in various countries can help to mobilize international public opinion, which is not always utterly useless in helping to reform national practice. For example, in the 1970s the

Commission played a major role in publicizing the human rights conditions in Chile, Israel, and South Africa. Furthermore, it is empowered by ECOSOC resolution 1503 (1970) to investigate communications (complaints) from individuals and groups that "appear to reveal a consistent pattern of gross and reliably attested violations of human rights."

The 1503 procedure, however, is at least as thoroughly hemmed in by constraints as are the other enforcement mechanisms that we have considered. Although individuals may communicate grievances, the 1503 procedure deals only with "*situations*" of gross and systematic violations, not the particular cases of individuals. Individuals cannot even obtain an international judgment in their particular case, let alone international enforcement of the human rights obligations of their government. Furthermore, the entire procedure remains confidential until a case is concluded, although the Commission does publicly announce a "blacklist" of countries being studied. In only four cases (Equatorial Guinea, Haiti, Malawi, and Uruguay) has the Commission gone public with a 1503 case. Its most forceful conclusion was a 1980 resolution provoked by the plight of Jehovah's Witnesses in Malawi, which merely expressed the hope that all human rights were being respected in Malawi.

In addition to this global human rights regime, there are regional regimes. The 1981 African Charter of Human and Peoples' Rights, drawn up by the Organization of African Unity, provides for a Human Rights Commission, but it is not yet functioning. In Europe and the Americas there are highly developed systems involving both commissions with very strong investigatory powers and regional human rights courts with the authority to make legally binding decisions on complaints by individuals (although only eight states have accepted the jurisdiction of the Inter-American Court of Human Rights).

Even in Europe and the Americas, however, implementation and enforcement remain primarily national. In nearly thirty years the European Commission of Human Rights has considered only about 350 cases, while the European Court of Human Rights has handled only one-fifth that number. Such regional powers certainly should not be ignored or denigrated. They provide authoritative interpretations in cases of genuine disagreements and a powerful check on backsliding and occasional deviations by states. But the real force of even the European regime lies in the voluntary acceptance of human rights by the states in question, which has infinitely more to do with domestic politics than with international procedures.

In sum, at the international level there are comprehensive, authoritative human rights norms that are widely accepted as binding on all states. Implementation and enforcement of these norms, however, both in theory and in practice, are left to states. The international context of national human rights practices certainly cannot be ignored. Furthermore, international norms may have an important socializing effect on national leaders and be useful to national advocates of improved domestic human rights practices. But the real work of implementing and enforcing human rights takes place at the national level. . . . Before the level of the nation-state is discussed, however, one final element of the international context needs to be considered, namely, human rights as an issue in national foreign policies.

HUMAN RIGHTS AND FOREIGN POLICY

Beyond the human rights related activities of states in international institutions such as those discussed in the preceding section, many states have chosen to make human rights a concern in their bilateral foreign relations.[3] In fact, much of the surge of interest in human rights in the last decade can be traced to the catalyzing effect of President Jimmy Carter's (1977–1981) efforts to make international human rights an objective of U.S. foreign policy.

In a discussion of human rights as an issue in national foreign policy, at least three problems need to be considered. First, a nation must select a particular set of rights to pursue. Second, the legal and moral issues raised by intervention on behalf of human rights abroad need to be explored. Third, human rights concerns must be integrated into the nation's broader foreign policy, since human rights are at best only one of several foreign policy objectives.

The international normative consensus on human rights noted above largely solves the problem of the choice of a set of rights to pursue, for unless a state chooses a list very similar to that of the Universal Declaration, its efforts are almost certain to be dismissed as fatally flawed by partisan or ideological bias. Thus, for example, claims by officials of the Reagan administration that economic and social rights are not really true human rights are almost universally denounced. By the same token, the Carter administration's serious attention to economic and social rights, even if it was ultimately subordinate to a concern for civil and political rights, greatly contributed to the international perception of its policy as genuinely concerned with human rights, not just a new rhetoric for the Cold War or neo-colonialism. Such an international perception is almost a necessary condition—although by no means a sufficient condition—for an effective international human rights policy.

A state is, of course, free to pursue any objectives it wishes in its foreign policy. If it wishes its human rights policy to be taken seriously, however, the policy must at least be enunciated in terms consistent with the international consensus that has been forged around the Universal Declaration. In practice, some rights must be given particular prominence in a nation's foreign policy, given the limited material resources and international political capital of even the most powerful state, but the basic contours of policy must be set by the Universal Declaration.

After the rights to be pursued have been selected, the second problem, that of intervention on behalf of human rights, arises. When state A pursues human rights in its relations with state B, A usually will be seeking to alter the way that B treats its own citizens. This is, by definition, a matter essentially within the domestic jurisdiction of B and thus outside the legitimate jurisdiction of A. A's action, therefore, is vulnerable to the charge of intervention, a charge that carries considerable legal, moral, and political force in a world, such as ours, that is structured at the international level around sovereign nation-states.

The legal problems raised by foreign policy action on behalf of human rights abroad are probably the most troubling. Sovereignty entails the principle of nonintervention; to say that A has sovereign jurisdiction over X is essentially equivalent to saying that no one else may intervene in A with respect to X. Because sovereignty is the foundation of international law, any foreign policy action that amounts to intervention is prohibited by international law. On the face of it at least, this prohibition applies to action on behalf of human rights as much as any other activity.

It might be suggested that we can circumvent the legal proscription of intervention in the case of human rights by reference to particular treaties or even the general international normative consensus discussed above. International norms per se, however, do not authorize even international organizations, let alone individual states acting independently, to enforce those norms. Even if all states are legally bound to implement the rights enumerated in the Universal Declaration, it simply does not follow, in logic or in law, that any particular state or group of states is entitled to enforce that obligation. States are perfectly free to accept international legal obligations that have no enforcement mechanisms attached.

Scrupulously avoiding intervention (coercive interference) thus still leaves considerable room for international action at improving the human rights performance of a foreign country. Quiet diplomacy, public protests or condemnations, downgrading or breaking diplomatic relations, reducing or halting foreign aid, and selective or comprehensive restrictions of trade and other forms of interaction are all actions that fall short of intervention. Thus in most circumstances they will be legally permissible actions on behalf of human rights abroad.

An international legal perspective on humanitarian intervention, however, does not exhaust the subject. Recently, several authors have argued, strongly and we believe convincingly, that moral considerations in at least some circumstances justify humanitarian intervention on behalf of human rights.[4] Michael Walzer, whose book *Just and Unjust Wars* has provoked much of the recent moral discussion of humanitarian intervention, can be taken as illustrative of such arguments.

Walzer presents a strong defense of the morality of the general international principle of nonintervention, arguing that it gives force to the basic right of peoples to self-determination, which in turn rests on the rights of individuals, acting in concert as a community, to choose their own government. Walzer has been criticized for interpreting this principle in a way that is excessively favorable to states by arguing that the presumption of legitimacy (and thus against intervention) should hold in all but the most extreme circumstances. Nonetheless, even Walzer allows that intervention must be permitted "when the violation of human rights is so terrible that it makes talk of community or self-determination . . . seem cynical and irrelevant,"[5] when gross, persistent, and systematic violations of human rights shock the moral conscience of mankind.

The idea underlying such arguments is that human rights are of such paramount moral importance that gross and systematic violations present a moral justification for remedial international action. If the international community as a whole cannot or will not act—and above we have shown that an effective collective international response will usually be impossible—then one or more states may be morally justified in acting ad hoc on behalf of the international community.

International law and morality thus lead to different and conflicting conclusions in at least some cases. One of the functions of international politics is to help to resolve such a conflict; political considerations will play a substantial role in determining how a state will respond in its foreign policy to the competing moral and legal demands placed on it. But the political dimensions of such decisions point to the practical dangers by moral arguments in favor of humanitarian intervention. . . .

Human rights may be moral concerns, but often they are not *merely* moral concerns. Morality and realism are not necessarily incompatible, and to treat them as if they always were can harm not only a state's human rights policy but its broader foreign policy as well.

Sometimes a country can afford to act on its human rights concerns; other times it cannot. Politics involves compromise, as a result of multiple and not always compatible goals that are pursued and the resistance of a world that more often than not is unsupportive of the particular objectives being sought. Human rights, like other goals of foreign policy, must at times be compromised. In some instances there is little that a country can afford to do even in the face of major human rights violations. . . .

If such variations in the treatment of human rights violators are to be part of a consistent policy, human rights concerns need to be explicitly and coherently integrated into the broader framework of foreign policy. A human rights policy must be an integral part of, not just something tacked on to, a country's overall foreign policy.

Difficult decisions have to be made about the relative weights to be given to human rights, as well as other foreign policy goals, and at least rough rules for making trade-offs need to be formulated. Furthermore, such decisions need to be made early in the process of working out a policy, and as a matter of principle. Ad hoc responses to immediate problems and crises, which have been the rule in the human rights policies of countries such as Canada and the United States, are almost sure to lead to inconsistencies and incoherence, both in appearance and in fact. Without such efforts to integrate human rights into the structure of national foreign policy, any trade-offs that are made will remain, literally, unprincipled.

Standards will be undeniably difficult to formulate, and their application will raise no less severe problems. Hard cases and exceptions are unavoidable. So are gray areas and fuzzy boundaries. Unless such efforts are seriously undertaken, however, the resulting policy is likely to appear baseless or inconsistent, and probably will be so in fact as well.

There are many opportunities for foreign policy action on behalf of human rights in foreign countries, but effective action requires the same sort of care and attention required for success in any area of foreign policy. . . .

CULTURE AND HUMAN RIGHTS

This view of the creation of the individual, with individual needs for human rights is criticized by many advocates of the "cultural relativist" school of human rights. They present the argument that human rights are a "Western construct with limited [universal] applicability."[6] But cultural relativism, as applied to human rights, fails to grasp the nature of culture. A number of erroneous assumptions underlies this viewpoint.

Criticism of the universality of human rights often stems from erroneous perceptions of the persistence of traditional societies, societies in which principles of social justice are based not on rights but on status and on the intermixture of privilege and responsibility. Often anthropologically anachronistic pictures are presented of premodern societies, taking no account whatsoever of the social change, we have described above. It is assumed that culture is a static entity. But culture—like the individual—is adaptive. One can accept the principle that customs, values, and norms do indeed glue society together, and that they will endure, without assuming cultural stasis. Even though elements of culture have a strong hold of people's individual psyches, cultures can and do change. Individuals are actors who can influence their own fate, even if their range of choice is circumscribed by the prevalent social structure, culture, or ideology.

Cultural relativist arguments also often assume that culture is a unitary and unique whole; that is, that one is born into, and will always be, a part of a distinctive, comprehensive, and integrated set of cultural values and institutions that cannot be changed incrementally or only in part. Since in each culture the social norms and roles vary, so, it is argued, human rights must vary. The norms of each society are held to be both valuable in and of their own right, and so firmly rooted as to be impervious to challenge. Therefore, such arguments are applicable only to certain Western societies; to impose them on other societies from which they did not originally arise would do serious and irreparable damage to those cultures. In fact, though, people are quite adept cultural accommodationists; they are able to choose which aspects of a "new" culture they wish to adopt and which aspects of the "old" they wish to retain. For example, the marabouts (priests), who lead Senegal's traditional Muslim brotherhoods, have become leading political figures and have acquired considerable wealth and power through the peanut trade.

Still another assumption of the cultural relativism school is that culture is unaffected by social structure. But structure does affect culture. To a significant extent cultures and values reflect the basic economic and political organization of a society. For example, a society such as Tokugawa Japan that moves from a feudal structure to an organized bureaucratic state is bound to experience changes in values. Or the amalgamation of many different ethnic groups into one nation-state inevitably changes the way that individuals view themselves: For example, state-sponsored retention of ethnic customs, as under Canada's multicultural policy of preserving ethnic communities, cannot mask the fact that most of those communities are merging into the larger Canadian society.

A final assumption of the cultural relativist view of human rights is that cultural practices are neutral in their impact on different individuals and groups. Yet very few social practices, whether cultural or otherwise, distribute the same benefits to each member of a group. In considering any cultural practice it is useful to ask, who benefits from its retention? Those who speak for the group are usually those most capable of articulating the group's values to the outside world. But such spokesmen are likely to stress, in their articulation of "group" values, those particular values that are most to their own advantage. Both those who choose to adopt "new" ideals, such as political democracy or atheism, and those who choose to retain "old" ideals, such as a God-fearing political consensus, may be doing so in their own interests. Culture is both influenced by, and an instrument of, conflict among individuals or social groups. Just as those who attempt to modify or change customs may have personal interests in so doing, so also do those who attempt to preserve them. Quite often, relativist arguments are adopted principally to protect the interests of those in power.

Thus the notion that human rights cannot be applied across cultures violates both the principle of human rights and its practice. Human rights mean precisely that: rights held by virtue of being human. Human rights do not mean human dignity, nor do they represent the sum of personal resources (material, moral, or spiritual) that an individual might hold. Cultural variances that do not violate basic human rights undoubtedly enrich the world. But to permit the interests of the powerful to masquerade behind spurious defenses of cultural relativity is merely to lessen the chance that the victims of their policies will be able to complain. In the modern world, concepts such as cultural relativity, which deny to individuals the moral right to make comparisons and to insist on universal standards of right and wrong, are happily adopted by those who control the state.

THIRD WORLD CRITICISMS

In recent years a number of commentators from the Third World have criticized the concept of universal human rights. Frequently, the intention of the criticisms appears to be to exempt some Third World governments from the standard of judgment generated by the concept of universal human rights. Much of the criticism in fact serves to cover abuses of human rights by state corporatist, developmental dictatorship, or allegedly "socialist" regimes.

A common criticism of the concept of universal human rights is that since it is Western in origin, it must be limited in its applicability to the Western world. Both logically and empirically, this criticism is invalid. Knowledge is not limited in its applicability to its place or people of origin—one does not assume, for example, that medicines discovered in the developed Western world will cure only people of European origin. Nor is it reasonable to state that knowledge or thought of a certain kind—about social arrangements instead of about human biology or natural science—is limited to its place of origin. Those same Third World critics who reject universal concepts of human rights often happily accept Marxist socialism, which also originated in the Western world, in the mind of a German Jew.

The fact that human rights is originally a liberal notion, rooted in the rise of a class of bourgeois citizens in Europe who demanded individual rights against the power of kings and nobility, does not make human rights inapplicable to the rest of the world. As we argue above, all over the world there are now formal states, whose citizens are increasingly individualized. All over the world, therefore, there are people who need protections against the depradations of class-ruled governments.

126

Moreover, whatever the liberal origins of human rights, the list now accepted as universal includes a wide range of economic and social rights that were first advocated by socialist and social-democratic critics of liberalism. Although eighteenth-century liberals stressed the right to private property, the 1966 International Human Rights Covenants do not mention it, substituting instead the right to sovereignty over national resources. . . . To attribute the idea of universal human rights to an outdated liberalism, unaffected by later notions of welfare democracy and uninfluenced by socialist concerns with economic rights, is simply incorrect.

The absence of a right to private property in the Covenants indicates a sensitivity to the legitimate preoccupations of socialist and postcolonial Third World governments. Conservative critics of recent trends in international human rights in fact deplore the right to national sovereignty over resources, as some of them also deplore any attention to the economic rights of the individual. We certainly do not share this view of rights; we believe that the economic rights of the individual are as important as civil and political rights. But it is the individual we are concerned with. We would like to see a world in which *every individual* has enough to eat, not merely a world in which every *state* has the right to economic sovereignty.

We are skeptical, therefore, of the radical Third Worldist assertion that "group" rights ought to be more important than individual rights. Too often, the "group" in question proves to be the state. Why allocate rights to a social institution that is already the chief violator of individuals' rights? Similarly, we fear the expression "peoples' rights." The communal rights of individuals to practice their own religion, speak their own language, and indulge in their own ancestral customs are protected in the Covenant on Civil and Political Rights. Individuals are free to come together in groups to engage in those cultural practices which are meaningful to them. On the other hand, often a "group" right can simply mean that the individual is subordinate to the group—for example, that the individual Christian fundamentalist in the Soviet Union risks arrest because of the desire of the larger "group" to enforce official atheism.

The one compelling use that we can envisage for the term "group rights" is in protection of native peoples, usually hunter-gatherers, pastoralists, or subsistence agriculturalists, whose property rights as collectivities are being violated by the larger state societies that encroach upon them. Such groups are fighting a battle against the forces of modernization and the state's accumulative tendencies. For example, native peoples in Canada began in the 1970s to object to state development projects, such as the James Bay Hydroelectric project in Quebec, which deprived them of their traditional lands. At the moment, there is no international human rights protection for such groups or their "way of life."

One way to protect such group rights would be to incorporate the group as a legal entity in order to preserve their land claims. However, even if the law protects such group rights, individual members of the group may prefer to move into the larger society in response to the processes of modernization discussed above. Both opinions must be protected.

If the purpose of group rights is to protect large, established groups of people who share the same territory, customs, language, religion, and ancestry, then such protection could only occur at the expense of states' rights. These groups, under international human rights law, do not have the right to withdraw from the states that enfold them. Moreover, it is clearly not the intention of Third World defenders of group rights to allow such a right to secession. A first principle of the Organization of African Unity, for example, is to preserve the sovereignty of all its member states not only against outside attack but also against internal attempts at secession. Group rights appear to mean, in practice, states' rights. But the rights of states are the rights of the individuals and classes who control the state.

Many Third World and socialist regimes also argue that rights ought to be tied to duties. A citizen's rights, it is argued, ought to be contingent upon his duties toward the society at large—privilege is contingent on responsibility. Such a view of rights made sense in nonstate societies in which each "person" fulfilled his roles along with others, all of the roles together creating a close-knit, tradition-bound group. But in modern state societies, to tie rights to duties is to risk the former's complete disappearance. All duties will be aimed toward the preservation of the state and of the interests of those who control it.

It is true that no human rights are absolute; even in societies that adhere in principle to the liberal ethos, individuals are frequently deprived of rights, especially in wartime or if they are convicted of criminal acts. However, such deprivations can legitimately be made only after the most scrupulous protection of civil and political rights under the rule of law. The difficulty with tying rights to duties without the intermediate step of scrutiny by a genuinely independent judiciary is the likelihood of wholesale cancellation of rights by the ruling class. But if one has rights merely because one is human, and for no other reason, then it is much more difficult, in principle, for the state to cancel them. It cannot legitimate the denial of rights by saying that only certain types of human beings, exhibiting certain kinds of behavior, are entitled to them.

One final criticism of the view of universal human rights embedded in the International Covenants is that an undue stress is laid on civil and political rights, whereas the overriding rights priority in the Third World is economic rights. In this view, the state as the agent of economic development—and hence, presumably, of eventual distribution of economic goods or "rights" to the masses—should not be bothered with problems of guaranteeing political participation in decision making, or of protecting people's basic civil rights. These rights, it is argued, come "after" development is completed. The empirical basis for this argument is weak. . . . Economic development per se will not guarantee future human rights, whether of an economic or any other kind. Often, development means economic growth, but without equitable distributive measures. Moreover, development strategies often fail because of insufficient attention to citizens' needs and views. Finally, development plans are often a cover for the continued violations of citizens' rights by the ruling class.

Thus we return to where we started: the rights of all men and women against all governments to treatment as free, equal, materially and physically secure persons. This is what human dignity means and requires in our era. And the individual human rights of the Universal Declaration and the Covenants are the means by which individuals today carry out the struggle to achieve their dignity. . . .

NOTES

1. The International Bill of Human Rights includes the Universal Declaration of Human Rights (1948), the International Covenant on Economic, Social and Cultural Rights (1966), the International Covenant on Civil and Political Rights (1966), and the Optional Protocol to the latter Covenant.

2. Howard Tolley, "The Concealed Crack in the Citadel: The United Nations Commission on Human Rights' Response to Confidential Communications," *Human Rights Quarterly* 6 (November 1984): 420–62.

3. This section draws heavily on Jack Donnelly, "Human Rights and Foreign Policy," *World Politics* 34 (July 1982): 574–95, and "Human Rights, Humanitarian Intervention and American Foreign Policy: Law, Morality and Politics," *Journal of International Affairs* 37 (Winter 1984): 311–28.

4. See, for example, Jerome Slater and Terry Nardin, "Nonintervention and Human Rights," *Journal of Politics* 48 (February 1986): 86–96; Charles R. Beitz, "Nonintervention and Communal Integrity," *Philosophy and Public Affairs* 9 (Summer 1980): 385–91; and Robert Matthews and Cranford Pratt, "Human Rights and Foreign Policy: Principles and Canadian Practice," *Human Rights Quarterly* 7 (May 1985): 159–88.

5. Michael Walzer, *Just and Unjust Wars* (New York: Basic Books, 1977), p. 90. For criticisms of Walzer see Slater and Nardin, "Nonintervention"; Beitz, "Nonintervention"; and David Luban, "The Romance of the Nation State," *Philosophy and Public Affairs* 9 (Summer 1980): 392–97.

6. Adamantia Pollis and Peter Schwab, "Human Rights: A Western Concept with Limited Applicability," in *Human Rights: Cultural and Ideological Perspectives*, Pollis and Schwab, ed. (New York: Praeger, 1979), pp. 1–18.

Reflections on Intervention

by Secretary-General Kofi Annan

It is a great honour for me to be asked to give the thirty-fifth annual Ditchley Foundation Lecture. I have carefully perused the list of your previous lecturers, and I may say I was somewhat intimidated to find myself following such a long line of presidents, prime ministers, cardinals ... and even central bankers. But I took heart when I saw that last year's speaker was my friend Bill Richardson. It is indeed reassuring that, after hearing from such an important and distinguished member of the United Nations Security Council, who is going on to become even more important and distinguished, you still think a mere Secretary-General might have something of interest to add.

Even so, I expect some of you are surprised by the title I have chosen for my talk. Or if not, you may think I have come to preach a sermon against intervention. I suppose that would be the traditional line for a citizen of a former British colony to take, in an address to senior policy makers and diplomats of the former imperial Power. And some people would also expect a sermon on those lines from the United Nations Secretary-General, whatever his country of origin.

The United Nations is, after all, an association of sovereign States, and sovereign States do tend to be extremely jealous of their sovereignty. Small States, especially, are fearful of intervention in their affairs by great Powers. And indeed, our century has seen many examples of the strong "intervening" – or interfering – in the affairs of the weak, from the Allied intervention in the Russian civil war in 1918 to the Soviet "interventions" in Hungary, Czechoslovakia and Afghanistan.

Others might refer to the American intervention in Viet Nam, or even the Turkish intervention in Cyprus in 1974. The motives, and the legal justification, may be better in some cases than others, but the word "intervention" has come to be used almost as a synonym for "invasion".

The Charter of the United Nations gives great responsibilities to great Powers, in their capacity as permanent members of the Security Council. But as a safeguard against abuse of those powers, Article 2.7 of the Charter protects national sovereignty even from intervention by the United Nations itself. I'm sure everyone in this audience knows it by heart. But let me remind you – just in case – that that Article forbids the United Nations to intervene "in matters which are essentially within the domestic jurisdiction of any State".

That prohibition is just as relevant today as it was in 1945: violations of sovereignty remain violations of the global order. Yet in other contexts the word "intervention" has a more benign meaning. We all applaud the policeman who intervenes to stop a fight, or the teacher who prevents big boys from bullying a smaller one. And medicine uses the word "intervention" to describe the act of the surgeon, who saves life by "intervening" to remove malignant growth, or to repair damaged organs. Of course, the most intrusive methods of treatment are not always to be recommended. A wise doctor knows when to let nature take its course. But a doctor who never intervened would have few admirers, and probably even fewer patients.

So it is in international affairs. Why was the United Nations established, if not to act as a benign policeman or doctor? Our job is to intervene: to prevent conflict where we can, to put a stop to it when it has broken out, or – when neither of those things is possible – at least to contain it and prevent it from spreading. That is what the world expects of us, even though – alas – the United Nations by no means always lives up to such expectations. It is also what the Charter requires of us, particularly in Chapter VI, which deals with the peaceful settlement of disputes, and Chapter VII, which describes the action the United Nations must take when peace comes under threat, or is actually broken.

The purpose of Article 2.7, which I quoted just now, was to confine such interventions to cases where the international peace is threatened or broken, and to keep the United Nations from interfering in purely domestic disputes. Yet even that article carries the important rider that "this principle shall not prejudice the application of enforcement measures under Chapter VII". In other words, even national sovereignty can be set aside if it stands in the way of the Security Council's overriding duty to preserve international peace and security. On the face of it, there is a simple distinction between international conflict, which is clearly the United Nations business, and domestic disputes, which are not. The very phrase "domestic dispute" sounds reassuring. It suggests a little local difficulty which the State in question can easily settle, if only it is left alone to do so.

We all know that in recent years it has not been like that. Most wars nowadays are civil wars. Or at least that is how they start. And these civil wars are anything but benign. In fact they are "civil" only in the sense that civilians – that is, non-combatants – have become the main victims. In the First World War, roughly 90 per cent of those killed were soldiers, and only 10 per cent civilians.

In the Second World War, even if we count all the victims of Nazi death camps as war casualties, civilians made up only half, or just over half, of all those killed. But in many of today's conflicts, civilians have become the main targets of violence. It is now conventional to put the proportion of civilian casualties somewhere in the region of 75 per cent. I say "conventional" because the truth is that no one really knows. Relief agencies such as the Office of the United Nations High Commissioner for Refugees (UNHCR) and the Red Cross rightly devote their resources to helping the living rather than counting the dead.

Armies count their own losses, and sometimes make boasts about the number of enemy they have killed. But there is no agency whose job is to keep a tally of civilians killed. The victims of today's brutal conflicts are not merely anonymous, but literally countless. Yet so long as the conflict rages within the borders of a single State, the old orthodoxy would require us to let it rage. We should leave it to "burn itself out", or perhaps to "fester". (You can choose your own euphemism.) We should leave it even to escalate, regardless of human consequences, at least until the point when its effects begin to spill over into neighbouring States, so that it becomes, in the words of so many Security Council resolutions, "a threat to international peace and security".

In reality, this "old orthodoxy" was never absolute. The Charter, after all, was issued in the name of "the peoples", not the governments, of the United Nations. Its aim is not only to preserve international peace – vitally important though that is – but also "to reaffirm faith in fundamental human rights, in the dignity and worth of the human person". The Charter protects the sovereignty of peoples. It was never meant as a licence for governments to trample on human rights and human dignity. Sovereignty implies responsibility, not just power.

This year we celebrate the fiftieth anniversary of the Universal Declaration of Human Rights. That declaration was not meant as a purely rhetorical statement. The General Assembly which adopted it also decided, in the same month, that it had the right to express its concern about the apartheid system in South Africa. The principle of international concern for human rights took precedence over the claim of non-interference in internal affairs.

And the day before it adopted the Universal Declaration, the General Assembly had adopted the Convention on the Prevention and Punishment of the Crime of Genocide, which puts all States under an obligation to "prevent and punish" this most heinous of crimes. It also allows them to "call upon the competent organs of the United Nations" to take action for this purpose.

Since genocide is almost always committed with the connivance, if not the direct participation, of the State authorities, it is hard to see how the United Nations could prevent it without intervening in a State's internal affairs.

As for punishment, a very important attempt is now being made to fulfil this obligation through the Ad hoc International Criminal Tribunals for the Former Yugoslavia and Rwanda. And 10 days ago in Rome, I had the honour to open the Conference which is to establish a permanent international criminal court. Within a year or two, I sincerely hope, this court will be up and running, with competence to try cases of war crimes and crimes against humanity wherever, and by whomsoever, they are committed.

State frontiers, ladies and gentlemen, should no longer be seen as a watertight protection for war criminals or mass murderers. The fact that a conflict is "internal" does not give the parties any right to disregard the most basic rules of human conduct. Besides, most "internal" conflicts do not stay internal for very long. They soon "spill over" into neighbouring countries.

The most obvious and tragic way this happens is through the flow of refugees. But there are others, one of which is the spread of knowledge. News today travels around the world more rapidly than we could imagine even a few years ago. Human suffering on a large scale has become impossible to keep quiet. People in far-off countries not only hear about it, but often see it on their TV screens.

That in turn leads to public outrage, and pressure on governments to "do something", in other words, to intervene. Moreover, today's conflicts do not only spread across existing frontiers. Sometimes they actually give birth to new States, which of course means new frontiers. In such cases, what started as an internal conflict becomes an international one. That happens when peoples who formerly lived together in one State find each other's behaviour so threatening, or so offensive, that they can no longer do so.

Such separations are seldom as smooth and trouble-free as the famous "velvet divorce" between Czechs and Slovaks. All too often they happen in the midst of, or at the end of, a long and bitter conflict, as was the case with Pakistan and Bangladesh, with the former Yugoslav republics, and with Ethiopia and Eritrea. In other cases, such as the former Soviet

Union, the initial separation may be largely non-violent, and yet it soon gives rise to new conflicts, which pose new problems to the international community. In many cases, the conflict eventually becomes so dangerous that the international community finds itself obliged to intervene. By then it can only do so in the most intrusive and expensive way, which is military intervention.

And yet the most effective interventions are not military. It is much better, from every point of view, if action can be taken to resolve or manage a conflict before it reaches the military stage. Sometimes this action may take the form of economic advice and assistance.

In so many cases ethnic tensions are exacerbated by poverty and famine, or by uneven economic development which brings wealth to one section of a community while destroying the homes and livelihood of another. If outsiders can help avert this by suitably targeted aid and investment, by giving information and training to local entrepreneurs, or by suggesting more appropriate State policies, their "intervention" should surely be welcomed by all concerned.

That is why I see the work of the United Nations Development Programme, and of our sister "Bretton Woods" institutions in Washington, as organically linked to the United Nations work on peace and security. In other cases, what is most needed is skilful and timely diplomacy.

Here in Europe I would cite the example of the Organization for Security and Cooperation in Europe (OSCE)'s High Commissioner on National Minorities, Max van der Stoel. You hardly ever see him on television or read about him in the newspapers, but that surely is a measure of his success. His job is to help European States deal with their minority problems quietly and peacefully, so that they never get to the stage of featuring in banner headlines or TV news bulletins around the world.

The United Nations also does its best to "intervene" in such effective but non-military ways. When I went to Baghdad in February of this year, I did so in search of a peaceful solution to a crisis that had brought us to the brink of a new war in the Gulf. I came back with an agreement which averted that crisis, at least for the time being.

The agreement was neither a victory nor a defeat for any one person, nation or group of nations. Certainly the United Nations and the world community lost nothing, gave away nothing and conceded nothing of substance. But by halting the renewal of military hostilities, it was a victory for peace, for reason, for the resolution of conflict by diplomacy.

It underscored, however, that if diplomacy is to succeed, it must be backed both by force and by fairness. The agreement was also a reminder to the entire world of why this Organization was established in the first place: to prevent the outbreak of unnecessary conflict; to seek to find international solutions to international problems; to obtain respect for international law and agreements from a recalcitrant party without destroying forever that party's dignity and willingness to cooperate.

Iraq is but one example of how, when the moment is ripe, diplomacy through the United Nations can achieve the will of the international community. We much prefer to see disputes settled under Chapter VI, rather than move to the drastic and expensive means available under Chapter VII.

For many years, the United Nations has been conducting successful peacekeeping operations – both of the traditional variety, monitoring ceasefires and buffer zones, as well as the more complex multidimensional operations that helped bring peace to Namibia, Mozambique and El Salvador.

And in recent years, there has been an increasing emphasis on the United Nations political work, as the size – though not the number – of peacekeeping operations has shrunk since its peak in the early 1990s. Early diplomatic intervention, at its best, can avert bloodshed altogether. But as you know, our resources are limited. And we are strong believers in the principle of "subsidiarity", which you Europeans are so fond of. In other words, we are more than happy if disputes can be dealt with peacefully at the regional level, without the United Nations needing to be involved.

We must assume, however, that there will always be some tragic cases where peaceful means have failed: where extreme violence is being used, and only forceful intervention can stop it. Even during the cold war, when the United Nations own enforcement capacity was largely paralysed by divisions in the Security Council, there were cases where extreme violations of human rights in one country led to military intervention by one of its neighbours. In 1971 Indian intervention ended the civil war in East Pakistan, allowing Bangladesh to achieve independence. In 1978 Viet Nam intervened in Cambodia, putting an end to the genocidal rule of the Khmer Rouge. In 1979 Tanzania intervened to overthrow Idi Amin's erratic dictatorship in Uganda.

In all three of those cases the intervening States gave refugee flows across the border as the reason why they had to act. But what justified their action in the eyes of the world was the internal character of the regimes they acted against. And history has by and large ratified that verdict. Few would now deny that in those cases intervention was a lesser evil than allowing massacre and extreme oppression to continue. Yet at the time, in all three cases, the international community was divided and disturbed. Why? Because these interventions were unilateral. The States in question had no mandate from anyone else to act as they did. And that sets an uncomfortable precedent.

Can we really afford to let each State be the judge of its own right, or duty, to intervene in another State's internal conflict? If we do, will we not be forced to legitimize Hitler's championship of the Sudeten Germans, or Soviet intervention in Afghanistan?

Most of us would prefer, I think – especially now that the cold war is over – to see such decisions taken collectively, by an international institution whose authority is generally respected. And surely the only institution competent to assume that role is the Security Council of the United Nations. The Charter clearly assigns responsibility to the Council for maintaining international peace and security. I would argue, therefore, that only the Council has the authority to decide that the internal situation in any State is so grave as to justify forceful intervention.

As you know, many Member States feel that the Council's authority now needs to be strengthened by an increase in its membership, bringing in new permanent members or possibly adding a new category of member. Unfortunately a consensus on the details of such a reform has yet to be reached.

This is a matter for the Member States. As Secretary-General I would make only three points. First, the Security Council must become more representative in order to reflect

Problems with SC

135

current realities, rather than the realities of 1945. Secondly, the Council's authority depends not only on the representative character of its membership but also on the quality and speed of its decisions. Humanity is ill served when the Council is unable to react quickly and decisively in a crisis. Thirdly, the delay in reaching agreement on reform, however regrettable, must not be allowed to detract from the Council's authority and responsibility in the meanwhile.

The Council in its present form derives its authority from the Charter. That gives it a unique legitimacy as the linchpin of world order, which all Member States should value and respect. It also places a unique responsibility on Council members, both permanent and non-permanent – a responsibility of which their governments and indeed their citizens should be fully conscious.

Of course the fact that the Council has this unique responsibility does not mean that the intervention itself should always be undertaken directly by the United Nations, in the sense of forces wearing blue helmets and controlled by the United Nations Secretariat. No one knows better than I do, as a former Under-Secretary-General in charge of peacekeeping, that the United Nations lacks the capacity for directing large-scale military enforcement operations.

At least for the foreseeable future, such operations will have to be undertaken by Member States, or by regional organizations. But they need to have the authority of the Security Council behind them, expressed in an authorizing resolution. That formula, developed in 1990 to deal with the Iraqi aggression against Kuwait, has proved its usefulness and will no doubt be used again in future crises. But we should not assume that intervention always needs to be on a massive scale.

There are cases where the speed of the action may be far more crucial than the size of the force. Personally, I am haunted by the experience of Rwanda in 1994: a terrible demonstration of what can happen when there is no intervention, or at least none in the crucial early weeks of a crisis. General Dallaire, the commander of the United Nations mission, has indicated that with a force of even modest size and means he could have prevented much of the killing. Indeed he has said that 5,000 peacekeepers could have saved 500,000 lives. How tragic it is that at the crucial moment the opposite course was chosen, and the size of the force reduced.

Surely things would have been different if the Security Council had had at its disposal a small rapid reaction force, ready to move at a few days' notice. I believe that if we are to avert further such disasters in the future we need such a capacity; that Member States must have appropriately trained stand-by forces immediately available, and must be willing to send them quickly when the Security Council requests it.

Some have even suggested that private security firms, like the one which recently helped restore the elected President to power in Sierra Leone, might play a role in providing the United Nations with the rapid reaction capacity it needs. When we had need of skilled soldiers to separate fighters from refugees in the Rwandan refugee camps in Goma, I even considered the possibility of engaging a private firm. But the world may not be ready to privatize peace.

In any case, let me stress that I am not asking for a standing army at the beck and call of the Secretary-General. The decision to intervene, I repeat, can only be taken by the Security

Council. But at present the Council's authority is diminished, because it lacks the means to intervene effectively even when it wishes to do so.

Let me conclude by coming back to where I started. The United Nations is an association of sovereign States, but the rights it exists to uphold belong to peoples, not governments. By the same token, it is wrong to think the obligations of United Nations membership fall only on States. Each one of us – whether as workers in government, in intergovernmental or non-governmental organizations, in business, in the media, or simply as human beings – has an obligation to do whatever he or she can to correct injustice. Each of us has a duty to halt – or, better, to prevent – the infliction of suffering.

Much has been written about the "duty to interfere" (*le devoir d'ingérence*). We should remember that the inventor of this phrase, Bernard Kouchner, coined it not as a minister in the French Government but when he was still running the charity Médecins du Monde. He argued that non-governmental organizations had a duty to cross national boundaries, with or without the consent of governments, in order to reach the victims of natural disasters and other emergencies. And their right to do this has since been recognized by two resolutions of the United Nations General Assembly – in 1988 (after the earthquake in Armenia) and again in 1991.

Both these resolutions, while paying full respect to State sovereignty, assert the overriding right of people in desperate situations to receive help, and the right of international bodies to provide it.

So when we recall tragic events such as those of Bosnia or Rwanda and ask "why did no one intervene?", the question should not be addressed only to the United Nations, or even to its Member States. Each of us as an individual has to take his or her share of responsibility. No one can claim ignorance of what happened. All of us should recall how we responded, and ask: What did I do? Could I have done more? Did I let my prejudice, my indifference, or my fear overwhelm my reasoning? Above all, how would I react next time?

And "next time" may already be here. The last few months' events in Kosovo present the international community with what may be its severest challenge in Europe since the Dayton agreement was concluded in 1995.

As in Bosnia, we have witnessed the shelling of towns and villages, indiscriminate attacks on civilians in the name of security, the separation of men from women and children and their summary execution, and the flight of thousands from their homes, many of them across an international border. In short, events reminiscent of the whole ghastly scenario of "ethnic cleansing" again – as yet on a smaller scale than in Bosnia, but for how long?

Of course there are differences – the crucial one being, precisely, that so far this conflict is being waged within the borders of a single State, recognized as such by the entire international community. I repeat: "so far". But when we witness the outflow of refugees into Albania; when we hear the insistence of Kosovar Albanian spokesmen that they will settle for nothing less than full independence; and when we remember the ethnic tensions in at least one neighbouring State, how can we not conclude that this crisis is indeed a threat to international peace and security?

This time, ladies and gentlemen, no one will be able to say that they were taken by surprise – neither by the means employed, nor by the ends pursued. This time, ethnically driven violence must be seen for what it is, and we know all too well what to expect if it is allowed to continue.

Recently, I recommended that the United Nations Preventive Deployment Force mandate be extended so as to sustain its success on the border of The former Yugoslav Republic of Macedonia and maintain stability. I have also been gratified by the clear determination expressed by the North Atlantic Treaty Organization (NATO) and its member governments to prevent a further escalation of the fighting, and I encourage all steps that may deter the further use of ethnically driven repression and the resort to violence by either side in Kosovo.

Of course, we all hope for a peaceful solution. And I particularly welcome the efforts of President Yeltsin to achieve this. But that only makes it more important to stop the violence now. And I feel confident that this time, if peaceful means fail to achieve this, the Security Council will not be slow to assume its grave responsibility.

A great deal is at stake in Kosovo today – for the people of Kosovo themselves; for the overall stability of the Balkans; and for the credibility and legitimacy of all our words and deeds in pursuit of collective security. All our professions of regret; all our expressions of determination to never again permit another Bosnia; all our hopes for a peaceful future for the Balkans will be cruelly mocked if we allow Kosovo to become another killing field.

Our theme is vast but the hour is late. Let me recall, in conclusion, that in French law there is a crime called "failure to assist a person in danger" (non-assistance a personne en danger).

I am sure this is what the late Francois Mitterrand had in mind in April 1991, when he congratulated the Security Council on its decision to intervene in the internal affairs of Iraq, in order to save the Kurds. "For the first time", President Mitterrand declared, "non-interference has stopped at the point where it was becoming failure to assist a people in danger". That, ladies and gentlemen, is what "intervention" is all about.

When people are in danger, everyone has a duty to speak out. No one has a right to pass by on the other side. If we are tempted to do so, we should call to mind the unforgettable warning of Martin Niemoller, the German Protestant theologian who lived through the Nazi persecution:

"In Germany they came first for the Communists. And I did not speak up because I was not a Communist. Then they came for the Jews. And I did not speak up, because I was not a Jew. Then they came for the trade unionists. And I did not speak up, because I was not a trade unionist. Then they came for the Catholics. And I did not speak up, because I was a Protestant. Then they came for me. And by that time there was no one left to speak up."

Third World Perspectives on Humanitarian Intervention and International Administration

by Mohammed Ayoob

Three points are fundamental to the understanding of third world perspectives on the international administration of war-torn territories. First, it must be recognized that Third World perspectives on this issue are linked in substantial measure to third world perspectives on humanitarian intervention. This does not mean that the former are automatically shaped by the latter regardless of context. What it amounts to is that the third world's generally suspicious orientation toward humanitarian intervention forms the starting point for most third world states' evaluation of cases of international administration. These assessments of individual cases are, however, also influenced by many other considerations, including geographic proximity, fear of spreading disorder in the neighborhood, amity or enmity among certain regimes and states, and ethnic and/or religious affinities. Second, while third world perspectives on these subjects may share substantial similarities, there is no single third world perspective on either humanitarian intervention or international administration. Third world states adopt stances in particular cases depending on a number of factors, and one can especially see differences between the perspectives of states situated in different continents and subregions within continents. Third, the selectivity demonstrated in the choice of cases both for humanitarian intervention and the installation of international administration has had a major impact on third world perspectives on these symbiotically linked enterprises. On the one hand, it has added to third world suspicions while, on the other hand, it has encouraged several third world states themselves to push for intervention in certain cases and oppose it in others. Consequently, not only has the exercise of double standards become somewhat rampant in the sphere of humanitarian intervention, it has provided the critics of such intervention with their most potent ammunition against this enterprise. In this article I analyze in turn each of these facets of the problem.

But, first, the term *third world* needs to be defined. In my definition, the term applies to all postcolonial states, including those—such as

Mohammed Ayoob, Selection from: "Third World Perspectives on Humanitarian Intervention," Global Governance, vol. 10, no. 1, pp. 99-104, 116-118.

Iran, Afghanistan, and Thailand—that may not have been directly colonized by the European powers but whose political geography and political economy were by and large determined by bargains among the European imperial powers. This definition also includes the post-Soviet states of Central Asia and the Caucasus, the latest additions to the category of postcolonial states. Such a definition goes beyond more restrictive terms such as *nonaligned countries*. States belong to the third world on the basis of their inherent political and economic characteristics, not because of particular foreign policy orientations. In short, third world states are the late entrants into the system of states and are in the early stages of state making and nation building. These are the two defining variables that also determine their economic and social characteristics—that is, economic dependence and lack of societal cohesion.[1] These political and socioeconomic attributes, which make such states acutely vulnerable to internal dissension and external interference, greatly influence their attitudes toward humanitarian intervention and international administration.

Humanitarian Intervention and International Administration

The close link between humanitarian intervention and international administration is demonstrated by the fact that international administration is usually a by-product or consequence of intervention justified on humanitarian grounds. Cambodia, East Timor, and Kosovo all testify to the veracity of this proposition. Therefore, the two phenomena cannot be divorced from each other. Consequently, reservations in the third world regarding humanitarian intervention are easily translated into initial skepticism about international administration as the beginning position regarding such ventures. This is particularly the case when intervention takes place without UN authorization or where the UN Security Council decision to authorize or endorse intervention is perceived to be the result of arm twisting on the part of the major powers, especially the United States.

At the most general level, third world reservations are related to the contested questions of what constitutes humanitarian intervention, how it should be authorized, and through what agents it should be implemented. All these boil down to the basic concern about the costs that states must pay in terms of the erosion of the principle of sovereignty in order to meet humanitarian ends and how much of this is justifiable in terms of the outcomes that such intervention seeks. Third world concerns in this context are much greater than those of the developed states of the global

North. Third world states are new states that have acquired the formal trappings of sovereignty only recently. Moreover, many of them are struggling to give this formal acquisition of juridical sovereignty greater substance.[2] As such, they are apprehensive of the new international activism and the developing norm of humanitarian intervention that could potentially threaten their sovereign status.[3]

This concern is heightened by the fact that the process of providing substance to the formal acquisition of sovereign statehood is usually accompanied by a certain amount of violence. State making, as the history of this enterprise in Europe demonstrates, is after all a "violent creation of order."[4] While one can hope to mitigate this violence to some extent, one cannot rule it out altogether. Many third world states feel that the inevitable occurrence of violence that accompanies the process of consolidating state power could leave them open to the charge of human rights violation and launch them on the slippery slope to external intervention and international tutelage. Many also perceive the recent decisions of the Security Council and, especially, the North Atlantic Treaty Organization (NATO) to engage in international intervention as a revival of the "standard of civilization" yardstick that was used in the nineteenth century to justify colonial subjugation.[5] This is not a fear that should be dismissed as a flimsy excuse for justifying human rights violation. It lies at the heart of much of the third world reaction to humanitarian intervention.

While some of these concerns are partially neutralized in the case of international administration, which often leads to the resuscitation of collapsing state structures and therefore serves state consolidation goals, the intervention that precedes the setting up of such administration continues to trouble many third world states—this despite the fact that such intervention is heralded by its supporters as the necessary first step toward the revival of legitimate and effective state authority. Third world concerns have become more acute as a result of the process through which decisions have been made since 1990 to identify targets for intervention and the way in which such decisions have been implemented. The arrogation by the Permanent Five (P-5)—some would argue the P-3 or the P-1—of the right to determine cases that are ripe for intervention and the subcontracting of interventionist ventures to coalitions of the "willing and the able" have made such interventions gravely suspect. The recent U.S.-led war against Iraq, which was justified partially on humanitarian grounds, is bound to heighten such suspicions immeasurably.[6]

This arrogation of international authority by the dominant coalition of North Atlantic states started with the decision to intervene in northern Iraq to create a safe haven for the Kurds. It was followed by the imposition of no-fly zones on northern and southern Iraq. Neither of these decisions, which virtually created a multinational "protectorate" in northern Iraq and seriously curtailed the sovereignty of the Iraqi state in the south of the country, was explicitly authorized by the UN Security Council. While the first could be justified by a tortuous process as an extension of UN Security Council Resolution 688, passed on 5 April 1991, the second had no justification in international law even if attempts were made to contrive such a justification.[7]

Moreover, interventions in Iraq and other locales left the distinct impression that the national interests of major powers determined such decisions. As S. Neil MacFarlane and Thomas Weiss, firm supporters of humanitarian intervention themselves, have pointed out,

> Military operations under chapter VII [undertaken for humanitarian purposes] are agreed largely on the basis of a calculus of shared interests or of tradeoffs among the five permanent members of the Security Council. In June 1994, for example, disparate interests resulted in separate council decisions to authorize interventions by the French in Rwanda, the Americans in Haiti, and the Russians in Georgia. Each of the three permanent members traded its vote for the favored intervention of the other in return for support of its own favored operation.[8]

Such bargaining among the major powers to enhance their respective strategic and economic interests in their spheres of influence had a substantial negative impact on third world perceptions of humanitarian intervention and detracted from their legitimacy in the long run.

The unrepresentative character of the Security Council and the threat of the veto that hangs over humanitarian decisions makes the Security Council a less-than-satisfactory medium for the determination of international will regarding humanitarian emergencies. Even the International Commission on Intervention and State Sovereignty (ICISS), which emphasized the central role of the Security Council in issues of humanitarian intervention, concluded, "It is unconscionable that one veto can override the rest of humanity in matters of grave humanitarian concern. Of particular concern is the possibility that needed action will be held hostage to unrelated concerns of one or more of the permanent members—a situation that has too frequently occurred in the past."[9]

Richard Falk has summed up the problems with regard to the legitimacy of actions authorized by the Security Council in the following words:

> Particularly confusing is the uncertainty regarding whether a Security Council decision involves a genuinely collective and community

interventionary judgement guided predominantly by considerations of public good. Uncertainty clouds the degree to which such a decision is little more than a legitimating rationale for use of force that would otherwise be more widely viewed as "illegal" if undertaken by a state on its own or in coalition with other states.[10]

When the Security Council's jurisdiction, itself open to question but nonetheless accepted by the majority of states, is circumvented in order to undertake interventions, as in the case of Kosovo, warning bells begin to ring louder in many third world capitals. In such cases, the dominant international coalition is perceived not merely as obstructing humanitarian action where it does not suit its interests, but also as promoting such action when it does. In the case of Kosovo, the North Atlantic powers were seen as actively undertaking intervention in defiance of the will of the international community, which is supposed to be expressed, in however a flawed manner, through the medium of the Security Council. It was in this context that the meeting of foreign ministers of the Nonaligned Movement (NAM) declared in its final communiqué, issued on 23 September 1999, that "we . . . reiterate our firm condemnation of all unilateral military actions or threats of military actions against the sovereignty, territorial integrity and independence of the members of [NAM] which constitute acts of aggression and blatant violations of the principle of non-intervention and non-interference."[11]

In the case of Kosovo, not only did NATO arrogantly arrogate to itself the power to determine international will, it added insult to injury by dumping the problem in the lap of the UN Security Council after it had militarily forced the withdrawal of Yugoslav authorities from the province. The Security Council was persuaded to provide international administration and to engage in state-building activities in Kosovo although the province's international legal status was not that of an independent state. Even the Independent International Commission on Kosovo, distinctly sympathetic to that particular intervention itself, was very uneasy about the precedent that the Kosovo intervention, which it described as "illegal, yet legitimate," was likely to set for the humanitarian enterprise.[12]

As a result of these multifaceted concerns about the legality and the legitimacy of these humanitarian interventions and the fact that such interventions did not take place in situations (such as Rwanda) that cried out for them, there is a substantial degree of suspicion regarding the real motives behind these interventions. Such reservations are likely to influence third world perspectives on international administrations that have been put in place following international interventions. Kosovo is the case that evokes the greatest amount of reservation. Many saw Cambodia as an attempt by the great powers to bring to an end an irritant from the days of the Cold War. It was also perceived as an attempt on the part of those powers, notably the United States and China, that had supported the genocidal Khmer Rouge to refurbish their image in the context of the changing international sensibility after the Cold War regarding human rights issues.

International action in East Timor is the least suspect, primarily because the UN and the vast majority of states did not recognize the Indonesian annexation of the territory. It was therefore not considered a part of Indonesia's sovereign territory except by Australia, paradoxically the country that led the international intervention into East Timor. Furthermore, East Timor's de-annexation returned it to its colonial borders, similar to the borders that are widely recognized in the third world as sacrosanct.[13] However, even here, Australian and U.S. actions were interpreted as self-serving because the former was the only major country that had recognized Indonesia's annexation of East Timor, and the latter had been Indonesia's principal great power patron during the Cold War.[14] It has been argued that Indonesia could not have consolidated its hold on East Timor without military hardware supplied by the United States and without a green signal from Washington. Australian worries about refugees reaching its shores with the collapse of Indonesian authority after the 1997 financial crisis and the removal of Suharto from power, and U.S. geopolitical maneuverings in Asia in the aftermath of the Cold War, were also credited for the international activism regarding East Timor.

Humanitarian interventions and the installation of international administrations are therefore looked upon with various degrees of suspicion around the third world. This perception is augmented by the selectivity with which such enterprises have been undertaken. I return to this subject after I have discussed regional variations in third world perceptions of both humanitarian intervention and international administration.

Notes

Mohammed Ayoob is University Distinguished Professor of International Relations, James Madison College, Michigan State University.

1. For details of this definition, see Mohammed Ayoob, *The Third World Security Predicament: State Making, Regional Conflict, and the International System* (Boulder: Lynne Rienner, 1995).

2. Robert Jackson, *Quasi-States: Sovereignty, International Relations and the Third World* (New York: Cambridge University Press, 1990).

3. For details of this argument, see Mohammed Ayoob, "Humanitarian Intervention and State Sovereignty," *International Journal of Human Rights* 6, no. 1 (spring 2002): 81–102.

4. For the intimate connection between violence and state making, see the seminal article by Youssef Cohen, Brian R. Brown, and A. F. K. Organski, "The Paradoxical Nature of State Making: The Violent Creation of Order," *American Political Science Review* 75, no. 4 (1981): 901–910.

5. Gerritt W. Gong, *The Standard of "Civilization" in International Society* (Oxford: Clarendon Press, 1984).

6. For details of this argument, see Mohammed Ayoob, "The War Against Iraq: Normative and Strategic Implications," *Middle East Policy* 10, no. 2 (summer 2003): 27–39.

7. See the text of Security Council Resolution 688, 5 April 1991, available online at http://www.un.org/Docs/scres/1991/688e.pdf. It makes no reference to Chapter VII of the charter. Derogation of a member state's sovereignty without specific reference to action undertaken under Chapter VII can have only dubious, if any, justification in international law.

8. S. Neil MacFarlane and Thomas Weiss, "Political Interest and Humanitarian Action," *Security Studies* 10, no. 1 (autumn 2000): 137.

9. International Commission on Intervention and State Sovereignty, *The Responsibility to Protect: Report of the International Commission on Intervention and State Sovereignty* (Ottawa: International Development Research Centre, 2001), p. 49.

10. Richard Falk, "The Complexities of Humanitarian Intervention: A New World Order Challenge," *Michigan Journal of International Law* 17 (winter 1996): 492–493.

11. Final Communiqué of the Meeting of Ministers for Foreign Affairs and Heads of Delegation of the Nonaligned Movement, held in New York on 23 September 1999, par. 8, available online at http://www.nam.gov.za/minmeet/newyorkcom.htm.

12. Independent International Commission on Kosovo, *The Kosovo Report: Conflict, International Response, Lessons Learned* (Oxford: Oxford University Press, 2000), p. 86.

13. James Cotton, "Against the Grain: The East Timor Intervention," *Survival* 43, no. 1 (spring 2001): 127–142.

14. According to James Cotton, "Both the United States and Australia had advance warning of the original invasion, but did nothing to prevent it, and took steps subsequently to deflect criticism from Jakarta for its policies. . . . Without US support, the annexation would not have taken place, and without U.S. materiel, the war against the Timorese resistance forces . . . would not have been successful." Cotton, ibid., p. 134.

15. Jusuf Wanandi, "Indonesia: A Failed State?" *Washington Quarterly* 25, no. 3 (summer 2002): 135.

16. Karin von Hippel, *Democracy by Force: U.S. Military Intervention in the Post–Cold War World* (New York: Cambridge University Press, 2000), p. 2.

17. James Dao, "In Quietly Courting Africa, U.S. Likes the Dowry: Oil," *New York Times*, 19 September 2002.

18. International Commission on Intervention and State Sovereignty, *The Responsibility to Protect: Research, Bibliography and Background* (Ottawa: International Development Research Centre, 2001), pp. 363–364.

19. Ibid. For the role of economics in the perpetuation of civil wars, see David Keen, *The Economic Functions of Violence in Civil Wars*, Adelphi Paper 320 (Oxford: Oxford University Press for IISS, 1998), and Mats Berdal and David M. Malone, eds., *Greed and Grievance: Economic Agendas and Civil Wars* (Boulder: Lynne Rienner, 2000).

20. Fund For Peace, "African Perspectives on Military Intervention: Conference Summary," *Regional Responses to Internal War, FfP Reports* 1 (December 2001), p. 6, available online at http://www.fundforpeace.org/programs/rriw/ffpr-africa_conference_report.pdf.

21. International Commission on Intervention and State Sovereignty, *The Responsibility to Protect*, pp. 387, 389.

22. Ibid., p. 392.

23. Ramesh Thakur, "Global Norms and International Humanitarian Law: An Asian Perspective," *International Review of the Red Cross* 83, no. 841 (March 2001): 34.

24. Ibid., pp. 38, 39.

25. Quoted in Hernan Vales, "The Latin American View on the Doctrine of Humanitarian Intervention," *Journal of Humanitarian Assistance* (February 2001): 4, available online at http://www.jha.ac/articles/a064.htm.

26. Quoted in Vales, ibid., p. 5.

27. Quoted in Vales, ibid., p. 7.

28. International Commission on Intervention and State Sovereignty, *The Responsibility to Protect*, p. 373.

29. The Arab participants in the ICISS roundtable in Cairo on 21 May 2001, made this very clear. They expressed their frustration that despite the fact that "The case of Palestine . . . involves a number of severe factors (disproportionate use of force, severe abuses of human rights, denial of the right to self-determination) . . . no international intervention is envisaged, despite appeals to the international community." For its part, the ICISS side agreed that "ICISS needs to seriously consider Arab experience in relation to double standards and

selectivity, with Palestine a good example." International Commission on Intervention and State Sovereignty, *The Responsibility to Protect*, pp. 375, 378.

30. Stephen Zunes, "United Nations Security Council Resolutions Currently Being Violated by Countries Other than Iraq," *Foreign Policy in Focus*, 2 October 2002, available online at http://www.fpif.org/commentary/2002/0210unres_body.html.

31. "U.S. Vetoes of UN Resolutions Critical of Israel (1972–2002)," *Jewish Virtual Library* (A Division of the American-Israeli Cooperative Enterprise), available online at http://www.us-israel.org/jsource/UN/usvetoes.html.

32. For example, see "Double Standards: Iraq, Israel and the UN," *The Economist*, 12 October 2002, pp. 22–24.

33. Fourth Geneva Convention, Art. 49, pars. 1, 6.

34. The UN General Assembly has constantly reiterated this position, most recently in its Resolution 56/61, passed on 10 December 2001.

35. Richard Falk and Burns H. Weston, "The Relevance of International Law to Palestinian Rights in the West Bank and Gaza: In Legal Defense of the Intifada," *Harvard International Law Journal* 32, no. 1 (winter 1991): 129–157.

36. Thalif Deen, "Third World Nations Split over Kosovo," *TWN Third World Network*, available online at http://www.twnside.org.sg/title/kosovo-cn.htm.

37. For a discussion of Hedley Bull's views on the role of the great powers in preserving order in the international system, see Bull, *The Anarchical Society: A Study of Order in World Politics* (New York: Columbia University Press, 1977), chap. 9.

The Veil Controversy

by Mark Allen Peterson

The practice of Muslim women wearing head coverings—ranging from head scarves, to gowns and veils covering the entire body—has become extremely controversial throughout the world. Belgium, France, Germany, Indonesia, the Netherlands, Tunisia, and Turkey have all instituted bans on some forms of Islamic dress in schools or other public places. Veiling has also sparked recent public debates in Denmark, Egypt, Italy, and the United Kingdom, and unveiling movements have sparked controversy in Iran and Saudi Arabia. Rather than being understood as a matter of cultural style—as jeans, saris, robes, and business suits usually are—these forms of dress have become symbols to much of the world of backwardness and oppression of women or, in some cases, as part of a clash of civilizations (Huntington 1993) between the West and the Islamic world. Getting an understanding of this worldwide debate requires a multidisciplinary approach.

There are many different kinds of face and head coverings that Western writers tend to collectively call "the veil." The simplest and most common is the *hijab*, a head scarf that covers the hair and neck. Some Middle Eastern Muslim women—wishing to distinguish themselves from Christian women, many of whom also wear the *hijab*—have begun adopting the *khimar*, a head-to-midriff covering with an oval for the face. The most thorough form of modest dress is the *niqab*, a dress that covers the entire body, accompanied by a face veil, gloves, and, in some places, an eye screen or sunglasses. A variation of this, the *burqa*, a head-to-foot pleated gown with an eye screen, is worn in parts of Afghanistan and Pakistan.

Although some Eastern European and Baltic countries have indigenous Muslim minorities, throughout most of Europe Islamic dress is inextricably linked with cultural concerns about immigration and pluralism. The most common concerns expressed about veiling involve secularism, integration, and security. In France, for example, *l'affaire du voile* (the affair of the veil) banning Islamic head coverings from public places has split the traditional political spectrum of right and left. Many side with the government's argument that the nation is inherently secular and that ostentatious displays of religion like the veil disrupt this principle. Others insist that religious freedom must include the right to dress as one wishes.

But for many, Islamic dress represents a deeper divide, one between secular Enlightenment values and something alien and backward. Some European feminists, for example, have argued that women are not truly free to choose the veil because they are oppressed by social pressures within their religious communities. Veiling advocates respond that social pressures for European and American women to dress seductively for men are just as strong and that banning the veil is just as oppressive as requiring it. Others decry a double standard that allows nuns to wear their habits in public spaces but refuses Muslim women the right to veil.

One response to this has been a claim that insistence on Islamic dress represents a refusal by migrants to integrate into their host societies. Even in countries like England, where the majority support the right of citizens to dress however they please as a civil liberties issue, the veil is widely seen as a "mark of separation," as former British prime minister Tony Blair put it, segregating Muslims from the British shared national culture (BBC 2006). Others have insisted that speaking to someone whose face is concealed is inherently undemocratic.

A major accusation leveled by anti-veiling activists in Europe and North America is that veiling is backward. In European history, Christian women wore veils or other head coverings in church, in accordance with a biblical injunction (1 Corinthians 11:4–10). Veils and head coverings were common in the European Middle Ages and the Renaissance. American and European notions of historical progress often draw on this history to see contemporary veiling by Muslims as an inappropriate remnant of history. But the history of veiling in the Middle East is quite different, and very complex. Historically, most of the world's Muslims have adopted whatever constituted modest dress in the areas in which they lived. Certainly this is true of the Middle East: head coverings and face veils were worn by Jews, Christians, and Zoroastrians before Islam. Ironically, veiling in the Islamic world seems to be rising in popularity largely through the influence of conservative Wahhabi and Salafi interpretations of Islam disseminated through global media using Saudi Arabian oil money, as a consequence of modern global migration patterns, and also as a result of twentieth-century economic patterns.

In many parts of the Middle East, veiling has long been a politically charged activity. In the 1920s and 1930s, Western-educated upper-class women in Egypt and elsewhere scandalized convention by publicly unveiling. At the same time, in Turkey and Iran, the government sought to ban veiling as a way to impose Western modernity on the populace. By the 1970s, in many parts of the region, the *hijab* and *niqab* were largely confined to older women and to Islamist students on college campuses. However, as the economic structural adjustment policies of the 1980s began to have financial consequences for middle- and working-class families, more and more women were forced into the workplace. For these women, adopting the veil was a way of showing that a woman could hold a job without compromising her morality as a wife and mother (Macleod 1991). Moroccan author Fatimah Mernissi reminds us that the *niqab* is like a one-way mirror. It conceals women from the gaze of the world, but it does not conceal the world from their gaze (Mernissi 2001). Many women who wear the *niqab*, or *burqa*, say that it offers them a sense of privacy in the most crowded conditions. Working women in particular say that it helps force men to pay attention to their minds rather than their bodies and allows them to be able to work with men without getting hit on. However, veiling has also been enforced on women by Islamist men through various means of coercion, including the horrific activity of throwing acid in the face of a Muslim woman who does not veil.

But many Westernized Arab governments were displeased with the widespread adoption of the veil in the 1980s and sought to curb it, seeing it as out of step with the modern secular ideologies they wanted to present. Egypt, for example, banned head scarves from college campuses (Eickelman and Piscatori 1996). This led to a protest in which large numbers of women began wearing head scarves to show solidarity with their fellow students and to send a message to the government not to meddle in domestic and religious issues. In the 1990s, the government tried again with regard to the *niqab*, only to achieve similar results. In Algeria, Tunisia, and Turkey "the new veiling" has also become an issue of political contention.

Why veiling? In Islam, the Qur'an requires men and women to dress modestly except in the presence of family members. What constitutes modest dress, and at what age it should be adopted, varies from community to community, and sometimes among people within a community. Worldwide, male modest dress has produced little or no controversy. It is only female modest dress that has sparked debate across parts of North America, Europe, Asia, and the Middle East.

The Qur'an itself is ambiguous about veiling. The term *hijab* is used only to refer to a curtain that provides privacy for the prophet's wives when guests were in the home. The text refers to neck scarves and cloaks (*jilbab*) for Muslim women when they go out so that they will be recognized as Muslims by nonmembers of the community. Several *hadith* extend the rules for women's modesty, but scholars are divided in their interpretations of these verses (Saleem 1996). Since Arab women of the prophet's era did not veil, many scholars believe that Arabs adopted veiling garments from the Zoroastrian Persians and Byzantine Christians in the decades following Muhammad's death (Esposito 2005, 98).

Saudi Arabia and Iran legally require veiling. Among Saudis, Muslim women must wear a loose robe called an *abaya*, a *hijab*, and *niqab*. Under the monarchy from the 1930s until 1979, it was illegal for Iranian women to wear veils or head coverings in public; since the revolution, it is illegal *not* to wear a *chador*, a loose-fitting cloak, and the *hijab*. Such laws are not the norm across the Middle East, however, and women choose to wear some form of head covering, or not, for any number of reasons.

There are practical reasons for wearing a head covering. Most people live in unheated and uncooled homes, and when they travel they are exposed to hot sunlight. The veil, like the traditional Arabian male head coverings, regulates the temperature of the head, keeping the sun off it and keeping it warm on cool nights and chilly mornings. Face veils protect the skin from sun and wind and keep dust off the face and out of the nose and mouth.

Many contemporary religious movements in the Middle East urge women to adopt the *hijab*, *khimar*, or *niqab* as a religious obligation. Among women whose families have not traditionally veiled, the decision to assume a head covering is often an important expression of religious piety. Adopting modest dress does not just show others you are devout; according to many teachers, it helps you become more devout by disciplining how you live your life.

Women who don't wear a veil because of personal piety may do so to reflect their family's respectability or to improve their chances of getting a husband in a conservative community. Many women begin to cover during specific life transitions: after first menses to show that a girl has become a marriageable woman, after marriage, after the birth of a first child, or after the death of a husband. And while women draw on family and community traditions in making these decisions, they are often also influenced by the twists and turns their own lives take.

Some women also argue that veiling is part of the erotic relationship between husbands and wives. When your husband is the only man who sees your hair and body (and, if he is faithful, yours is the *only* female body he sees) the act of unveiling at home becomes sexually charged. Certainly, Victoria's Secret does a thriving business in Riyadh (although men are banned from working there), and even decades-old regional department stores like Cairo's Omar Effendi have erotic lingerie sections.

Veiling also has significant economic advantages. Secular middle- and working-class women in Muslim countries may wear the *hijab* simply because it is cheaper than having their hair done. The shampoos, conditioners, blow dryers, and other home hair-care equipment Americans and Europeans take for granted are out of reach for all but a small percentage of most of the world's population. Yet if secular women may wear the veil for economic reasons, many religious leaders tout the *niqab* as offering a spiritual liberation from materialism. When every woman wears identical garb, they claim, women meet one another as equals, without external signs of wealth or status.

In many places, though, this logic completely fails. As the *hijab* and *khimar* have become more popular among upper classes throughout the Muslim world, they are increasingly seen as stylish. Many women choose their head scarves as carefully as they do their purses, shoes, belts, and other accessories. Chanel and other global fashion designers have begun offering elegant designer veils for Muslim women who can afford them. Islamic fashion for women is rapidly becoming a global industry.

Why do women veil? The reasons are many, and there is no universal meaning of veiling throughout the Middle East or in the Islamic world. Nor do European, American, and Asian governments agree about what the veil means and if they should do something about it. Many apologists of veiling in the Middle East and elsewhere ask why governments think they should *do* anything. Why, they ask, is the custom so arresting to Americans and Europeans that they talk of "liberating" Muslim women from the veil but rarely about liberating women from poverty, illness, and malnutrition—serious problems throughout the Islamic world (Abu-Lughod 2002).

References

Abu-Lughod, Lila. 2002. "Do Muslim Women Really Need Saving?" *American Anthropologist* 104, no. 3: 783–790.

BBC. 2006. "Blair's Concerns over Face Veils." BBC News. October 17. http://news.bbc.co.uk/1/hi/uk_politics/6058672.stm.

Eickelman, Dale, and James Piscatori. 1996. *Muslim Politics*. Princeton, NJ: Princeton University Press.

Esposito, John. 2005. *Islam: The Straight Path*, 3rd ed. New York: Oxford University Press.

Huntington, Samuel P. 1993. "The Clash of Civilizations?" *Foreign Affairs* 72, no. 3: 22–49.

Macleod, Arlene. 1991. *Accommodating Protest: Working Women, the New Veiling, and Change in Cairo*. New York: Columbia University Press.

Mernissi, Fatimah. 2001. *Scheherazade Goes West: Different Cultures, Different Harems*. New York: Simon & Schuster.

Saleem, Shehzad. 1996. "The Qur'anic Concept of Hijab." *Renaissance* 6, no. 11: http://www.renaissance.com.pk/index.html.

Required Readings Available Online

Universal Declaration of Human Rights (UNDR). United Nations. 1948. http://www.un.org/en/universal-declaration-human-rights/.

Bajoria, Jayshree. 2013. "The Dilemma of Humanitarian Intervention." *Council on Foreign Relations Backgrounder,* http://www.cfr.org/humanitarian-intervention/dilemma-humanitarian-intervention/p16524.

Additional Works Cited

Donnelly, Jack. 2003. *Universal Human Rights in theory and Practice*, Second Edition. Ithaca and London: Cornell University Press.

Iriye, Akira, Petra Goedde and William Hitchcock eds. 2012. *The Human Rights Revolution*. New York: Oxford University Press.

Waltz, Susan. 2008. "Who Wrote the Universal Declaration?" in Human Rights. Washington: U.S. Department of State Bureau of International Information Programs.

IV. MODULE FOUR:

Global Health and Environment

Global Health

Health is intricately linked to other issues of global scope and significance. In order to understand major trends in health, it is therefore necessary to also consider processes of globalization (the topic of the first module), government policy (a topic in the second module), economic development (the topic of the next module), as well as progress in medicine and science. Expanding our frame of reference beyond the science in general or medicine in particular will enable us to understand the biological, behavioral, economic, social, and political determinants of health.

Epidemiologists[8] have observed that with an increase in wealth, mortality and disease patterns make a corresponding shift. Pandemics and infectious disease are gradually replaced as the main causes of death by self-chosen or lifestyle diseases that result from poor exercise and food choices. Therefore, while people in more developed, wealthier nations are more likely to die of lifestyle diseases like heart disease, people in less developed parts of the world are more likely to die of infectious diseases. The socioeconomic gains of a society can have a great impact on population health (Delaet and Delaet. 2012: 30). However, this doesn't protect people in less wealthy countries from acquiring lifestyle diseases like obesity, heart disease etc. These, too, are being globalized, leading to new burdens of disease around the world. These global inequalities, and strategies for reducing them, will be explored in more depth in the next module.

The development of medicine and global health is not a one-way exchange with people in the developing world as beneficiaries of discoveries and developments in the so-called global North. To foreshadow the topic of indigenous peoples we will explore in the last module, the majority of the worlds' medications have been developed from plants, and much of the knowledge that has permitted these discoveries comes from indigenous knowledge. There are contentious debates about how indigenous people might be compensated for their knowledge. There are many court cases to remedy the fact that indigenous people are rarely paid for the information they share.

When it comes to health, globalization is a double edged sword. On one hand, it facilitates the rapid spread of disease. Further, global competition can weaken local health care systems. On the other hand, globalization also brings international organizations like the World Health Organization to rebuild these systems, disseminate effective treatment and address inequities.

---

[8] "Epidemiologists are public health professionals who investigate patterns and causes of disease and injury in humans. They seek to reduce the risk and occurrence of negative health outcomes through research, community education, and health policy. "United States Department of Labor Bureau of Labor Statistics http://www.bls.gov/ooh/life-physical-and-social-science/epidemiologists.htm

Readings

In "Key Concepts in Global Health" **Delaet** and **Delaet** provide a useful overview of the economic, social, and biologic determinants of health. These authors teach us the meaning of terms needed to be conversant in the field of public and global health. For example, the demographic and the epidemiological transition are concepts that are especially needed because they provide a way to understand the relationship between socio-economic gains and population health. This is foundational for appreciating the very real benefits to be gained from the human development project.

Key Concepts in Global Health

by Debra DeLaet and David DeLaet

Introduction

This chapter introduces key concepts in global health. It provides an introduction to the determinants of health, including biological and behavioral factors as well as economic, social, and cultural determinants. It introduces the key indicators of health and provides an overview of commonly used measures of burden of disease. The chapter describes the relative burden of various diseases among different populations and in different geographic regions. Lastly, the chapter covers the concepts of demographic transition and epidemiological transition as they relate to the economic development of a population and the associated variations in the health status and age composition of that population.

Determinants of Health

In studying global and comparative population health, it is critical for students to first understand the key variables that contribute to the well-being of any individual, regardless of geographic location. As this chapter shows, the overall health status of an individual is determined by a complex interaction of both individual variables and social, cultural, and environmental factors.

Historically, the health sciences have focused on a **biomedical model of health**, which emphasizes individual-level determinants of health, including genetics, individual behaviors, and direct exposure to harmful particles and organisms.[1] However, marked population differences in health status between countries—for example, 2007 data reveal the average life expectancy at birth is 83 years in Japan versus 42 years in Afghanistan—clearly suggest that individual factors alone cannot explain health outcomes, thus dictating the need for a more complex model.[2] **Social epidemiology** emerged as a field in which scholars and practitioners attempt to explain factors external to the individual that contribute to health outcomes.[3] These factors include, but are not limited to, socioeconomic status, education, culture, the physical environment, and access to health care services. The purpose of this section is to review the major determinants of health. In doing so, the chapter demonstrates that a complex interplay of both individual and external variables provides the best explanation for most health outcomes.

Biological Determinants of Health

Individual

Genetic makeup is one innate factor that determines the health of an individual. Certain diseases occur only among individuals who inherit specific gene variants. For example, sickle cell anemia, a condition characterized by abnormally functioning red blood cells, manifests only when an individual inherits an abnormal gene from both parents. Though the severity

KEY CONCEPTS IN THE DETERMINANTS OF HEALTH

Biomedical Model of Health: a model of health that emphasizes individual-level determinants of health, including genetics, individual behaviors, and direct exposure to harmful particles and organisms.

Demographic Transition: the shift of a population from one of high levels of both fertility and mortality and a low rate of population growth to one of low levels of both fertility and mortality and a low rate of population growth.

Epidemiological Transition: a change in mortality and disease patterns whereby a society experiences a shift from a period of high and fluctuating mortality rates largely attributable to communicable diseases to a period of lower and more stable mortality rates primarily due to chronic, noncommunicable diseases.

Gender: social roles and categories associated with men and women that are based on culturally prevailing constructs of presumed "normal," "appropriate," or "ideal" behavior and identities of men (masculinity) and women (femininity).

Social Capital: a broad range of economic, cultural, and personal resources attained through the social relationships of individuals living and interacting together in communities.

Social Epidemiology: a field in which scholars and practitioners attempt to explain factors external to the individual, including socioeconomic status, levels of education, culture, and access to health care, that contribute to health outcomes.

---

of the disease may vary from one person to another, all individuals inheriting two abnormal gene variants will exhibit some features of the condition, while those with one or no abnormal gene variant will not develop the disease. More commonly, however, diseases with a genetic predisposition do not present in such an all-or-none fashion. Rather, the inheritance of gene variants places an individual at increased risk for a specific condition, but whether a susceptible person develops the disease depends on other factors. For example, although Type II diabetes mellitus has a substantial genetic component, whether a genetically susceptible individual develops the disease is also strongly influenced by factors such as obesity. Similarly, an individual's risk for cardiovascular disease is significantly increased if there is a family history of the disease, but other factors—such as

smoking, age, biological sex, and the presence or absence of other medical conditions such as diabetes mellitus, hypercholesterolemia (high cholesterol), hypertension (high blood pressure), and obesity—contribute to the development of disease.[4]

Another innate determinant of health is biological sex. Social and cultural determinants of health often impact men and women differently. However, biological sex also contributes to the development of specific diseases. Certain cancers are possible in only one gender—ovarian and cervical cancer in women and prostate cancer in men. A perhaps less obvious example is the sex-specific risk of cardiovascular disease. Among individuals less than 60 years of age, men have a twofold risk of cardiovascular disease as compared with women, a disparity that decreases with age until the disease rate is equivalent between genders, by the eighth decade of life.[5]

Age is another biological variable that determines individual health. For example, children are much more likely to succumb to diarrheal illnesses, particularly in lesser developed countries where access to appropriate rehydration therapy may be limited.[6] Conversely, chronic illnesses such as osteoarthritis, hypertension, and Type II diabetes mellitus by their very nature cause increasing morbidity and mortality with the increasing age of an individual. As previously referenced, advancing age is also a risk factor for cardiovascular disease, with risk increasing after 45 years of age for men and 55 years of age for women.[7]

Behavioral Determinants of Health

The health of an individual is also determined by personal behaviors. Individual choices about whether to use seat belts, child restraints, or motorcycle helmets have obvious health implications. Sexual behaviors affect the likelihood of acquiring sexually transmitted diseases such as human immunodeficiency virus (HIV), viral hepatitis, syphilis, gonorrhea, and *Chlamydia*. Chronic alcohol abuse increases one's risk for developing liver disease. As a final example, physical inactivity and smoking can greatly increase an individual's risk of developing cardiovascular disease.[8]

Although personal behaviors have clear effects on health outcomes, it is important to note that political, social, and, in some instances, genetic variables shape individual behaviors with health consequences. In the case of motor vehicle safety, governmental policies and educational outreach can fundamentally shape individual behavior, leading to much-improved health outcomes. Similarly, education regarding safe sexual practices is critical in preventing sexually transmitted diseases. In the case of health risks associated with alcohol abuse, research suggests a strong genetic predisposition to alcoholism. Social factors can greatly influence one's physical activity level. Smoking behavior is influenced by

socioeconomic status as well as by the behavior of others. Individuals of lower income and educational attainment are more likely to smoke, and it has also been demonstrated that children of smokers are more likely to smoke.[9] As these examples indicate, personal behaviors are not entirely "individualized." Rather, behavioral determinants of health are rooted in a social and political context.

In a similar vein, it is important to consider the manner in which individual behavior influences not only individual health outcomes but also population health outcomes. By adhering to safe motor vehicle practices, an individual impacts his or her own well-being as well as that of others. As another example, secondhand smoke exposure among children has been shown to increase the risk of sudden infant death syndrome, respiratory and middle ear infections, and more frequent and severe asthma attacks. The most intimately shared environment is that of the pregnant mother and the developing fetus, and thus the health status and behavioral choices of the mother obviously have a profound impact on the immediate and future health of the fetus. Smoking during pregnancy has been shown to increase the risk of a child being born prematurely and of small birth weight. Such birth outcomes not only affect early child health and development but may also increase the risk of adverse health outcomes as an adult, including an increased risk of cardiovascular disease.[10]

Economic, Social, and Political Determinants of Health

Social factors, including socioeconomic status, employment, and education, have a significant impact on health. Poverty greatly influences one's risk of developing specific diseases. As an example, transmission of HIV is much greater among individuals living in developing countries.[11] It has been shown that even in more developed countries, poverty is the single most important risk factor associated with HIV infection among heterosexuals living in urban settings.[12] Individuals of lower-income status

161

are more likely to smoke, thus increasing their risk of conditions such as cancer and cardiovascular disease while posing a risk of secondhand smoke exposure to close contacts.

Another social factor that shapes health outcomes is the employment status of an individual. Employment obviously contributes directly to one's financial well-being, which itself has effects on health. Employment status often determines health insurance coverage in specific countries. Variables related to employment, occupation, and unpaid labor can have negative consequences on one's health, and certain occupations increase the risk of exposure to potential physical health hazards.

Work-related health risks are often unequally distributed according to gender. For example, in developing countries, women are often responsible for unpaid tasks of maintaining the home, such as providing water and fuel. These responsibilities have been shown to increase the risk of exposure to waterborne illnesses such as schistosomiasis as well as mosquito-borne illnesses such as malaria.[13] Cooking on open stoves in such settings also increases women's risk of burns and illnesses due to smoke pollution.[14] In more developed countries, women often constitute a higher percentage of the labor force in industries such as textiles and clothing manufacturing, and thus they also suffer higher rates of asthma and allergies due to exposure to dust in the workplace.[15] Conversely, men are more likely to suffer accidents in the workplace.[16] Further, men in developed countries report greater occupational exposure than women to noise, vibrations, extreme temperatures, chemicals, and physical stress and are thus more likely to suffer illnesses associated with such exposures.[17]

Employment can influence health outcomes in more subtle ways. For example, the Whitehall study in Britain demonstrated that, among British civil servants, employment grade was associated with adverse cardiovascular outcomes in a continuous and downward-sloping gradient.[18] In other words, individuals with a lower job rank were more likely to have cardiovascular disease; when comparing groups of workers across job rank categories, workers in the lower job rank category consistently had higher rates of heart disease than workers in the next highest ranking group. As the study was conducted among civil servants, all of whom earned above living wage and had access to health care services, the implication is that psychosocial pathways contributed to this increased cardiovascular risk.

One's educational attainment also determines health outcomes in both direct and indirect ways. Directly, appropriate educational interventions can lead to the adoption of healthy lifestyle practices. As previously referenced, education regarding safe sexual practices has been shown to reduce the transmission of sexually transmitted diseases such as HIV/AIDS. Educational interventions also have been associated with decreased tobacco use among adolescents. Indirectly, higher educational attainment typically leads to better employment with associated higher income and social status. This, in turn, impacts health in ways previously described in this section.

One's physical environment also has clear implications for health. As an example, individuals living in developing countries have less consistent access to clean water supplies, with the resultant increased risk of waterborne illnesses. These populations also are at increased risk for respiratory illnesses associated with higher rates of indoor air pollution. Highlighting the fact that individual health determinants do not operate in isolation, young children in these populations are particularly vulnerable to these adverse health outcomes.[19] Studies have suggested that one's environment has an important effect on health outcomes in developed countries as well. As an example, one's risk of developing respiratory conditions such as asthma increases if there is early postnatal exposure to common allergens such as dust mites and cockroaches,[20] and asthma severity is often impacted by outdoor air pollution.[21]

UNDER THE MICROSCOPE

Determinants of Cardiovascular Disease

The likelihood that an individual will develop a specific disease state and the severity with which that disease will manifest in an individual are determined by many interdependent risk factors, risks often unevenly distributed by gender, race, and socioeconomic status. A review of the determinants of the development of cardiovascular disease illustrates the complex interplay among individual, behavioral, social, and political determinants of health.

An individual's likelihood of developing cardiovascular disease is influenced by biological factors such as genetic susceptibility and gender. Risk increases with advancing age. Interestingly, gender discrepancies noted among younger individuals are not seen when comparing elderly males and females. It has been suggested that individual biological risk of cardiovascular disease may be increased by prematurity and low birth weight, the risk of which is, in turn, impacted by maternal health status, behavior, and access to appropriate health care.

The development of cardiovascular disease is further influenced by individual behaviors such as level of physical activity and smoking, behaviors that are not only influenced by educational interventions but also often shaped by the behavior patterns of the members of one's family and community. Further, the community-level behavior patterns can be influenced by availability of green space, access to healthy foods, and perceived safety of the neighborhood—factors that are themselves shaped by complex economic and political determinants. As was shown in the previously discussed Whitehall study, even the employment grade of an individual can increase his or her risk of cardiovascular disease.

Additionally, whether one has access to affordable and appropriate health care can contribute not only to the development of disease but also to the severity of disease expression. As there are many underlying medical conditions that serve as risk factors for the development of cardiovascular disease (for example, hypertension, Type II diabetes mellitus, and hypercholesterolemia), consistent access to health care for individuals with these conditions is critical in the prevention of cardiovascular disease. Social and political factors also play an important role in shaping the risk of cardiovascular disease. For example, access to appropriate care for cardiovascular disease may be limited for both women and minority groups. Historically, even research studies of interventions for cardiovascular management have been biased against women and minority groups.

The example of cardiovascular disease clearly demonstrates the complicated interplay among individual, social, and political variables that determine the health of an individual in regard to a specific health condition.

One's local environment and community can affect health outcomes in other ways as well. In the past several decades, considerable research has been done on the concept of **social capital**. Social capital suggests that individuals gain access to a broader range of economic and cultural resources through the social relationships they create.[22] Studies have suggested that higher levels of individual-level social capital are associated with better self-rated health.[23] Conversely, it has been suggested that social mistrust is closely associated with higher rates of mortality and violent crime.[24] Other studies have highlighted the effect that neighborhoods have on disease states such as obesity, Type II diabetes mellitus, hypertension, and mental health disorders.[25] As one specific example, it has been shown that obesity is associated with poor access to healthy foods and neighborhood green space for exercise.[26]

Finally, governmental policies shape individual and population health outcomes in significant ways. National health policy may lead to more efficient and effective spending of health care dollars, resulting in a greater number of individuals having access to affordable health care services. Further, economic and taxation policies may contribute to more uniform distribution of national wealth, and educational policy may ensure better access to appropriate educational and vocational opportunities for individuals. In this way, public policy can result in better living conditions for a greater number of individuals in a given population. National and local legislation can also directly shape individual behaviors in a manner that results in better health outcomes. As previously mentioned, adoption of safe motor vehicle practices can be influenced by legislation. As an additional example, smoke-free air laws have been shown to reduce secondhand smoke exposure among nonsmoking youth.

Population Health Assessment

Whereas the prior section addressed the determinants of individual health, this section introduces concepts pertinent to **population**

health. In order to evaluate the health status of populations, one must have an understanding of the key indicators of population health as well as measures commonly used to assess the burden that specific diseases place on a population. Additionally, knowledge of these concepts is critical to inform national, state, and local policy-setting in ways likely to improve the health of a specific population. To this end, this section provides definitions for commonly used indicators of population health and measures of disease burden. Additionally, the section provides an overview of global trends of comparative population health.

Key Indicators of Population Health

When assessing population health, it is imperative to have available a set of key indicators of health that can be consistently applied such that reliable comparisons might be made between various populations. These indicators should also be able to provide insight into variants of health by gender and age within and across populations.

The **mortality rate** is one of the most basic indicators used in studies of population health. Simply stated, a mortality rate is an estimate of the proportion of a population that dies during a specified period. A mortality rate can be determined for any population or subpopulation (for example, **adult mortality rate**) for any defined period of time, based on the specific health outcomes one wishes to assess. Another commonly employed health indicator is **life expectancy at birth**, defined as the average number of years that a newborn is expected to live if mortality patterns at the time of its birth were to prevail throughout the child's life. A similar health indicator is the **health-adjusted life expectancy (HALE)**, defined as the average number of years that a person can expect to live in full health by taking into account the years the person is in less than full health due to disease and/or injury. Current estimates of these population health indicators for the six World Health

164

KEY INDICATORS OF HEALTH

Adult Mortality Rate: the probability of dying between the ages of 15 and 60 years (per 1,000 population) per year among a hypothetical cohort of 100,000 people who would experience the age-specific mortality rate of the reporting year.

Health-adjusted Life Expectancy (HALE): the average number of years that a person can expect to live in full health by taking into account the years the person is in less than full health due to disease and/or injury.

Infant Mortality Rate: the probability of a child born in a specific year or period dying before reaching the age of one, if subject to age-specific mortality rates of that period.

Life Expectancy at Birth: the average number of years that a newborn is expected to live if mortality patterns at the time of its birth were to prevail throughout the child's life.

Maternal Mortality Ratio: the annual number of female deaths from any cause related to or aggravated by pregnancy or its management (excluding accidental or incidental causes) during pregnancy and childbirth or within 42 days of termination of pregnancy, irrespective of the duration or site of the pregnancy, per 100,000 live births, for a specified year.

Mortality Rate: an estimate of the proportion of a population that dies during a specified period. The numerator is the number of persons dying during the period; the denominator is the total number of people in the population, usually estimated as the midyear population.

Neonatal Mortality Rate: the number of registered deaths in the neonatal period (the first 28 completed days of life) per 1,000 live births in a given year or period of time.

Under-five Mortality Rate: the probability (expressed as a rate per 1,000 live births) of a child born in a specific year or period dying before reaching the age of five, if subject to age-specific mortality rates of that period.

Organization (WHO) global regions are presented in Table 2.1, along with the gross national income per capita of those regions. As the data demonstrate, poverty is associated with poorer health outcomes for each of these key health indicators. Also, it appears that these poorer health outcomes are particularly noteworthy for women and young children living in poverty, as evidenced by the somewhat greater disparity between higher- and lower-income regions for **maternal mortality ratio** and **neonatal, infant, and under-five mortality rates** as compared with the other key health indicators. The reasons for these contrasting health outcomes are likely multifactorial. An introduction to the factors that lead to disparate health outcomes was provided in the previous section on the determinants of health, and Chapter 6 explores this topic in greater depth.

TABLE 2.1 Key Indicators of Population Health, by WHO Region, 2008

	Africa	Americas	Southeast Asia	Europe	Eastern Mediterranean	Western Pacific
Neonatal mortality rate (per 1,000 live births)	40	9	34	7	35	11
Infant mortality rate (per 1,000 live births)	85	15	48	12	57	18
Under-five mortality rate (per 1,000 live births)	142	18	63	14	78	21
Maternal mortality ratio[a] (per 100,000 live births)	900	99	450	27	420	82
Adult mortality rate (per 1,000 population)	392	126	218	149	203	113
Life expectancy at birth (years)	52	73	63	71	63	72
Health-adjusted life expectancy (HALE) at birth[b] (years)	45	67	57	67	56	67
Gross national income per capita (PPP int. $)	2,279	24,005	3,043	22,849	3,805	8,958

[a]2005 data
[b]2007 data

Source: World Health Organization, "Part II: Global Health Indicators," *World Health Statistics 2010.* Available online at: http://www.who.int/whosis/whostat/EN_WHS10_Part2.pdf.

Common Measures of Disease Burden

In evaluating population health, it is important to assess not only the health status of that population but also the diseases that most significantly contribute to mortality, morbidity, and disability for that population. To do so, one must be familiar with commonly used measures of **burden of disease**. This section introduces these measures and provides a brief overview of the categories of diseases. Additionally, this section highlights data on the global burden of disease.

Individual **mortality**, **morbidity**, and **disability** may occur due to injury or the presence of disease. Typically, diseases are broadly categorized as either communicable or noncommunicable. **Communicable diseases** are transmitted directly or indirectly from one individual to another via a microbial agent such as a virus, bacteria, parasite, or fungus. Key examples of

a communicable disease include tuberculosis, malaria, and HIV. Conversely, **noncommunicable diseases**, such as Type II diabetes mellitus, occur in the absence of such infectious agents and are not transmissible between individuals. Communicable diseases and noncommunicable diseases are explored in much greater detail in Chapters 4 and 5, respectively.

Measures commonly used to describe disease burden include prevalence, incidence, and cause-specific mortality rates. **Prevalence** is defined as "the number of affected persons present in the population at a specific time divided by the number of persons in the population at that time."[27] Typically, this measure is applied as *point prevalence*, with the assessment made at one specific point in time rather than over a period of time. **Incidence** is "the number of new cases of a disease that occur during a specified period of time in a population at risk for developing the disease."[28] Whereas prevalence measures the current burden of disease in a population, incidence reflects the current risk of developing the disease in those not currently affected by the disease. These two measures are related in that, as disease incidence increases, so too does disease prevalence. Prevalence also increases with improvements in disease management that allow an individual to survive a specific illness for a greater duration of time. Conversely, prevalence decreases if individuals are cured of the illness or die. Population disease burden can also be assessed using **cause-specific mortality rates**, an estimate of the proportion of a population that dies during a specified period as a result of a specific disease or injury. For example, the WHO routinely includes cause-specific mortality rates for tuberculosis, malaria, and HIV/AIDS in its updated global health reports.

These measures are useful in demonstrating how commonly a specific disease or injury occurs within a population as well as the contribution of that disease or injury to the overall mortality rate of a population. However, these are imperfect measures of disease burden in that they fail to capture the contribution of a specific disease or injury to morbidity and disability within a population.[29] Therefore, measures of population health have been developed that allow for the combined impact of death, disability, and morbidity to be considered simultaneously.[30] The most commonly used of these measures is the **disability-adjusted life year (DALY)**. The DALY is defined as the sum of years of potential life lost due to premature mortality and the years of productive life lost due to disability; in essence, it "measures the difference between a current situation and an ideal situation where everyone lives up to the age of standard life expectancy, and in perfect health."[31]

Applying this measure, the WHO periodically determines the leading causes of disease burden to global populations. The most recently published estimates for the ten leading causes of disease burden, stratified by country income, are presented in Table 2.2. As can be seen, communicable diseases contribute the majority of disease burden in low-income countries, whereas high-income countries are much more likely to suffer morbidity, disability, and mortality as a result of noncommunicable diseases. Disease burden in middle-income countries appears to more closely parallel that of high-income countries than low-income countries, with the exception that communicable diseases such as lower respiratory infections and HIV/AIDS are significant contributors to morbidity, disability, and

TABLE 2.2 Leading Causes of Burden of Disease (DALYs), Countries Grouped by Income, 2004

Disease or injury	DALYs (millions)	Percentage of total DALYs	Disease or injury	DALYs (millions)	Percentage of total DALYs
World			**Low-income countries**		
Lower respiratory infections	94.5	6.2	Lower respiratory infections	76.9	9.3
Diarrheal diseases	72.8	4.8	Diarrheal diseases	59.2	7.2
Unipolar depressive disorders	65.5	4.3	HIV/AIDS	42.9	5.2
Ischemic heart disease	62.6	4.1	Malaria	32.8	4.0
HIV/AIDS	58.5	3.8	Prematurity and low birth weight	32.1	3.9
Cerebrovascular disease	46.6	3.1	Neonatal infections	31.4	3.8
Prematurity and low birth weight	44.3	2.9	Birth asphyxia and birth trauma	29.8	3.6
Birth asphyxia and birth trauma	41.7	2.7	Unipolar depressive disorders	26.5	3.2
Road traffic accidents	41.2	2.7	Ischemic heart disease	26.0	3.1
Neonatal infections	40.4	2.7	Tuberculosis	22.4	2.7
Middle-income countries			**High-income countries**		
Unipolar depressive disorders	29.0	5.1	Unipolar depressive disorders	10.0	8.2
Ischemic heart disease	28.9	5.0	Ischemic heart disease	7.7	6.3
Cerebrovascular disease	27.5	4.8	Cerebrovascular disease	4.8	3.9
Road traffic accidents	21.4	3.7	Alzheimer's and other dementias	4.4	3.6
Lower respiratory infections	16.3	2.8	Alcohol use disorders	4.2	3.4
Chronic obstructive lung disease	16.1	2.8	Hearing loss, adult onset	4.2	3.4
HIV/AIDS	15.0	2.6	Chronic obstructive lung disease	3.7	3.0
Alcohol use disorders	14.9	2.6	Diabetes mellitus	3.6	3.0
Refractive errors	13.7	2.4	Trachea, bronchus, lung cancers	3.6	3.0
Diarrheal diseases	13.1	2.3	Road traffic accidents	3.1	2.6

Source: Reproduced from the World Health Organization, *The Global Burden of Disease: 2004 Update.* Available online at: http://www.who.int/healthinfo/global_burden_disease/GBD_report_2004update_full.pdf.

mortality in middle-income countries. Careful inspection of the data in Table 2.2 provides further insights. For one, it can be seen that in low-income regions, considerable disease burden results from pregnancy- and birth-related disease and injury, again highlighting that women and young children living in poverty are particularly vulnerable to poor health outcomes. Additionally, the data demonstrate that with socioeconomic advances, populations are faced with increasing morbidity and mortality associated with advancing age, such as dementia and chronic illnesses such as ischemic heart disease, chronic obstructive lung disease, and cancers.

Demographic and Epidemiological Transitions

This chapter would be incomplete without a discussion of the two distinct yet closely related concepts of epidemiological transition and demographic transition. As described earlier in this chapter, individual health is determined by the interplay among individual, social, and political variables. Further, population health is closely linked with economic, social, and political determinants. The concepts of epidemiological transition and demographic transition serve as examples of how these variables interact to shape not only the health of populations but also population growth, as well as the relative burden of specific diseases within populations. This section provides a brief review of these two concepts and discusses the implications of these transitions for specific populations.

Epidemiological Transition

The concept of **epidemiological transition** was first described in 1971 by Abdel Omran as a transition of a population in which "a long shift occurs in mortality and disease patterns whereby pandemics of infection are gradually displaced by degenerative and man-made diseases as the chief form of morbidity and primary cause of death."[32] In essence, a population moves from a period when mortality rates are high and fluctuating, with death largely attributable to famine and infectious diseases, to a state of lower and more stable mortality rates, with morbidity and mortality largely due to chronic, noncommunicable diseases.

The determinants that influence this transition are complex. However, most research has suggested that cultural and socioeconomic factors leading to improvements in living conditions, nutrition, and hygiene have contributed most significantly to this transition, particularly for most Western populations that began this transition in the 19th century. Advances in public health and medicine, including improved public sanitation, immunizations, and development of therapies such as antibiotics, have played an additional role in populations undergoing this transition more recently.[33]

Most developed countries have undergone such a transition, with relatively low and more stable mortality rates and disease burden attributable most significantly to noncommunicable diseases. Conversely, many developing countries exhibit higher mortality rates with significant disease burden due to infectious diseases, suggesting the epidemiological transition has not yet been completed.

Demographic Transition

The **demographic transition** represents the shift of a population from one of high levels of fertility and mortality and a low rate of population growth to one of low levels of fertility and mortality and a low rate of population growth.[34] Socioeconomic, public health, and medical advances within a population result in decreased mortality rates for that population, particularly improving health outcomes for infants and young children. As depicted in Figure 2.1, the decline in mortality leads to a resultant increase in the population growth rate, particularly among younger members of the population. After some time, there is a subsequent decline in the fertility rate of the population, with a resultant slowing of population growth until there is again a zero, or sometimes negative, population growth rate.

The reasons for the decline in population fertility rates are unclear yet likely multifactorial. In part, this decline is presumably attributable to the fact that, with the realization of a greater likelihood of child survival to adulthood, there is an associated parental desire for fewer births with a greater financial investment in the health and education for each child.[35] Also, it is likely that, in addition to reducing infant and child mortality rates, the socioeconomic advances of a population also allow for greater educational and employment opportunities for women and, in turn, a desire for fewer children.[36] As many populations began the demographic transition in the late 18th and 19th centuries, the role of such medical advances as contraception in the decline in fertility rates is likely minimal, though access to contraceptives may play a

FIGURE 2.1 The Demographic Transition

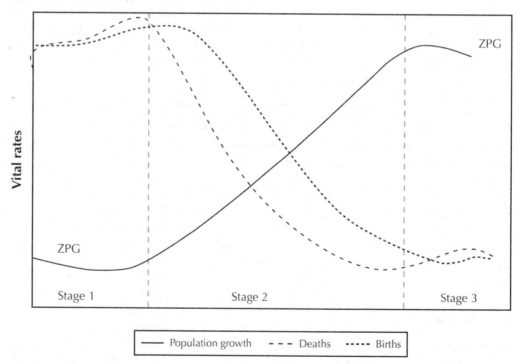

ZPG = zero population growth

Source: Adapted from the Australian Department of Families, Housing, Community Services and Indigenous Affairs, *Policy Research Paper No. 13.* Available online at: http://www.facs.gov.au/about/publicationsarticles/research/socialpolicy/Documents/prp13/sec1.htm.

greater role in populations more recently entering this transition period.[37]

As represented in Figure 2.2, the most notable result of this transition is ultimately a shift in the age composition of the involved population, represented by a greater ratio of older to younger members. In stage 1 of the demographic transition, populations experience high levels of fertility and mortality and a relatively low rate of population growth. In stage 2, high levels

FIGURE 2.2 Population Pyramids Representing the Stages of Demographic Transition

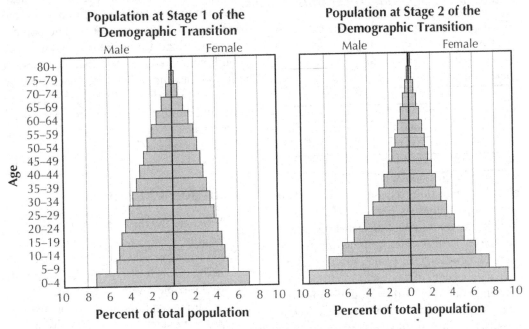

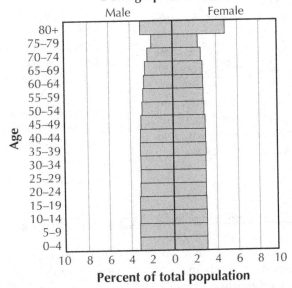

Source: Adapted from U.S. Census Bureau, "International Population Reports WP/02," *Global Population Profile: 2002* (Washington, DC: U.S. Government Printing Office, 2004). Available online at: http://www.census.gov/prod/2004pubs/wp-02.pdf.

of fertility coupled with decreasing mortality rates lead to relatively high rates of population growth. Finally, in stage 3, populations experience low rates of population growth as fertility rates decline to match lower mortality rates.

Implications of the Demographic and Epidemiological Transitions

The demographic and epidemiological transitions have several key implications for population health. The socioeconomic gains of a society have considerable positive influence on population health, typically more so than advances in medicine. Investments made in improving living conditions, sanitation, nutrition, and hygiene lead to a decrease in infectious disease burden and, thus, reduced mortality of members of the population typically most vulnerable to infectious diseases, namely, infants and young children. As infant and child mortality falls, and prior to the anticipated subsequent decline in fertility rates, population growth, particularly among the young, necessitates further investments in resources to support the care and education of these younger members of the population. When fertility rates decline, population shifts ultimately lead to an aging population that will be faced with the morbidity associated with chronic, noncommunicable diseases. This shift tends to occur at the same time that fewer young adults are entering the workforce. Thus, governments facing these implications of the demographic transition are faced with the challenges of taking care of larger aging populations—for example, by funding pension plans and expanding health care—at the same time that their tax base may be decreasing due to a smaller workforce.

Conclusion

A wide variety of individual, social, and political variables shape human health across the globe. Notably, these variables do not operate in isolation. Rather, a complex interplay among personal behaviors, social environment, and public policy is responsible for variations in individual and population health outcomes. Poverty and levels of national economic development also are critical in determining the distribution of disease within particular countries and the overall health of a given population, as Chapter 6 will discuss in greater detail. The epidemiological transition and the demographic transition demonstrate the ways in which improvements in the socioeconomic status of a population as well as advances in medicine affect not only the distribution of disease within particular countries but also the demographic composition of specific populations. In turn, the demography of a given population has important consequences for national health policies and health outcomes in specific countries. Thus, it is critical for students of global and comparative health to have a solid understanding of the determinants of health as well as the interrelated effects among them.

Discussion Questions

1. What are the major determinants of health?
2. Do you agree with the assertion that health is largely determined by individual-level variables? Why or why not?
3. What populations appear to be disproportionately burdened by disease? What indicators of population health and measures of disease burden support your conclusions?
4. How does the DALY differ from other measures of disease burden?
5. How is the age composition of a population altered by the demographic transition? What would be the expected impact of the epidemiological transition on the burden of disease within a population? How might this shape economic and health care policy for the impacted population?

Web Resources

WHO The Determinants of Health: http://www.who.int/hia/evidence/doh/en/
WHO Global Burden of Disease: http://www.who.int/healthinfo/global_burden_disease/en/
WHO Statistical Information System: http://www.who.int/whosis/whostat/en/

Environment

The environment is experiencing a number of very serious challenges. Desertification, deforestation, deteriorating water quality, and many other problems result from unbalanced interactions between people and their environments. It is beyond the scope of this volume to cover all of these issues. A better strategy is to concentrate on one issue in depth: climate change. Climate change is believed to be

one of humanity's most significant challenges.[9]

The impact of global warming is not shared equally among nations. The less developed nations are the hardest hit because their economies are more reliant on agriculture, and because they lack the capital for technological innovations. This is particularly unfortunate considering that it is the developed nations that are primarily responsible for the damage.

The international and interdisciplinary perspective we strive for in this volume requires us to recognize that climate change may lead to cultural change. Global warming is especially challenging to the lives of people in the circumpolar north. For example, the Sami people of northern Scandinavia have found that their reindeer herds are threatened (Smallman and Brown 2011: 341). Because indigenous peoples often rely on the natural environment for their livelihood, they are particularly vulnerable to being hurt by climate change. The themes in this module will be carried into the next because the issues that stem from the effects of climate change and issues of health and well-being are problems that human development is designed to address.

Readings

"The Scientific Consensus" provides a concise explanation of the science behind human-caused climate change. This understanding is necessary to make effective policy, the topic of the following reading in this volume.

Bulkeley and **Newell** provide a history of the response to climate change, detailing actors, institutions, and progress in policy making. A large part of the challenge is balancing the different risks, needs, and resources in the global North and South.

---

[9] Elliot, Larry, "Climate change disaster is biggest threat to global economy in 2016" The Guardian, 14 January, 2016. https://www.theguardian.com/business/2016/jan/14/climate-change-disaster-is-biggest-threat-to-global-economy-in-2016-say-experts

The Scientific Consensus

by Michael D. Mastrandrea and Stephen H. Schneider

SINCE THE SECOND HALF OF THE NINE-teenth century, global temperatures have been on the rise. The increase in global average surface temperature, as estimated by the IPCC, is around 0.75°C (~1.4°F). Twelve of the thirteen years leading up to 2009 are the twelve warmest years on record. There is now overwhelming scientific evidence of a human fingerprint on this global warming.

Many impacts of warming can be—and have been—observed: the melting of mountain glaciers, the Greenland ice sheets and parts of the West Antarctic ice sheets, and northern polar sea ice; rising and increasingly acidic seas; increasing severity of droughts, heat waves, fires, and hurricanes (the intensity and/or frequency of extreme events can change substantially with small changes in average conditions); and changing lifecycles and ranges of plants and animals. The primary driver, particularly of the rapid warming since the 1970s, is emissions of greenhouse gases, such as carbon dioxide and methane, generated by human activities. The burning of fossil fuels is the greatest contributor of greenhouse gases, but agricultural practices, deforestation, and cement production also play a role.

The Warming Planet

The greenhouse effect and its intensification by human-induced emissions are well understood and solidly grounded in basic science. The potential of carbon dioxide in the atmosphere to trap radiant heat was proposed as early as 1827 by the French mathematician and physicist Joseph Fourier. In 1896 the Swedish chemist Svante Arrhenius dubbed this the *greenhouse effect*. Arrhenius was the first to argue that anthropogenic increases in the level of carbon dioxide in the atmosphere could significantly affect surface temperature.

So how does it work? Earth's atmosphere is moderately transparent to visible light. About half of the radiant energy from the sun penetrates the atmosphere and is absorbed by the Earth's surface. The other half either is absorbed by the atmosphere or reflected back to space by clouds, atmospheric gases, aerosols, and the Earth's surface. The absorbed energy warms the surface and atmosphere, which re-emit energy as infrared radiation. To stay in energy balance, the Earth must radiate back to space as much energy as it absorbs, but the atmosphere is much less transparent to infrared radiation.

Carbon dioxide and other greenhouse gases and clouds absorb 80-90 percent of the infrared radiation emitted at the surface and re-emit energy in all directions, both up to space and back toward the Earth's surface.

Thus, some infrared radiant energy is trapped, heating the lower layers of the atmosphere and warming the surface further. As it warms, the surface emits infrared radiation upward at a still greater rate, and so on, until the infrared radiation emitted to space is in balance with the absorbed radiant energy from sunlight and the other forms of energy coming and going from the surface (for example, rising plumes of convective energy, or evaporated water vapor that carries a great deal of latent chemical energy from the surface to the clouds where it is released in the condensation process).

The natural greenhouse effect makes our planet much more habitable—about 33°C warmer than it otherwise would be. But human activities are increasing the concentrations of greenhouse gases in the atmosphere directly and indirectly, thus intensifying the greenhouse effect. The indirect effect primarily stems from the extra evaporation of water from a warmed surface, a feedback that adds more water vapor—a greenhouse gas—to the atmosphere, warming the surface further. These amplifying influences are called *positive feedbacks in radiative forcing*, since the net effect of the addition of greenhouse gases when averaged over the globe is to trap extra heat, which in turn increases temperatures in order to restore energy balance. Greenhouse gases commonly emitted in human activities include carbon dioxide, methane, nitrous oxide, and a host of industrial gases such as chlorofluorocarbons that do not appear naturally in the atmosphere. Indirectly, humans also generate ozone in the lower atmosphere. The concentration of ozone, a health-damaging component of smog, is increasing with atmospheric warming and continued burning of fossil fuels.

These same activities—fuel combustion, and, to a lesser extent, agricultural and industrial processes—also produce emissions of aerosol particles. Many aerosols directly reflect incoming solar energy upward toward space, a *negative radiative forcing*, or cooling effect. Aerosol particles also affect the color, size, and number of cloud droplets, in aggregate, a negative forcing. Some dark aerosols, such as soot, absorb solar energy, a positive forcing if they darken the planet enough to cause more sunlight to be absorbed. Another indirect effect is soot falling on snow and ice, darkening it and thus accelerating melting. Many land-use activities, such as deforestation, contribute to greenhouse-gas emissions, a positive forcing, but they also can change the Earth's albedo, or reflectivity, in aggregate, again, a negative forcing. However, deforested surfaces may warm locally due to the removal of evapo-transpiring vegetation that cools the surface.*

The best available estimate of the combined influence of all human activities to date is strongly positive. Its magnitude is roughly equivalent to the positive radiative forcing of increased carbon dioxide concentrations alone, with the positive forcing of the non-carbon dioxide greenhouse gases and dark aerosols roughly offset by the negative forcing of direct and indirect aerosol effects and land-use changes, though the many uncertainties involved mean that precise estimates are not yet possible with high confidence. However, we can be highly confident that the overall effect is positive, and thus that human activities are contributing to observed warming.

---

* For more on radiative forcing, aerosols, albedo feedbacks, and other details, see the resources in the "Further Reading" section.

What besides human activities could be at work in the warming of the planet? Many natural processes affect the Earth's energy balance and therefore climate, which varied a great deal in the distant past. Aerosols ejected from large explosive volcanic eruptions can remain in the stratosphere for several years, all the while cooling the lower atmosphere by a few tenths of a degree. Changing solar output can alter temperatures by similar amount over the course of decades, and the sunspot cycle has a small, but discernible effect on solar output (~0.1 percent). Some scientists and interested parties champion these natural processes as the primary sources of warming in our own era. But natural processes alone do not cause a sufficiently sustained radiative forcing to explain more than a small fraction of the observed warming of the past 40 years. On the other hand, anthropogenic forces can explain a much higher fraction of what has been observed over that period.

Examining climates of the more distant past allows scientists to compare the current changes to earlier natural ones. Scientists use proxies that provide a window into those natural fluctuations. Proxies such as tree rings and pollen percentages in lake beds indicate that current temperatures are the warmest of the millennium and that the rate and magnitude of warming likely have been greater in the past 150 years than during the rest of this period. Ice cores bored in Greenland and Antarctica provide estimates of both temperature and atmospheric greenhouse gases going back hundreds of thousands of years, spanning several cycles of warmth (5,000-20,000 year "interglacials") separated by ice ages up to 100,000 years in duration. Not only do the samples indicate a strong correlation between temperature and atmospheric greenhouse-gas concentrations—particularly carbon dioxide and methane—the samples also indicate that current levels of carbon dioxide and other greenhouse gases in the atmosphere are far above any seen in at least the past 650,000 years. Ice cores also provide information about volcanic eruptions and variations in solar energy, furthering understanding of these natural forcing mechanisms described above.

There are many other lines of evidence of the human "fingerprint" on observed warming trends. To give one more example, the Earth's stratosphere has cooled while the surface has warmed, an indicator of increased concentrations of atmospheric greenhouse gases and stratospheric ozone-depleting substances rather than, for example, an increase in the energy output of the sun, which should warm all levels of the atmosphere. Combined, the present-day observations and the data provided by proxies have led the IPCC to conclude that it is *very likely* (there is at least a 90 percent chance) that human activities are responsible for most of the warming observed over the twentieth century, particularly that of the last 40 years.

Nevertheless, the future course of climate change is deeply uncertain because we don't know how much more greenhouse gases humans will emit or exactly how the natural climate system will respond to those emissions. Policy decisions can strongly influence the first source of uncertainty (future emissions), but will have little influence on the second (climate response to emissions).

Modeling Climate Change

This uncertainty means that projecting future climate change is a complex, imprecise task. There is a range of plausible futures. Using computer models that describe mathematically the physical, biological, and chemical processes that determine climate, scientists try to project the response of the climate to future scenarios of greenhouse-gas emissions. The ideal model would include all processes known to have climatological significance and would involve spatial and temporal detail sufficient to model phenomena occurring over small geographic regions and over short time periods.

Today's best models strive to approach this ideal but still rely on many approximations because of computational limits and incomplete understanding of climatically important small-scale phenomena, such as clouds. The resolution of current models is limited to a geographic grid-box of roughly 50-100 kilometers horizontally and one kilometer vertically. Because all physical, chemical, and biological properties are averaged over each grid-box, it is impossible to represent "sub-grid-scale" phenomena *explicitly* within a model. In other words, the specific climatic goings-on within the grid-box must be approximated.

But sub-grid-scale phenomena can be incorporated *implicitly* by a parametric representation. This "parameterization" connects sub-grid-scale processes to explicitly modeled grid-box averages via semi-empirical rules designed to capture the major interactions between these scales. Developing and testing parameterizations to assess the degree to which they can reliably incorporate sub-grid-scale processes is one of the most arduous and important tasks of climate modelers. The best models reproduce approximately, although not completely accurately, the detailed geographic patterns of temperature, precipitation, and other climatic variables seen on a regional scale, and can project changes in those patterns given scenarios for future greenhouse-gas emissions.

IPCC AR4, of which both of us were authors, includes climate-model projections based upon six "storylines," possible future worlds that come about under different assumptions about population growth, levels of economic development, and technological advancement and deployment. In one scenario, the IPCC assumes heavy reliance on fossil fuels and significantly increasing emissions during the century, and projects further global average surface warming of 2.4-6.4°C by the year 2100. In a second scenario, emissions grow more slowly, peak around 2050, and then fall, with expected warming of 1.1-2.9°C by the year 2100. The difference between the temperature ranges for the first and second scenarios reflects the influence of different trajectories for future greenhouse-gas emissions and climatic responses to those emissions: how much will temperatures increase for a given increase in concentrations (how sensitive is the climate to radiative forcing)? And how will the carbon cycle and the uptake of carbon dioxide by the ocean and by terrestrial ecosystems be altered by changing temperature and atmospheric greenhouse-gas concentrations?

These different projections for warming imply very different climate-change risks, affecting other climate variables (for example, precipitation patterns) as well as the likelihood of severe impacts. Warming at the high end of the range could have widespread catastrophic consequences and very few benefits, save the viability of shipping routes across an ice-free Arctic Ocean, or the possibility of expanded oil exploration in that sensitive region. Five to seven degrees Celsius of warming on a globally averaged basis is about the difference between an ice age and an interglacial period; in this case, the change would occur in merely a century or so rather than over millennia as in the paleo-climatic history of ice-age cycles not influenced by human activities.

Warming at the low end of the range (a few degrees Celsius) would be less damaging, but would still be significant for some communities, sectors, and natural ecosystems. Human civilization has grown in an age in which global temperatures were never more than a degree or two warmer than now, thus warming exceeding a degree or two is unprecedented in our entire historical experience. Indeed, some systems have already shown worrisome responses to the ~0.75 °C warming over the past century. Alarmingly, actual emissions of the past ten years (except for a year or so of temporary decline during the economic recession of 2008-9) exceed the assumptions of even the highest of the IPCC scenarios, which were crafted in 2000. This suggests that large increases in greenhouse-gas concentrations are in store in the next several decades unless rapid action is taken to reduce emissions.

Governing Climate Change

by Harriet Bulkeley and Peter Newell

Although we often assume that the high profile that climate change now enjoys means that it is a new political issue, in fact it has a much longer legacy. In this chapter we provide a brief history of the politics of climate change. We analyze the key issues and conflicts in the international negotiations, from the negotiation of the 1992 United Nations Framework Convention on Climate Change (UNFCCC) through to the Kyoto Protocol in 1997 and up to the present state of negotiations towards the Copenhagen summit in 2009. The discussion is organized around three features of climate governance which have characterized this period: the role of science and the scientific community in the governance of climate change, the role of North–South politics, and finally the increasing marketization of climate governance. Before examining these key issues in turn, we provide a brief overview of how climate policy is made at the international level.

Making policy on climate change

Actors and institutions

The international negotiations on climate change are organized around a number of key actors, institutions, and decision-making processes that it is necessary to understand to follow the discussion that follows. In terms of international organizations, three institutions are critical to the process of negotiating climate change policy. First, there is the secretariat of the UNFCCC, based in Bonn since 1996, which organizes and oversees the negotiations, prepares the necessary documentation and is responsible for overseeing reporting of emissions profiles and projects funded through the Kyoto Protocol. Guided by the parties to the Convention, it provides organizational support and technical expertise to the negotiations and institutions, and facilitates the flow of authoritative information on the implementation of the Convention. It has a key and often underestimated role to play in shaping the outcomes of the negotiations.[1] It has an executive secretary who has the responsibility of trying to guide the negotiations towards a successful conclusion. Second, there is the Conference of the Parties (COP) to the UNFCCC and Kyoto Protocol, which meets annually to review progress on commitments contained in those treaties and to update them in the light of the latest scientific advice. This is the ultimate decision-making body in the climate negotiations. Third, there are the Subsidiary Bodies on Implementation (SBI) and Scientific and Technological Advice (SBSTA) and the Ad Hoc Working Groups that take forward negotiations on specific issues which the COP ultimately has to approve. For example, at the moment there is an Ad Hoc Working Group on Further Commitments for Annex 1 parties under the Kyoto Protocol.

In order to shape this process, governments often organize themselves into blocs and negotiating coalitions to enhance their influence and to advance common agendas. These key coalitions and negotiating blocs emerged early on in the negotiations, but have evolved significantly since then as the issues have changed and their levels of economic development have dramatically altered.[2] At one end of the spectrum the Organization of Petroleum Exporting Countries (OPEC) grouping quickly emerged as the coalition of states most hostile to action on climate change. With revenues almost entirely dependent on the export of oil, that opposition was unsurprising. This bloc affected the pace and course of the negotiations, with calls for greater scientific certainty before action could take place, the formation of alliances with businesses opposed to action,[3] and the use of wrecking tactics such as the call for compensation for loss of oil revenues in response to the call from many low-lying developing countries for economic compensation for impacts suffered as a result of climate change.

At the other end of the spectrum the Alliance of Small Island States (AOSIS), a coalition of island states most vulnerable to the effects of sea-level rise, has been the most strident of the negotiating coalitions in its demands for far-reaching and stringent emissions reductions targets. In 1995 it proposed its own protocol to the agreement mandating a 20 percent cut in 1990 emissions by 2005. The AOSIS group works closely with the London-based legal group Foundation for International Environmental Law and Development (FIELD) that provides legal advice on the negotiating text. Indeed, FIELD was attributed a key role in drafting the AOSIS protocol proposal, suggesting the fragility of rigid distinctions about who exercises power and authority in the governance of climate change.[4]

In between these two polarities lay the G77 of less developed countries + China coalition that emphasized the North's primary contribution to the problem of climate change and sought to deflect calls for the South to make commitments and to ensure that funds committed to achieve the Convention's goals were genuinely additional to existing money for aid. The G77, which as we will see below is now less cohesive, continues to provide a platform for shared concerns about climate change policy. The European Union, meanwhile, has been keen to see a stronger agreement, while the United States, particularly during the administrations of presidents George H. W. Bush and George W. Bush, was resolutely opposed to legally binding cuts in GHG. Japan has adopted a position between these two as host to the summit that produced the Kyoto Protocol, but has often been a reluctant leader because of high levels of industry pressure to not over-commit. Both the United States and Japan were part of the JUSCANZ grouping (Japan, United States, Canada, Australia, and New Zealand) which argued for maximum flexibility in how countries are expected to meet their commitments.

Alongside the formal negotiations organized in plenary sessions and working groups that meet in parallel to discuss specific issues, a bewildering array of non-governmental, business and other organizations are registered to participate in the process. Though they do not have formal voting rights, they are allowed to make interventions and are often admitted onto government delegations where they have access to all the meetings taking place. In many ways, these actors are non-governmental "diplomats" that perform many of the same functions as state delegates: representing the interests of their constituencies, engaging in information exchange, negotiating, and providing policy advice.[5]

We can see, therefore, that the process of making climate policy involves international organizations and institutional structures established for this purpose, coalitions and blocs of state actors, and a range of non-state actors who have sought to influence the process of negotiation in a variety of ways. Before turning to discuss particular aspects of this process in detail, we first consider the main policy milestones that have shaped the current state of international climate policy.

Climate change policy milestones

The governance of climate change as a global political issue has progressed from being a cause for concern among a growing number of scientists to gaining recognition as an issue deserving of a collective global effort orchestrated by the United Nations (UN) (Box 1.1). Over time there has been a deepening of cooperation and a firming-up of obligations to act; a process common to many international negotiations on the environment where a general agreement identifies the need for action and a subsequent protocol contains concrete, legally binding emissions reductions commitments. What is also notable, a theme to which we return below, is the increasing use of market or flexible mechanisms to achieve emissions reductions.

Box 1.1 The global governance of climate change: a short chronology

1988   World Conference on the Changing Atmosphere: politicians and scientists conclude that "humanity is conducting an unintended, uncontrolled, globally pervasive experiment whose ultimate consequences could be second only to nuclear war." The conference recommends reducing CO_2 emissions by 20 percent by 2005.

1990   IPCC publishes its *First Assessment Report*.

1991   The Intergovernmental Negotiating Committee is set up to oversee negotiations towards an international agreement.

1992   154 countries sign the UNFCCC at the United Nations Conference on Environment and Development in Rio, which aims to stabilize emissions at 1990 levels by the year 2000 as part of an overall goal to stabilize GHG "concentrations in the atmosphere at a level that would prevent dangerous interference with the climate system."[1]

1994   The UNFCCC enters into force on 21 March.

1995   The first COP agrees in Berlin that binding commitments by industrialized countries are required to reduce emissions.

1995   The IPCC publishes its *Second Assessment Report*, which establishes that "The balance of evidence suggests a discernible human influence on global climate."[2]

1996   The second COP in Geneva sees the United States agree to legally binding targets to reduce emissions as long as emissions trading is included in an agreement.

Box continued on next page.

1997　More than 150 countries sign the Kyoto Protocol which binds 38 industrialized (Annex 1) countries to reduce GHG emissions by an average of 5.2 percent below 1990 levels during the period 2008–12.

2000　The negotiations at the sixth COP in The Hague collapse amid disagreements, principally between the United States and Europe, about the use of the Kyoto Protocol's flexibility mechanisms.

2001　US president George W. Bush announces that his country is to withdraw from the Kyoto Protocol.

2001　In Marrakesh the final elements of the Kyoto Protocol are worked out, particularly the rules and procedures by which the flexible mechanisms will operate.

2005　On 16 February the Kyoto Protocol becomes law after Russian ratification pushes the emissions of ratified Annex 1 countries over the 55 percent mark.

2004　The Buenos Aires Programme of Work on Adaptation and Response Measures is agreed at COP 10.

2005　The first Meeting of the Parties to the Kyoto Protocol takes place in Montreal at COP 11.

2006　At the Second Meeting of the Parties (COP 12), the Nairobi Work Programme on Adaptation and the Nairobi Framework on Capacity-Building for the CDM are agreed.

2007　The IPCC publishes its *Fourth Assessment Report*.

2007　At COP 13 the Bali Action Plan is agreed, which calls for a long-term goal for emissions reductions; measurable, reportable, verifiable mitigation commitments including nationally appropriate mitigation actions by LDCs; enhanced adaptation, action on technology development and transfer, and financial resources and investment to support the above.

2009　The COP 15 takes place in Copenhagen amid concerns that time is running out to create an international agreement that could enter into force by 2012, when the current Kyoto Protocol target period ends.

Notes:
1 Article 2 of the UNFCCC (1992): http://unfccc.int/resource/docs/convkp/conv eng.pdf
2 IPCC, *Second Assessment Report* (Cambridge: Cambridge University Press, 1995).

The UNFCCC was agreed at the United Nations Conference on Environment and Development (UNCED) summit in Rio in 1992. As the first major milestone in the history of climate diplomacy, the UNFCCC provided a framework for global action on the issue. It sought to emulate the apparent success of the ozone regime, which first produced the Vienna Convention establishing the nature of the problem and the basis for action on it, and subsequently the Montreal Protocol which agreed a phase-out of the most damaging ozone-depleting chemicals. Given the sharp differences of opinion described above and the relative lack of momentum behind the issue at the time, the fact the UNFCCC was agreed at all can be considered a considerable achievement. The agreement set the goal of "avoiding dangerous interference in the climate system," defined as aiming to stabilize concentrations of GHG in the atmosphere, and listed some of the policies and measures that countries might adopt to achieve that end. Acknowledging the vast differences in contributions to the problem, the Convention established the principle of "common but differentiated responsibility"[6] and recognized that developing countries were not yet in a position to assume their own obligations. Efforts they could make towards tackling the issue were made dependent on the receipt of aid and technology transfer from Northern countries that were meant to be "additional" to existing aid budgets.

Attention then turned to how to realize the general nature of the commitments contained in the UNFCCC. With scientific assessments of the severity of climate change becoming increasingly common and growing awareness of the inadequacy of existing policy responses, momentum built for a follow-up to the Convention.[7] The 1995 Berlin Mandate at the first COP sought to promote Quantifiable Emissions Limitations and Reduction Obligations (QELROs), and negotiations thus began towards a protocol which would set legally binding targets to reduce GHG emissions. The Kyoto Protocol concluded in 1997 was the outcome of this. Signed by more than 150 countries, it binds 38 industrialized (Annex 1) countries to reduce GHG emissions by an average of 5.2 percent below 1990 levels during the period 2008–12 (see Box 1.2). It fixes differentiated targets for industrialized countries, while setting in train a process to further elaborate joint implementation schemes, set up an emissions trading scheme (ETS) and create a Clean Development Mechanism (CDM). We discuss these further below.

The process for finalizing the rules and operational details of the Protocol was agreed at COP 4 in 1998 as part of the Buenos Aires Plan of Action. In November 2000 parties met in The Hague at COP 6 to try and complete these negotiations, but failed to do so amid a growing rift between the European Union and United States in particular.[8] Having been party to the negotiations and lobbied hard for the inclusion of market-based mechanisms which would allow industrialized countries maximum flexibility, in 2001 the United States then walked away from the Kyoto Protocol. We will see below that part of the United States' refusal to ratify Kyoto was because its economic competitors in the developing world were not required to reduce their emissions. Without the involvement of the United States, many assumed the inevitable demise of the Kyoto Protocol. If the largest contributor to the problem and most powerful economy in the world was not on board, what incentive was there for others to sign up? In fact, the absence of the United States served to galvanize the European Union and G77 + China into further action, and with the Russian ratification of the Kyoto Protocol in 2005 it entered into force.

Subsequent negotiations have focused on detailed issues concerning the implementation and enforcement of Kyoto and, increasingly, what might come in its place as the end of the implementation period (2012) draws ever closer. At COP 7 the Marrakesh Accords were agreed, which established the rules and procedures for the operation of the flexible mechanisms, including the CDM, as well as details on reporting and methodologies. Importantly, they also established three new funds: the Least Developed Countries Fund, the Special Climate Change Fund, and the Adaptation Fund. This work was continued through to the Buenos Aires Programme of Work on Adaptation and Response Measures agreed at COP 10 in 2004. This was followed at COP 11 in Montreal with the creation of the Ad Hoc Working Group on Further Commitments for Annex 1 parties under the Kyoto Protocol. At COP 12 in Nairobi, dubbed the "Africa COP," there was significant discussion about financing issues and how to increase the number of CDM projects being hosted by the poorest regions of the world, most notably sub-Saharan Africa. The meeting produced the Nairobi Work Programme on Adaptation, and the Nairobi Framework on Capacity-Building for the CDM.[9] The Bali Action Plan agreed a year later at COP 13 has set the path for negotiations towards Copenhagen, calling for a long-term goal for emissions reductions; measurable, reportable, verifiable mitigation commitments including nationally appropriate mitigation actions by Least Developed Countries (LDCs); as well as enhanced adaptation, action on technology development and transfer and financial resources, and investment to support the above.[10] We will see in Chapter 2 how these complex questions of responsibility, and who pays for action on climate change, have come to dominate the negotiations.

Box 1.2 The Kyoto Protocol in brief[1]

Commitments

- Industrialized countries are required to reduce their collective emissions of GHG by an average of 5.2 percent below 1990 levels in the commitment period 2008–12.[2]
- The USA must reduce its emissions by an average of 7 percent; Japan by an average of 6 percent and the EU by an average of 8 percent. Other industrialized countries are permitted small increases, while others are obliged only to freeze their emissions.
- Developed countries are obliged to provide:

  - "new and additional financial resources to meet the agreed full costs incurred by developing country parties in advancing the implementation of existing commitments."
  - "such financial resources, including transfer of technology, needed by the developing country parties to meet the agreed and full incremental costs of advancing the implementation of existing commitments," and
  - "financial resources for the implementation of Article 10, through bilateral, regional and other multilateral channels" which developing country parties can avail of.

Instruments

- Clean Development Mechanism—The aim of this body is to assist developing countries in achieving sustainable development and at the same time to help developed countries "in achieving compliance with their quantified emission limitation and reduction commitments." In effect its purpose is to oversee the implementation of projects funded by developed states wanting to accrue credits for emissions achieved overseas. Participation is voluntary and procedures and modalities for auditing and verifying projects were worked out later in the negotiations. Reduction credits are certified by the CDM to ensure that projects add value to savings that would have been made in their absence (Article 12). In addition, a "share of the proceeds from the certified activities

Box continued on next page.

is used to cover administrative expenses as well as to assist the developing country parties that are particularly vulnerable to the effects of climate change to meet the costs of adaptation."

- Joint Implementation/Actions Implemented Jointly—These activities have to be "additional to any that would otherwise occur" and "supplemental to domestic actions." Scope is provided to include "verifiable changes in stocks of sinks" in parties' assessment of their net GHG emissions (Article 6).
- Emissions Trading (Article 17).
- Implementation is via national reports overseen by teams of experts nominated by the parties.

Notes:
1 Peter Newell, "Who CoPed Out at Kyoto? An Assessment of the Third Conference of the Parties to the Framework Convention on Climate Change," *Environmental Politics* 7, no. 2 (2008): 153–159.
2 Parties are expected to have demonstrated progress in reaching this target by the year 2005. Cuts in the three important gases (CO_2, CH_4, and NO_2) will be calculated against a base year of 1990, and cuts in the long-lived industrial gases (hydroflurocarbons, perflurocarbons and sulfur hexafluride) can be measured against a base year of either 1990 or 1995.

Climate becomes political: science and climate governance

As we have seen above, the process of making climate policy has been shaped by a complex mix of institutions and actors. One of the key issues has been the interface between science and policy, which provided the first impetus for international agreement and continues to be central to global climate politics.

The greenhouse effect—in which particular atmospheric gases, so-called greenhouse gases, act to increase the amount of energy retained in the earth's atmosphere—was discovered by Joseph Fourier in 1824. Other scientists, such as the physicist John Tyndall, helped to further identify the relative radiative forcing values of the different greenhouse gases before the greenhouse effect was first investigated quantitatively by Svante Arrhenius in 1896. The basic science behind the greenhouse effect is graphically portrayed in the diagram below (Figure 1.1). This is a naturally occurring phenomenon. However, by increasing the proportion of GHG in the atmosphere, human activities can exacerbate this effect, leading to higher globally average temperatures and changes

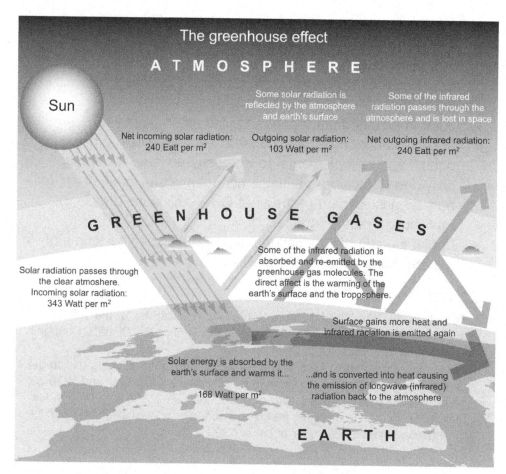

Figure 1.1 The greenhouse effect and climate change.

in the climate. Despite the early discoveries noted above, it was not until the late 1970s, according to climate scientist Bert Bolin, that this "possibility of human-induced change of climate first caught the attention of politicians."[11] During the early 1980s the first international assessment of climate change was convened, supported by the International Council of Scientific Unions and the World Meteorological Organization (WMO), which concluded with the Villach conference in 1985 and an appeal to the international community to address the issue seriously.

The IPCC was then established in 1988 to provide expert input into the climate negotiations, but was to be directed in its mandate by governmental representatives. It was formed by the WMO and the United Nations Environment Programme (UNEP). The IPCC is an expert body made up of the world's leading climate scientists in areas such as oceanography, climatology, meteorology, and economics to produce reports, subject to widespread peer review, on the latest scientific understanding of climate change. Successive reports by the body issued in

1990, 1995, 2001, and 2007 have provided a substantive and consolidated knowledge base about three dimensions of the climate change problem: (i) the science and the basic causal mechanisms, (ii) impacts, and (iii) response strategies: economic, technical and policy implications. Working groups have been created to provide policymakers with the latest research in each of these areas.

Though charged with the responsibility of providing independent and objective advice on the latest scientific understanding of all aspects of the problem of climate change, the IPCC's work has been heavily politicized from the very outset. Science has been a key battleground in the debate about climate change: the severity of the threat, the nature of the causal mechanisms and probable impacts and economic costs associated with taking action. Scientific knowledge is used by all actors in climate governance to advance and defend their position and to confer legitimacy upon it. It is the perception of science as objective and above politics that makes it attractive to actors who believe it provides them with a trump card over the claims of others. However, decisions about whose knowledge counts, who wields authority, and how knowledge is presented and framed are deeply political processes that imply the exercise of power. As Foucault argues, "we should admit ... that power and knowledge directly imply one another; that there is no power relation without the correlative constitution of a field of knowledge, nor any knowledge that does not at the same time presuppose and constitute power relations."[12]

It is unsurprising that the process of accumulating and presenting scientific evidence and advice about the climate change issue has been so political. There is a lot at stake. We see this with the production of policymakers' summaries of the latest IPCC reports, the mostly widely read part of the report. Business, NGOs, and government representatives are allowed to participate in the drafting of these summaries and actively seek to shape their content to reflect their views of the severity of climate change: highlighting uncertainties in the case of those opposed to action or drawing attention to warnings about the potential for dramatic feedback effects by those wanting more stringent near-term action. As former IPCC chairman Bert Bolin reflects: "the Summary for Policy-makers is approved in a plenary session of the respective working groups ... [these] become the occasions when the scientists engaged by the IPCC are confronted with political views and even attempts to clothe special interests in scientific terms."[13]

Recognizing the interwoven nature of power and knowledge challenges the assumption that science interacts with policy in a fairly linear way where governments and international institutions are dependent on experts—sometimes labeled epistemic communities—to advise them on political actions in conditions of uncertainty.[14] In practice, however, the worlds of science and politics overlap. One of the key roles of scientists is to act as "knowledge brokers,"[15] translators of abstract scientific findings into policy messages, intermediaries between lab and law. The fact that scientists are also often dependent on government money for their research has led some to claim that the alleged urgency of the threat posed by climate change has been deliberately exaggerated by a scientific community keen to attract research funding for further work in the area.[16] Once established in a well-resourced and high-profile policy network, so this argument goes, scientists develop their own self-interests in maintaining that position and securing funding for their work. Another source of potent criticism has been that important uncertainties in the science and modeling have been downplayed or ignored altogether. This has been the line of attack of a relatively small but vocal group of so-called climate skeptics who either doubt that global warming results from anthropogenic influences or suggest that the scale of that influence has been overestimated.[17] Given the contentious ground which the IPCC occupies, it is also unsurprising that senior appointments within the IPCC have also been a source of controversy. For example, the US government successfully vetoed the re-appointment of Bob Watson as head of the IPCC amid claims he was pursuing a personal agenda which was interpreted at the time as being too outspoken an advocate of climate action.[18]

One of the key issues here is not only that politics get played out through science, but the way science is used politically. While the UNFCCC refers to the prevention of "dangerous anthropogenic interference in the climate system"[19] as the overall goal of the agreement, defining what counts as "dangerous" is a political act, a judgment about risk: how much risk we as a society are willing to take and who bears the consequences. A key battleground in the negotiations towards the UNFCCC was whether sufficient scientific consensus existed to warrant global collective action. Those against more strident forms of action demanded more science, as if that was the key obstacle to action. As the NGO newsletter *ECO* declared at the Geneva climate meeting back in 1990, "all the computer models in the world will not make a Swiss Franc of difference to governments who simply want to sell all the oil the world can be persuaded to buy."[20] Part of the reason the interface between science and policy is so contested is because of the political significance of recommendations that are made for identifying and allocating responsibility. This has been a highly contested issue between developed and developing countries, and it is to this issue that we now turn.

The poverty of climate governance: North–South politics

The second dimension of climate governance which cuts across this history of climate diplomacy is the importance of North–South politics. Climate change in many ways highlights more starkly the North–South divisions which characterize other global environmental threats such as ozone depletion and biodiversity.[21] Early battles about the need to differentiate between the "survival" emissions of the South and the "luxury" emissions of the North[22] have been compounded by claims of carbon colonialism and climate injustice, as we will see in Chapter 2. Underpinning this conflict is the fact that while climate change has been largely caused by the wealthy industrialized parts of the world, it is the least developed areas of the world that will suffer its worst consequences. This makes climate change first and foremost an issue of social justice and equity.

Early discussions of the climate change issue demonstrated a clear polarity of positions between developed countries and developing countries, with the latter arguing that the former, as leading contributors to the problem, were duty-bound to accept responsibility and take action. The language in the UNFCCC embodies this notion of "common but differentiated responsibility,"[23] the idea that everybody has a responsibility to act but some have more responsibility than others. In so far as developing (or non-Annex 1) countries have responsibilities under the Convention, these are conditional on the receipt of aid and technology transfer from more developed countries. Aid and technology transfer provide what economists would refer to as side-payments: inducements to cooperate in tackling a problem to which, historically speaking, they have contributed very little.

Debate has focused on the governance of aid and technology transfer; which institution will oversee these and on whose terms. While developed countries were keen to see the Global Environment Facility (GEF) play a key role, the institution's close association with the World Bank was a source of concern for many developing countries that were distrustful of the organization.[24] Many developing countries also expressed reservations about the levels and types of aid that would be forthcoming. They sought forms of financial assistance that were "additional" to existing aid budgets and not drawn from budget lines targeted for other development priorities.

The presentation of a united front by the G77 on these key issues always disguised a spectrum of diverse national and regional differences. Over time, however, divisions among developing countries have become more apparent and more clearly defined. Increasing emphasis in the global debate on the use of flexible market mechanisms, endorsed by the Kyoto Protocol, forced developing countries to assess how they might benefit from engagement with such mechanisms. Interest in the role of forests as carbon sinks for which credits might be earned and finance provided to developing countries, has drawn biodiverse countries, particularly many Latin American countries, further into the realm of joint actions.[25] At the same time, the newly industrializing powerhouses of China, India, Brazil, Malaysia, Mexico, and South Korea now make their own significant contribution to the problem, raising further questions about how the principle of "common but differentiated responsibilities" should be put into practice.

In this context, there is an ongoing debate about whether, and if so, in what form, developing countries should take on their own emissions reductions commitments. There is a perception among some developed countries that rapidly industrializing competitors will be able to free-ride on the sacrifices made by Annex 1 parties. The related concern is that industries will uproot and relocate to areas of the world not covered by the provisions of the Kyoto Protocol, resulting in "carbon leakage."[26] Increasing recognition of this new geography of responsibility prompted demands from leading polluters—such as the United States and Australia—to draw their competitors into a global regime of regulation and controls on GHG. Most dramatically, at the time of the Kyoto negotiations in 1997, Senator Chuck Hagel drafted the Bryd-Hagel resolution (Senate Resolution 98) which made US acceptance of the terms of the Kyoto Protocol conditional on agreement from leading developing countries to reduce their own emissions. Given the sensitivity about the issue of legally binding emissions reductions obligations for developing countries, this strategy was aimed at causing maximum divisions, stalling progress, and most importantly tying the hands of US negotiators by showing that the Senate would not ratify any deal which did not contain developing country commitments. Indeed, it was this issue in part that led the United States, under George W. Bush, to withdraw from the Kyoto Protocol in 2001.

Besides the issue of responsibility, there is also a clear North–South dimension in terms of vulnerability to the effects of climate change (particularly sea-level rise and changes to agricultural systems). In terms of impacts of climate change, developing countries are in a weaker position to protect themselves from the adverse effects of climate change. Sea defenses, and other means available to wealthier nations to ensure that land is not flooded and that population displacement is not necessary, are not affordable to many developing countries. Their reliance for agricultural production in many low-lying areas that are especially prone to flooding from sea-level rise, makes them particularly vulnerable to the effects of climate change. This is an issue we return to in Chapter 2.

These uneven patterns of responsibility for emissions of GHG and vulnerability to the effects of climate change have profoundly affected efforts to secure global agreements on climate change. The broader historical and contemporary features of the unequal relationship between the developed and developing world run through virtually all aspects of climate governance. Scientists from developing countries are poorly represented in the expert bodies that provide the knowledge base for policy. Poorer groups within these countries are disproportionately vulnerable to the effects of climate change, even if they contribute little to the problem. In many cases, developing country governments lack the capacity to attend, let alone shape and influence, negotiating processes that are heavily dominated by developed countries with the resources to attend all meetings and the legal and scientific capacity to shape developments according to their preferences. The politics of North–South relations have, therefore, both explicitly and implicitly shaped the history of international climate policy, with profound implications for how the issue is addressed. We return to this debate in Chapter 2.

The marketization of climate governance

The third notable feature of climate governance which cuts across this history is the increasing emphasis on market-based solutions. Often referred to as "flexibility mechanisms," the right of countries to meet their obligations through funding emissions reductions elsewhere through the joint implementation of projects or through the buying and selling of permits has been asserted forcefully by the world's most powerful country, the United States. As we can see in Box 1.2, the Kyoto Protocol that was agreed in December 1997 embodied a commitment to constructing such flexible mechanisms.

The support for market-based approaches as the preferred means of climate governance reflects a number of factors. The endorsement of emissions trading in particular built on the apparent effectiveness of other similar schemes, most notably the United States' sulfur dioxide trading scheme. Such approaches reflect the primacy of efficiency as the guiding policy principle of climate governance. In this vein, advocates have argued that it makes no difference where in the world a tonne of carbon is reduced and therefore it makes sense to create mechanisms which allow countries to pay for reductions where it is most cost-effective to do so.

In terms of domestic politics, such mechanisms make emissions reductions easier to sell to electorates wary of burdening domestic industry with additional obligations. Such tools were also seen as a valuable way of bridging some of the North–South conflicts discussed above. They could imply resource transfers to developing countries, potentially on a significant scale, and because emissions are being reduced in these countries they draw them further into the climate regime, pacifying concerns about them free-riding on the sacrifices made by industrialized countries.

That the world of climate governance has become a laboratory for experiments in market-based approaches to regulation is unsurprising, given that climate politics have risen to prominence during an era of heightened neo-liberalism. This broader political context is important in explaining why some solutions are seen as valid, legitimate and plausible, and others are not. It helps us to understand why, for example, command-and-control state-led regulatory approaches are out of favor, or why in a context of globalization and the mobility of capital, it becomes more important than ever to address potential carbon leakage. The emphasis in contemporary neo-liberalism on the creation of (carbon) markets, the allocation of property rights (in this case through allocating permits), the political preference for voluntary partnership-based approaches (such as the Asia Pacific Partnership on Clean Development and Climate (APP)) and voluntary efforts by industry, is clearly apparent in all aspects of contemporary climate governance, as we will see in Chapter 5. The irony, of course, was that having insisted on the inclusion of market-based mechanisms, the United States then refused to ratify the Kyoto Protocol. The European Union, meanwhile, which had initially been hostile to the idea of emissions trading, went on to develop the most advanced emissions trading scheme of its kind, the EU Emissions Trading Scheme.[27]

Despite the prevalence of the idea that markets deliver outcomes more efficiently and effectively than governments, each of the market-based mechanisms mentioned here relies on institutional backing. Governments have to decide who can participate in carbon markets (which sectors and actors) and set limits on the number of permits that are to be traded to create the necessary scarcity to incentivize emissions reductions. Markets, in other words, have to be governed. The 2001 Marrakesh Accords agreed rules, procedures, and modalities for the operation of the CDM, for example (Chapter 2). Furthermore, in order to guarantee the worth of the Certified Emissions Reduction units that are allocated, a range of governance actors have to be enrolled to verify baselines and methodologies, to demonstrate beyond doubt that emission reductions are "additional" (that they would not otherwise have been achieved by other means). Project developers help set up projects and a CDM executive board approves methodologies and projects. Harnessing the market to the goal of climate protection is one thing, but it does not do away with the need for inputs from traditional actors in climate governance, such as states, and international institutions.

Governance issues and challenges

This chapter draws our attention to a number of general features of climate governance. First, though climate change is often talked about as a global governance challenge, those countries whose actions directly determine the shape and effectiveness of the regime are relatively few in number. Deal-brokering unsurprisingly tends to focus on those actors. Traditionally, these have been the United States, the European Union, and Japan. The rising economic power of countries like China, India, Brazil, and South Africa means that they also are increasingly privy to head-to-head closed meetings in which negotiators attempt to establish the basic contours of agreement within which cooperation might be possible. The key deal-brokers in climate governance have changed in a way which reflects shifts in economic power in the global economy. The scope and nature of the negotiations mirrors broader geopolitical and economic shifts in another way too: the support for market mechanisms as the preferred way of governing climate change. Climate governance cannot be understood as separate from the ideology, institutions, and material interests that predominate within the wider global economy in which climate politics exists and with which it seeks to engage.

Second, although traditional approaches to understanding global environmental politics focus on bargaining between nation-states at the international level, they often neglect the importance of domestic politics. Various researchers have revealed the dynamic relationship whereby what happens in the domestic arenas of global powers carries global repercussions, just as what is agreed in global fora reconfigures domestic politics.[28] We have seen in this chapter, particularly in relation to the role of the United States, how global arenas are also a site of domestic politics and domestic politics get played out globally. Analytical distinctions which attempt to neatly separate the two are poorly served by the reality of networks, coalitions, and messy politics that cut across these levels of analysis. Importantly, as we will see in Chapter 2, the effectiveness of traditional climate governance in the form of national regulation and the forms of public international law described here, and the spaces and places where it is said to take place (within states and international institutions), is contingent on the ability and willingness of these governance actors and processes to engage with and seek to transform the everyday practices of climate governance that go by the name of energy policy, development policy, trade, industry, and agricultural policy. These are blind spots or areas of active neglect in the governance of climate change, whose future path will determine whether our collective responses to climate change are up to the challenge.

Third, non-state actors are central to the governance of climate change. Even in the relatively closed world of inter-state diplomacy, non-state actors are on delegations, in the conference rooms, talking to the media and protesting outside the negotiations. The neat distinctions that underpin the official roles and status ascribed to non-state actors describe poorly the reality of actors and individuals that move in and out of these categories, constructing and participating in coalitions and network formations that bypass traditional "levels of analysis," and producing climate governance in their wake. Whether it is the scientific community, business lobbies, or environmental groups, each of these actors plays a role and draws on assets that go beyond what governments and international institutions, the traditional agents in climate politics, can deliver alone.[29] As carbon markets assume increasing importance in the delivery of emissions reductions, business actors in particular play a more important role than ever before. NGOs are increasingly enrolled as project developers, monitors, and watchdogs. Indeed, with so many governance sites beyond the international regime, the UN faces a struggle to retain relevance, and some non-state actors have moved their sights elsewhere. While there are many competing explanations about why the international climate change regime takes the form it does, some of which we discuss in the Introduction (knowledge-based, interest-based and power-based regime theories), the increasing role of non-state actors and the importance of broader (non-regime) economic factors and forces in particular have changed the way we conceive of the whereabouts of the global politics of climate change, how they are conducted and for whom.[30] We return to discuss these issues in more depth in Chapters 3, 4 and 5.

Endnotes

by Harriet Bulkeley and Peter Newell

1 Governing climate change: a brief history

1 Joanna Depledge, *The Organization of the Global Negotiations: Constructing the Climate Regime* (London: Earthscan, 2005).

2 Matthew Paterson and Michael Grubb, "The International Politics of Climate Change," *International Affairs* 68, no. 2 (1992): 293–310.

3 Peter Newell, *Climate for Change: Non-State Actors and the Global Politics of the Greenhouse* (Cambridge: Cambridge University Press, 2000).

4 Bas Arts, *The Political Influence of Global NGOs: Case Studies on the Climate and Biodiversity Conventions* (Utrecht, Netherlands: International Books, 1998); Peter Newell, *Climate for Change*.

5 Michele Betsill and Elisabeth Corell, eds, *NGO Diplomacy: The Influence of Nongovernmental Organizations in International Environmental Negotiations* (Cambridge, Mass.: MIT Press, 2008), 3.

6 United Nations, *United Nations Framework Convention on Climate Change*, Bonn, Germany: UNFCCC Secretariat, 1992, http://unfccc.int/resource/docs/convkp/conveng.pdf

7 Michael Grubb with Christiaan Vrolijk and Duncan Brack, *The Kyoto Protocol: A Guide and Assessment* (London: Earthscan and the Royal Institute of International Affairs, 1999).

8 Michael Grubb and Farhana Yamin, "Climatic Collapse at The Hague: What Happened, Why, and Where Do We Go from Here?" *International Affairs* 77, no. 2 (2001): 261–76.

9 Chukwumerije Okereke, Phillip Mann, and Andy Newsham, "Assessment of Key Negotiating Issues at Nairobi Climate COP/MOP and what It Means for the Future of the Climate Regime," *Tyndall Centre Working Paper* 106 (2007).

10 Benito Muller, "Bali 2007: On the Road Again! Impressions from the Thirteenth UN Climate Change Conference," www.oxfordclimatepolicy.org/publications/Bali2007Final.pdf; Jennifer Morgan, "Towards a New Global Climate Deal: An Analysis of the Agreements and Politics of the Bali Negotiations. E3G," www.e3g.org/images/uploads/Bali_Analysis_Morgan_080120.pdf

11 Bert Bolin, "Scientific Assessment of Climate Change," in *International Politics of Climate Change: Key Issues and Actors*, ed. Gunnar Fermann (Oslo, Norway: Scandinavian University Press, 1997), 99.

12 Michel Foucault, *Power/Knowledge: Selected Interviews and Other Writings 1972–77* (New York: Pantheon books, 1980), 27.

13 Bolin, "Scientific Assessment of Climate Change," 102.

14 Peter Haas, *Saving the Mediterranean: The Politics of International Environmental Cooperation* (New York: Columbia University Press, 1990).

15 Karen Litfin, *Ozone Discourses* (New York: Columbia University Press, 1994).

16 Sonia Boehmer-Christiansen, "Global Climate Protection Policy: The Limits of Scientific Advice—Part 1," *Global Environmental Change* 4, no. 2 (1992): 140–59.

17 Among the most prominent "climate skeptics" are Fred Singer (George Mason University) and Richard Linzen (MIT).

18 "US Reportedly Seeking to Sink Watson as IPCC Head," www.unwire.org/unwire/20020402/25249_story.asp

19 Article 2 of the UNFCCC (1992): http://unfccc.int/resource/docs/convkp/conveng.pdf

20 *ECO* NGO Newsletter, issue 7, Geneva, 1990.

21 Adil Najam, Saleemul Huq, and Youba Sokona, "Climate Negotiations Beyond Kyoto: Developing Countries' Concerns and Interests," *Climate Policy* 3, no. 3 (2003): 221–31; Michele Williams, "The Third World and Global Environmental Negotiations: Interests, Institutions and Ideas," *Global Environmental Politics* 5, no. 3 (2005): 48–49.

22 Anil Argwal and Sunita Narain, *"Global Warming in an Unequal World: A Case of Environmental Colonialism,"* (New Delhi, India: Centre for Science and the Environment/WRI, 1991).

23 Article 3 of the UNFCCC (1992): http://unfccc.int/resource/docs/convkp/conveng.pdf

24 Zoe Young, *A New Green Order? The World Bank and the Politics of the Global Environment Facility* (London: Pluto Press, 2002).

25 Sjur Kasa, Anne Therese Gullberg, and Gørild Heggelund, "The Group of 77 in the International Climate Negotiations: Recent Developments and Future Directions," *International Environmental Agreements: Politics, Law and Economics* 8, no. 2 (2008): 113–27.

26 Scott Barrett, "Montreal Versus Kyoto: International Cooperation on the Global Environment," in *Global Public Goods*, eds Inge Kaul, Isabelle Grunberg, and Marc Stern (New York: Oxford University Press, 1999), 192–220.

27 Jan-Peter Voss, "Innovation Processes in Governance: the Development of 'Emissions Trading' as a New Policy Instrument," *Science and Public Policy* 34, no. 5 (2007): 329–43; Jon Birger Skjærseth and Jørgen Wettestad, *EU Emissions Trading: Initiation, Decision-Making and Implementation* (Aldershot, UK: Ashgate, 2008).

28 Miranda Schreurs and Elizabeth Economy, eds, *The Internationalization of Environmental Protection* (Cambridge: Cambridge University Press, 1997); Peter Newell "The Political Economy of Global Environmental Governance," *Review of International Studies* 34 (July 2008): 507–29.

29 Newell, *Climate for Change.*

30 David Levy and Peter Newell, eds, *The Business of Global Environmental Governance* (Cambridge, Mass.: MIT Press, 2005); Chukwumerije Okereke, Harriet Bulkeley, and Heike Schroeder, "Conceptualizing Climate Governance Beyond the International Regime," *Global Environmental Politics* 9, no. 1 (2009): 58–78.

Additional Works Cited

Smallman, Shawn and Kimberley Brown. 2011. *Introduction to International and Global Studies*. University of North Carolina Press.

V. MODULE FIVE:

Human Development

One of the first things students may notice when reading about development is a multitude of categories: in order to discuss development, scholars and policy makers have found it necessary to divide nation-states into categories based on their level of development. At best, these categories fail to explain. At worst, the categories perpetuate harmful stereotypes.

Unhelpful dichotomies previously used for heuristic purposes are gradually being refined as a result of an increasingly nuanced understanding of the interconnectedness of more and less prosperous regions. Both the World Bank and the United Nations now use four categories.

Economic growth increases our potential to reduce poverty, but indicators of wealth like Gross Domestic Product (GDP) don't provide enough information about quality of life or allocation of resources within a nation. A crucial distinction in this module is therefore between "development" and "human development." While the former term refers to advances in material wealth and focuses on economic growth, human development encompasses human security. Human development can include any activity that improves lives. Scholars and policy makers have worked hard to develop indexes that can quantify this more holistic notion of development. Human development is now assessed with complex algorithms that measure health, education, and life expectancy. As a way to enhance people's ability to live long and creative lives, human development is closely tied to political freedoms and human rights.

While the field of human development has many advocates and continues to grow, some take a critical perspective. In fact, the project of human of human development has been criticized from two important angles. The first set of criticisms revolves around the way that human development is being measured. In general, these critics hold that the index uses the wrong variables and that it does not reflect the idea of human development accurately. For example, Sagar and Najam (1998) went so far as to say that the HDI presents a "distorted" image of the world. Others argue that the HDI presents an oversimplified account that should be questioned because it relies on low quality data (Kovacevic 2010). As a result of these limitations, critics take the view that the HDI does not offer much in addition to the GDP.

A more serious set of criticisms has to do with the outcomes of the development project itself. While development was envisioned as a project that would make the world a better place, the way it has been carried out has not always been successful. Ernesto Sirolli argues that the chief problem with the project of development is not taking the knowledge, expertise, and goals of locals sufficiently into account.[i] In "Dead Aid," Dambisa Moya challenges the most basic assumptions that have informed development projects. She argues that the billions of dollars that have flowed into African nations kept developing nations in a state of dependency (Moyo 2009). Amartya Sen, who influenced the formulation of the Human Development Report and won the 1998 Nobel Prize in Economics, is another well-known critic of traditional approaches to development. He takes the view that development instigated from the top down will tend to eclipse human rights. His alternative is to start thinking about development as "capacity" and development as "freedom." (Sen 1999).

Readings

In "Underdevelopment and Diversity in the Global South," **Baker** offers conceptual tools for understanding both the similarities and differences among countries in the global South. They provide a definition of what we mean when we say "less developed country" and, in alignment with the comparative interdisciplinary approach of international studies, explore the economic, social, and political aspects of underdevelopment. In this reading, you will find an important discussion of the causes of poverty, as well as explanations of important terms like Gross Domestic Product or GDP.

Kennedy Odede offers a very personal perspective on the same underdevelopment discussed by Baker. Odede has a Kenyan perspective on "Slum Tourism," a practice in which people from the developed world see – and try to understand - poverty first-hand. His observations add valuable perspective to academic readings such as the chapter by Baker. Odede questions whether slum tourism truly promotes greater social awareness or begins to address poverty. In his experience, it turns poverty into entertainment.

In "The Danger of a Single Story," **Chimanda Ngozi Adichie** explores how it is we often come to have a single story about countries other than our own. She writes from the perspective of a Nigerian with a middle-class childhood. In her view, stereotypes are easy to fall into, but undermine the ability to understand.

Underdevelopment and Diversity
in the Global South

by Andy Baker

Nathalie of the Democratic Republic of Congo. Nathalie is an eight-year-old girl residing in the world's poorest country, the Democratic Republic of Congo. She lives in a remote rural village in the eastern province of South Kivu. Nathalie has five siblings, and another died in childbirth. Tragically, her mother also died during this stillborn birth. For the most part, Nathalie is now being raised by her aunts and a grandmother. Her family and fellow villagers grow their own food and thus have a precarious food supply. Nathalie, in particular, is malnourished. She is listless and undersized—given her height and weight, she would be mistaken for a six-year-old if in the United States.

Nathalie goes to school in a small building with forty-six other children and one teacher. In a few years, Nathalie's schooling will be done. Few girls are expected to be educated past thirteen, the age at which many of their fathers arrange for them to be married. She is absent from school quite frequently. Twice a week she misses school to walk four miles round-trip to fetch clean drinking water. (Although she struggles to carry and balance three gallons of water on her head, Nathalie's brothers stay in school and are not expected to perform this task.) Nathalie also misses school quite frequently due to illness. She sleeps with her siblings under a mosquito net given to her family by a foreign humanitarian group, but every year Nathalie still suffers a few bouts of malaria sickness—chills, fever, vomiting, and headache. Even when in school, malnourishment complicates her ability to pay attention. Despite the schooling, Nathalie cannot read a simple text.

Nathalie's province has been troubled by war for years. Marauding bands of rebels, some of them from neighboring Rwanda, are known to sweep through the provinces' villages, stealing supplies, ransacking homes, and raping women and girls. Nathalie's village has been spared from the violence, yet she knows about the potential threat from adult villagers. They are debating whether to abandon the village and move to a refugee camp that would be a twelve-hour walk through thick forest and over muddy roads. The prospect terrifies Nathalie, as she has never been more than ten miles from her village. Despite the ongoing violence and potential threat in the province, Nathalie has never seen a Congolese soldier or police officer.

Priya of India. Dharavi, a neighborhood in the city of Mumbai (India), is considered by some to be Asia's largest slum. About the size of a large U.S. college campus, Dharavi has 1 million residents. Many of the homes in Dharavi are small wooden shacks with dirt floors that become muddy, like the unpaved streets outside, during the heavy rains of the summer monsoon. Few have toilets, so public restrooms are shared by hundreds of families. To avoid the wait at these latrines, some neighbors put their waste in a bag that is then hurled onto the street or nearby creek—so-called flying toilets. The neighborhood is seen by many as unsafe, and few parents allow their children to go outside after dark.

Priya is a twenty-eight-year-old Dalit woman who moved to Dharavi from a small rural village when she was six. Her parents had just died and her new caretakers, her aunt and uncle, moved with her to the city in search of better economic opportunities. Priya dropped out of school to marry around the age of sixteen and has since birthed three daughters. She works as a maid for a middle-class family and gets paid in cash the equivalent of US$22 per month. Her husband works a steadier manufacturing job, earning US$54 per month, but every day he endures an hour-long commute on crowded trains. Once off the train, he has to compete with hundreds of other commuters to hail an auto rickshaw to carry him the last two kilometers. On these combined wages, Priya's family rarely lacks for food, although their diet is not incredibly diverse or rich

in protein. Still, their income is not always sufficient to cover other expenses for items such as medicine, the family cell phone, train tickets, and entertainment for the girls. To supplement, Priya occasionally borrows money at about 15 percent monthly interest from a grocer who owns a small store down the street, and she remains indebted to him. She also keeps some extra savings in a bag under her bed, holding it for health emergencies or her daughters' weddings.

Priya's house contains two rooms—one bedroom for Priya, her husband, and oldest daughter; and a second multipurpose room with a stove, dining table, TV, and couches where everyone else sleeps. This includes an unrelated single man who pays them US$11 per month in rent. The home does have electricity, but it draws from an illegal hookup that is potentially unsafe and not monitored by the utility company. Although Priya's home is meager, she is concerned about losing it. The Mumbai municipal government, which Priya voted against in the last election, would like to develop the area with modern housing, infrastructure, and amenities. If this development project occurs, a family like Priya's, which simply built its home without first securing ownership of the land beneath it, might have to leave Dharavi without receiving any compensation for its lost residence. While the government promises to give each dispossessed family a small flat (about 300 square feet) in the redeveloped neighborhood, Priya is doubtful. Without proof of ownership, there are no guarantees, and with no real sense of their future in Dharavi, Priya's family is hesitant to ever improve their home.

Cheng of China. With a sense of foreboding, Cheng looks over his sixteen-year-old son's shoulder as he works on the family computer. His son is filling out applications for admission to some of the top universities in China. He is a talented student who attends an elite private prep school,

208

but Cheng silently worries about his son's chances for admission. A year earlier, Cheng became an unlikely environmental activist and critic of local officials in the Chinese Communist Party. He thinks that, in having doing so, he may have derailed his son's educational aspirations. Cheng fears that the government could covertly keep the boy out of top schools.

Cheng's entry into Chinese politics was sudden and unexpected. After all, he is a forty-two-year-old computer engineer whose salary affords his three-person family an apartment in a luxury high-rise complex, a car, a flat-screen television, a personal computer, and other modern amenities. Such comforts are not usually a recipe for political dissidence, but Cheng became a vocal critic of the ruling party when its environmental policy hit home. Cheng lives on the outskirts of the city of Wuxi near the shores of Lake Tai, long known as a haven for fishermen and, because of its natural beauty, tourists. Lake Tai in recent decades has become a hotbed of manufacturing activity. Local political officials encouraged industry as a means to raise the region's gross domestic product, and it dramatically boosted their tax revenues and the region's economic living standards. However, the boom around Lake Tai came with a dramatic cost, one that spurred Cheng's political activity: environmental degradation. Lake Tai is now heavily polluted. The thousands of chemical factories on its shores dump toxic industrial waste into its waters. Most fish and many other aquatic species have died off along with the lake's attraction to potential tourists. Most notoriously, the lake periodically experiences algal blooms, or overgrowths of toxic algae that literally turn the lake a fluorescent green color and emit a noxious odor that can be detected up to one mile away.

During one algal bloom, Wuxi's tap water turned yellowish-green and became undrinkable. Residents who showered in it smelled for the rest of the day. Cheng and other citizens queued for hours at shopping malls to buy bottled drinking water, which quickly became very expensive and was ultimately rationed by store owners. At nearly the same time, Cheng's mother died from cancer, a condition he suspected was caused by toxins in the city's water, food, and air. In response to both incidents, Cheng decided to organize small meetings with family and friends and even one street protest against pollution. He also investigated nearby factories to determine who was dumping waste, informing local political officials of his findings in the hopes that they might shut down or at least enforce regulations against polluting factories. His complaints were ignored and, in actuality, he has been followed and verbally intimidated by police. Cheng has kept his job, but he fears for his son's academic future.

Defining the Developing World

What do an African peasant girl, an Indian maid, and a Chinese software engineer have in common?[1] At first glance, seemingly very little. Nathalie and Priya are poor, yet Cheng leads a comfortable middle-class lifestyle. Nathalie is often hungry, but Priya and Cheng are not. Cheng resides in an authoritarian country, Priya lives in a democracy, and Nathalie lives in a place where the government has virtually no presence at all. Nathalie is rural, Priya is urban, and Cheng is suburban. Their very different life experiences would seem to undermine any attempt to lump them or the countries in which they live together, and yet Nathalie, Priya, and Cheng are united in the fact they are all residents of the developing world. Not all of them are poor themselves, but their lives are shaped by the fact that they live in a less developed country.

Naming the Developing World

A developing or **less developed country** (LDC) is one in which a large share of the population cannot meet or experiences great difficulties in meeting basic material needs such as housing, food, water, health care, education, electricity, transport, communications, and physical security. For a society, the state of experiencing these deprivations is called **underdevelopment**, and the gradual process of shedding them is called development. Less developed countries are different from developed countries like the United States, since U.S. citizens have a relatively high average income and are largely able to meet basic needs. In sum, whether or not a country is defined as less developed depends on material factors of an economic and social nature.

The use of these terms and classification scheme is not always straightforward. The term "developing country" itself is imperfect because, as a descriptor, it is often inaccurate. Many poor countries are not developing. For example, Nathalie's DR Congo has become less prosperous, not more so, over the last fifty years. The notion of a less developed country is thus more accurate because it does not imply economic progress, yet even this seemingly innocuous term has its critics. In particular, the word "developed" offends some who see it as betraying a sense that rich countries and their peoples are more evolved, perfected, and superior to underdeveloped ones.

Other commonly used labels for poor countries also have shortcomings. Two are "global South" or just "the South." These terms make use of the geographical fact that the wealthiest countries are in the northern hemisphere with poorer countries to their south: Latin America is to the south of the United States, Africa and the Middle East are south of Europe, and the poorer regions of Asia are south of industrialized Russia. Like the others, these terms are imperfect. For example, wealthy Australia and New Zealand are among the southernmost countries of the world. Moreover, these terms obfuscate the classification issue by using a locational label for what is an economically and socially defined category of countries.

Another term frequently used is "Third World." French anthropologist Alfred Sauvy coined the term in 1952 to give identity to the many countries that, during the Cold War, were not formally allied with either the wealthy capitalist First World countries of the West (meaning the U.S. and Western Europe) or the Second World communist countries of the East. Thus, at its inception, the term Third World had a political and not an economic or social meaning. However, since the world's nonaligned countries also tended to be non-industrialized, the term eventually took on the economic meaning that has stuck to this day. Few users of the term today realize that some of today's so-called Third World nations, most notably China, were not originally classified as such. Because of this inaccuracy, along with the fact that many dislike the term because it implicitly ranks the quality of countries on a scale from one to three, "Third World" is largely avoided in this textbook. In the end, although each of the terms has its flaws and slightly divergent connotations, this textbook uses "less developed countries," "LDCs," "developing countries," "underdeveloped countries," "global South," and "South" interchangeably.

Delineating the Developing World

The map inside this book's front cover identifies the world's developing countries. Those classified as something other than less developed are shaded in gray. LDCs are colored by the five geographical regions that comprise the developing world: East Asia and the Pacific, Latin America and the Caribbean, the Middle East and North Africa, South Asia, and sub-Saharan Africa. To provide a point of contrast, information for the traditionally defined developed countries will often be described and summarized as the "High-income OECD" category. (The Organisation for Economic Co-operation and Development, or OECD, is an international organization that has included only rich countries since its inception in 1961.)[2] As is clear from the map, the vast majority of countries are less developed, and in fact about 80 percent of humanity resides in an LDC. Underdevelopment is thus much more prevalent than prosperity as a context of the human experience.

Furthermore, a large minority of humans are themselves impoverished. Many experts treat US$2 per day as the global poverty line, and anyone below US$1.25 per day is classified as extremely poor. In 2008, about 2.5 billion people, or 35 percent of the world's population, were below the poverty line, and 18 percent of humanity, or about 1.2 billion people, were below the extreme poverty line. As a region, South Asia has the largest number of these global poor, although sub-Saharan Africa stands as the world region with the highest share of its population below the extreme poverty line. Table 1.1 summarizes some of these economic and poverty statistics for each of the six world regions.[3]

The simple label "less developed" disguises a vast array of prosperity levels throughout the developing world. To better illustrate this diversity, Map 1.1 places LDCs into one of three categories based on the average economic living standards of their populations. The four categories are delineated by levels of gross national income (GNI) per capita. GNI per capita, along with the closely related gross domestic product (GDP) per-capita statistic, is the most commonly used measure of a country's overall economic prosperity. (See Understanding Indicators: Measuring Prosperity

with Gross Domestic Product.) For a given country, it can be thought of as the average citizen's income. According to the World Bank, low-income countries have an annual GNI per capita of US$995 or less. At this cutoff, the average citizen has an income of about US$3 per day. Lower-middle-income countries have average incomes between US$996 and US$3,945, or about US$3 and US$10 per day, respectively. Upper-middle-income countries are between US$3,946 and US$12,195. In contrast, high-income or developed countries are those with an average annual income greater than US$12,196. Map 1.1 makes it clear that less developed countries span everything from the many low-income countries of sub-Saharan Africa to numerous upper-middle income countries scattered throughout all five regions.

As indicated by these maps, this textbook does not include the countries of the former Soviet Union among its contents. These former members of the Second World have economic and social characteristics that are distinct from the traditionally defined less developed countries. In particular, they became independent countries in 1991 (much more recently than virtually all LDCs), with higher levels of industrialization, equality, educational attainment, and life

Table 1.1   **Poverty and Income Statistics in Six World Regions**

Region	Average Income	Percentage and Number Living in Poverty	Percentage and Number Living in Extreme Poverty
East Asia and the Pacific	US$2,720	33 percent (640 million)	14 percent (270 million)
Latin America and the Caribbean	US$6,860	12 percent (68 million)	6 percent (34 million)
Middle East and North Africa	US$3,380	14 percent (45 million)	3 percent (10 million)
South Asia	US$964	71 percent (1.1 billion)	36 percent (575 million)
Sub-Saharan Africa	US$1,100	69 percent (560 million)	48 percent (390 million)
High-Income OECD	US$40,000	<1 percent	<1 percent

Source: Compiled from World Development Indicators, 2008, http://data.worldbank.org/data-catalog/world-development-indicators.

Notes: Average income is GNI per capita, Atlas method. Percentage and number living in poverty are those < US$2 per day. Percentage and number living in extreme poverty reflects those < US$1.25 per day.

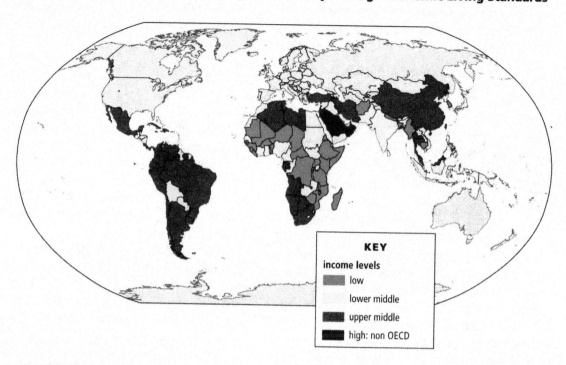

KEY

income levels

low

lower middle

upper middle

high: non OECD

Source: Modified by author from data at the World Bank, World Development Indicators, http://data.worldbank.org/data-catalog/world-development-indicators.

expectancy than standard LDCs. To be sure, many still have major pockets of poverty and social underdevelopment, giving them some shared characteristics with less developed countries. On most grounds, however, they are treated as a case apart. Throughout the book, readers will find data on LDCs and developed countries contrasted in tables and figures. In some figures, case study countries and some developed countries are labeled to make comparisons easier. A list of these country code labels is in the book's Appendix.

Economic, Social, and Political Characteristics

Given its diversity, the developing world defies simple summary. Few individuals in the developing world actually match the horrific images—such as the naked, starving child with the bloated belly or the illiterate child soldier—that are often seen in Western media and characterize many Westerners' notions of life in the developing world. Still, there are certain economic, social, and political commonalities that characterize most developing countries and that distinguish them from developed ones. All of these characteristics mentioned in this section are described in greater detail in subsequent chapters of this book.

Economic Characteristics

To say that LDCs tend to have relatively high rates of poverty or low per-capita GDPs is merely a starting point in describing their economies and economic characteristics. Another defining economic feature of the developing world is low productivity. In any given day, a typical person in the developing world produces fewer goods and services of value than does an average person in the developed world. Indeed, asking why a country is poor is nearly equivalent to asking why it is not productive: "Prosperity is the increase in the amount of goods and services you can earn with the same amount of work."[4] This is why gross domestic *product* is such a popular proxy for prosperity.

It is important to point out that, in describing people in the developing world as less productive, they are not being characterized as inherently lazy or deficient. It is not personal ability or effort but people's surroundings—the general characteristics of the economies in which they live—that largely determine how productive and thus how wealthy they are. The importance of economic context is most evident in the fact that, worldwide, a person's country of residence is more than three times as important for determining their income than are all of their individual characteristics, including innate ability and effort.[5] Rich countries have the technologies and institutions in place that make their citizens' efforts highly productive. For example, most of the things that make successful U.S. engineers rich are well beyond their making: the schools they attended, the banks that gave them loans for their education, the companies that hired them, the many customers rich enough to afford their services, the roads they use to get to work, the computer and telecommunications technologies they use at their work, the police force and legal system that protect their ownership of their earnings and home, and so on. In contrast, Nathalie and her family from this chapter's opening stories remain poor because, despite working hard to grow food and collect water, they toil in a context that does not provide them with these things. They lack modern farming equipment, roads and security to transport crops to markets, good schools, banks from which to borrow, a pool of well-off potential customers, and, of particular import to Nathalie's productivity, a clean water tap nearby.

Another feature of economies in the developing world is poor **infrastructure**, a term that refers to the facilities that make economic activity and economic exchange possible. Infrastructure is generally divided into four sectors: transport, communications, energy, and water. Roads, telephones, electricity, and indoor plumbing are all examples of infrastructure. The opening vignettes to this chapter provide numerous examples of poor infrastructure in the developing world. Priya's husband wriggles onto a crowded train every morning and often cannot hail a rickshaw to complete his journey. Priya lives on muddy streets, has no toilet, and must use an illegal electricity hookup. Throughout India, only two-thirds of the population even has access to electricity. Nathalie lives far from any paved roads and has never seen a telephone. In her country, there are less than 2,000 miles of paved roads, and less than 20 percent of the population has a telephone.[6] Cheng is deeply affected by the polluted drinking water in his city, and China has some of world's most polluted freshwater sources.

As another economic characteristic, a large portion of economic activity in LDCs is concentrated in the primary sector, which is largely comprised of farming activities, and in unskilled labor. Less than 5 percent of the workforce in developed countries is in agriculture, yet in LDCs the amount is typically far greater than this. The vast majority of Nathalie's compatriots reside, like her, in rural areas and farm small plots of land for survival. The same applies to more than 40 percent of the Chinese and Indian populations. For those who do not work in agriculture, unskilled labor in the secondary (manufacturing) or tertiary (services) sectors is likely. As a maid, Priya provides manual labor in the services sector and her husband, as a factory worker, in the secondary sector. Skill-oriented jobs and economic activities that require a high degree of specialization and education are rarer in LDCs than in developed countries.

Finally, less developed economies have large informal sectors. The informal sector is comprised of economic activity that occurs outside the monitoring and legal purview of the government. Between 30 percent and 60 percent of all economic activity in most LDCs takes place in the informal sector. In developed countries, where this percentage ranges

A set of indicators all closely related to **gross domestic product (GDP)** contains the most widely used and recognized yardsticks of a country's prosperity. This includes the GNI per-capita figures used by the World Bank to classify countries into the groups reported in Map 1.1. Roughly speaking, a country's GDP for a given year is the total value added in the production of goods and services by all residents of that country, and the value of a good or service is determined by its price in the local currency. (GNI differs only in that it also includes income earned by citizens from assets or jobs they have abroad.) Dividing the total GDP by population size yields the GDP per-capita measure, which is the total value produced by the average citizen in the relevant year. GDP per capita is the most widely used measure of a country's average level of material well-being. Scholars convert GDP per-capita figures that are denominated in local currency to U.S. dollars (using the prevailing exchange rate) to make international comparisons of well-being more straightforward. In turn, a final adjustment that facilitates cross-national comparison of these dollar amounts is the purchasing power parity (PPP) fix. A dollar goes farther in a country with a low cost of living, so, to better measure its average level of material prosperity, its raw GDP per capita figures can be adjusted upward to reflect the greater purchasing power of a dollar in its economy. In the end, of the various indicators within the GDP family, the GDP per capita at PPP measure allows for the most informative cross-national comparisons of citizens' well-being and will be frequently used in this book.

All that said, the heavy reliance on GDP-related measures to gauge human well-being has generated a number of criticisms. First, GDP equates the value of an economic activity or product to its price and thus does not accurately gauge its worth to quality of life. GDP excludes the many activities that contribute to a sense of fulfillment and purpose but that have no market price: volunteer activity, time spent with one's family, leisure activities, physical and mental wellness, intellectual fulfillment, political freedoms, happiness, cultural belonging, social connectedness, natural beauty, clean air, personal efficacy, and so on. Meanwhile, GDP gives value to many things that do not enhance quality of life. For example, traffic jams (which increase the demand for gasoline), rising crime (which raises demand for lawyers and security personnel), threats to national security (military hardware), natural disasters (construction materials and services), unnecessary medical procedures (health equipment and doctors), and environmental catastrophes (cleanup services) all boost GDP.

Second, GDP overlooks the sustainability of production. For instance, politicians incentivized to grow short-term GDP figures have repeatedly created bubble economies driven by unsustainable debt that eventually implode in recession or depression. Similarly, it ignores what is destroyed in the production process. GDP makes no accounting for the depletion of natural resources used in production or for their availability to future generations. Environmental damage, greenhouse gas emissions (unless they are priced), and deaths caused by modern technologies are unaccounted for. As one example, the conversion of tropical rain forest to agricultural land by felling trees boosts a country's GDP since it makes the land more economically productive, yet this has devastating consequences for the local and global environment.

Finally, GDP per capita is indifferent to equality—that is, how dispersed the gains from production are around the average income. Decreases in inequality do not register as higher GDP, and GDP figures grow even when much of the newfound wealth accrues to the wealthy. Subsequent chapters in this book will introduce inequality measures and raise alternatives to GDP.

- Despite its shortcomings, why is GDP per capita so widely used as a measure of prosperity?

- What might be some better ways to measure human well-being than GDP?

---

from the single digits to the teens, governments register, regulate, and tax most businesses, workers, and major assets. In doing so, governments can provide a variety of benefits and services to citizens. Priya's story provides three examples of informality and its costs. First, she is paid at her maid job in cash, or under the table. This means that she receives none of the side benefits, such as an eventual retirement pension or unemployment insurance, that are typically offered workers in developed countries. Also, since her workplace is unregulated, there are no safety standards or rules against her dismissal in the event of illness or pregnancy. In India, an estimated 80 percent of nonagricultural jobs are informal.[7] Second, Priya's ownership of her home is neither recognized nor protected by the government. She thus has no means to protect this asset from theft, damage, or expropriation by other citizens or by the government itself. Third, Priya relies on informal channels to manage her cash flow. Priya stashes money in her house, making it susceptible to loss, theft, and depreciation through inflation. She also borrows from a nearby storekeeper at a very high interest rate. In India, less than 10 percent of the poor have formal bank accounts, and the average annual interest rates they pay on loans are more than five times the rates on offer in the developed world.[8]

Table 1.2 illustrates some of these features of less developed economies by summarizing information by world region about infrastructure (paved roads as a percentage of all roads), the primary sector (share of labor force working in agriculture), and informality (share of economic activity that is informal).

Social Characteristics

Underdevelopment is more than just an economic characteristic. Social underdevelopment is also a common feature in the global South. A society with poor social development fails to deliver educational and health amenities to large shares of its population. The systematic exclusion and disempowerment of major groups is also an aspect of social underdevelopment.

In the area of health, LDCs fall short of developed countries on a long list of indicators. Life expectancies are shorter, as deaths from diseases that are easily curable or preventable in the West are more common. Recall that both Nathalie and Priya had parents who died at a relatively young age. Moreover, Nathalie herself contracts malaria a few times year, a disease that children in the West almost never get. All told, average life expectancy is only in the high forties in DR Congo and the mid-sixties in India. Infant mortality rates are also higher. Again, the tragedy of Nathalie's sibling, who died at birth, attests to this. Nearly one in six children die before their fifth birthday in the DR Congo, and in India the figure is one in seventeen. Furthermore, nearly one woman in twenty dies in childbirth in the DR Congo. Even in China, where average life expectancies and infant mortality rates are closer to

Table 1.2 **Economic Characteristics in Six World Regions**

Region	Paved Roads (as a percentage of all roads)	Share of Labor Force Working in Agriculture	Size of the Informal Sector (as a percentage of total economy)
East Asia and the Pacific	30.7 percent	39.6 percent	32.3 percent
Latin America and the Caribbean	22.5 percent	14.3 percent	41.2 percent
Middle East and North Africa	75.2 percent	27.2 percent	28.0 percent
South Asia	53.9 percent	53.5 percent	33.2 percent
Sub-Saharan Africa	18.8 percent	65.0 percent	40.8 percent
High-Income OECD	79.7 percent	3.3 percent	3.3 percent

Sources: Data on paved roads and labor force compiled from World Development Indicators, 2004–2009, http://data.worldbank.org/data-catalog/world-development-indicators; informal sector from Friedrich Schneider, Andreas Buehn, and Claudio E. Montenegro, "Shadow Economies All over the World," *World Bank Policy Research Working Paper*, no. 5326 (2010).

Western standards, the poor quality of the environment poses an ongoing health threat.

Moreover, in LDCs, levels of educational attainment and the quality of schooling tend to be lower, while literacy rates are often higher. Nathalie has little hope of being educated past primary school. What she is able to attain is of low quality, as she is in a classroom with more than forty children and can herself barely read. In DR Congo, only about one half of children complete primary education, and a third of adults are illiterate. Similarly, Priya did not complete secondary school in India, where only a minority of people do so. The same is true in China, Cheng's advanced degree notwithstanding.[9]

Social exclusion based on group status is also a common characteristic of underdevelopment in LDCs. Various forms of gender discrimination are particularly pernicious in many parts of the global South. Nathalie, not her brothers, is expected to fetch water and miss school because of it. She will also have a limited say over who her eventual marriage partner is. Cheng's only child is a son in a country where many parents strongly prefer sons to daughters and are willing to have sex-selective abortions to achieve this goal. Moreover, rural dwellers also tend to suffer higher degrees of exclusion than city dwellers

in LDCs. Worldwide, about 75 percent of those living in extreme poverty are residents of rural areas, even though less than 60 percent of LDC residents are rural.[10] Health and educational services, as well as infrastructure, are much less likely to reach rural areas than urban ones. Although urban slums such as Priya's Dharavi are often portrayed as the context for developing world poverty, Nathalie's rural reality is a much more common setting for the global poor.

Table 1.3 illustrates some of the social deficits that exist between rich and less developed countries. It reports regional averages for indicators of health (infant mortality), the social exclusion of rural populations (rural/urban gap in access to sanitation facilities), and gender discrimination (female/male gap in literacy).

Political Characteristics

Providing broad characterizations of the political systems of the less developed world is more difficult than describing its economic and social characteristics. After all, the very term "less developed" refers to an economic and social state of being, not a political one. Still, there are some tendencies that make political systems in LDCs different on average from

Table 1.3 **Social Characteristics in Six World Regions**

Region	Infant Mortality Rate	Rural Population with Improved Sanitation	Urban Population with Improved Sanitation	Female Literacy Rate	Male Literacy Rate
East Asia and the Pacific	17.0	57 percent	76 percent	91 percent	97 percent
Latin America and the Caribbean	16.2	59 percent	84 percent	91 percent	92 percent
Middle East and North Africa	26.1	59 percent	80 percent	68 percent	84 percent
South Asia	48.3	28 percent	59 percent	50 percent	73 percent
Sub-Saharan Africa	69.4	23 percent	42 percent	55 percent	72 percent
High-Income OECD	4.6	99 percent	99 percent	100 percent	100 percent

Source: Compiled from World Development Indicators, 2010, http://data.worldbank.org/data-catalog/world-development-indicators.

Notes: Infant mortality rate is deaths per 1,000 live births.

those in developed countries. The most important is that **political regimes**—that is, the set of rules that shape how a society is governed—tend to be more authoritarian and less democratic than regimes in developed countries. The developed countries of Europe and North America are democracies with free and fair elections, alternations in power among competing political parties, and legal protections of basic civil rights and liberties. In contrast, many of the top political leaders throughout the developing world are not selected through free and fair elections, nor do they uphold and respect their citizens' fundamental civil and political rights. All told, only about forty percent of LDCs are democracies, and virtually all of the political systems of the Middle East, as well as many in Africa and Asia, are authoritarian, including Cheng's China. Even in the LDCs where democracy does prevail, such as Priya's India, it is likely the case that the country became a democracy only in recent decades. By comparison, most Western countries have been democracies for nearly a century or more.

LDCs also experience more political instability than developed countries. Political instability exists when there is high uncertainty about the future existence of the current political regime. Wholesale changes in the political regime happen with some frequency in the developing world. Events that fall slightly short of this—widespread protest, political assassinations, terrorism, armed insurgencies, frequent turnover of the chief executive, failed efforts to change the government through illegal means (*coup d'état* attempts)—but that nonetheless indicate that the existing regime is under threat are also more prevalent in the developing world. The violence propagated by the armed bands in Nathalie's DR Congo is one indicator of political instability. By contrast, in the democracies of the developed world, alternations in power occur through election-based competition, and regime change and political violence are rare.

Another feature of LDC political systems is that they tend to have lower state capacity. State capacity is the degree to which a state is able to successfully and efficiently carry out its designated responsibilities and provide high-quality public goods and services. For example, many governments in LDCs are entirely ineffective at providing a safe environment for their citizens to live in. Recall that Nathalie has never seen a police officer or Congolese army soldier, despite the fact that she lives in a war-stricken province. Priya worries about safety because her city is deficient in preventing crime and lacks a legal system that can prosecute criminals. At the extreme, low state capacity can manifest as complete state failure, in which a state has no presence or ability to govern at all in most of its territory.

Finally, the vast majority of today's LDCs are former colonies. Colonialism is the governing of a territory by individuals and institutions from outside the territory, with the colony being the territory that is governed by foreigners. In the early 1500s, Spain and Portugal colonized much of Central and South America, commencing a five-hundred-year era of Western imperialism during which European powers took and held much of the non-Western world as their colonial possessions. Great Britain, France and the Netherlands were the other major Western colonizers during this era. Most of Africa, Asia, and the Western Hemisphere fell under Western colonial rule at various points during the era, which did not completely end until the decolonization of Africa in the 1960s and 1970s. For example, parts of Priya's India were colonized by various European powers—Netherlands, Denmark, France, Portugal, Great Britain—in the sixteenth and seventeenth centuries, and colonial rule of the entire Indian subcontinent was centralized under the British in the nineteenth century until Indian independence in 1947. Nathalie's DR Congo was colonized by King Leopold II of Belgium and then Belgium itself starting in the late 1800s, and European powers occupied many of the cities in Cheng's China during the nineteenth century.

Table 1.4 illustrates a number of these political features by contrasting regional averages on three political indicators: regime type (percentage of

Table 1.4	Political Characteristics in Six World Regions		
Region	**Democratic Countries**	**Failed and Successful Coups since 1946**	**Average Government Effectiveness Score***
East Asia and the Pacific	8 (of 16)	57	−.02
Latin America and the Caribbean	19 (of 24)	130	−.06
Middle East and North Africa	2 (of 18)	68	−.42
South Asia	3 (of 7)	29	−.23
Sub-Saharan Africa	19 (of 48)	226	−.82
High-Income OECD	30 (of 30)	13	1.33

Sources: Data on countries that are democratic is compiled from Polity IV Project: Political Regime Characteristics and Transitions, 1800–2010, www.systemicpeace.org/polity/polity4.htm; failed and successful coups, Monty Marshall and Donna Ramsey Marshall, "Coup D'État Events 1946–2011," Center for System Peace, http://www.systemicpeace.org/inscr/CSPoupsCodebook2011.pdf; government effectiveness, World Governance Indicators, 2011, http://info.worldbank.org/governance/wgi/index.asp.

*-2.5 is least effective and +2.5 is most effective

countries that are democracies), political instability (number of failed and successful coups), and state capacity (government effectiveness score assigned by the World Bank).

A Brief History of Economic Development

When looking at all of human history, the existence of less developed parts of the world is actually a rather recent occurrence, since modern economic growth and a set of more developed countries emerged just 250 years ago. A brief overview of this history helps put modern development and underdevelopment into context.

The Pre-Industrial Eras

Homo sapiens as a species has existed in its modern physiological form for about 200,000 years. For the first 190,000 (or 95 percent) of those years, humans lived as hunter-gatherers in small bands of a dozen to a few dozen people. Hunter-gatherers lived by foraging for edible plants, hunting live animals, and nomadically moving from place to place when food sources in one area became exhausted. The distribution of well-being across the human population was extremely equitable, as most food findings were shared within bands and there were no technologies or assets such as machinery or homes to make some bands wealthier than others.

Around 10,000 years ago, a variety of **agricultural revolutions**, defined as the invention and dissemination of farming, occurred in different pockets of the world and ushered in the Neolithic Era. The domestication of plants and animals enabled humans to exert greater control over the production of food. This increased food yields dramatically and freed up a minority of individuals in each society to take up professions—such as priest, merchant, engineer, inventor, soldier, politician, or artist—that did not directly involve food production. Farming also tied people to particular plots of land, removing the need for

nomadism and leading to sedentary societies. The first civilizations (Sumerian, Egyptian, Indus Valley) were stable settlements whose emergence was made possible by the agricultural revolution. The emergence of new specializations and the associated division of labor, along with variations in productivity across different farmers, introduced wealth inequalities into the human experience.

After the agricultural revolution spread to most human societies, economic experience remained defined by and fixed to agriculture for millennia. Up until the late 1700s, the vast majority of individuals worldwide were small-time farmers. Many were peasants engaged strictly in subsistence agriculture, growing themselves what they and their families ate and rarely, if ever, having a surplus to sell to others. Even in the most advanced civilizations of the 1700s, such as those of Europe and China, nonfarmers comprised at most 20 percent of the population. Average living standards, especially in comparison to modern ones, were very low. Famine was common, and even in times of plenty most people ate a nutrition-poor and undiversified diet. Most humans died of highly curable (by today's standards) infectious diseases or malnutrition in their thirties. Housing was primitive, with entire families sharing sleeping quarters and often, if fortunate enough to not sleep on a dirt floor, a single bed. Cities did not have underground sewage and indoor plumbing, so human waste ran everywhere in urban centers. Neither people nor information moved faster than horses could carry them, and individuals rarely travelled from their city or town. By the early 1700s, the ratio of average income in the world's richest societies to the world's poorest was a modest three to one.[11] In a sense, everyone yet no one lived in the developing world. In other words, all humans lived in poor societies, yet because there was no developed world to speak of, there was no *less* developed world to speak of.

The Industrial Revolution

These conditions began to change very gradually in a few societies with the advent of the

Industrial Revolution in the late eighteenth century. The Industrial Revolution ushered in a new stage in economic history, the era of "modern economic growth," which has only been in existence for the last 0.1 percent of human history. This was not the first time that human economic activity grew more productive, but it was the first time that growth was so rapid and sustained. To illustrate, world GDP growth between 1500 and 1820 was .04 percent per year, but from 1820 to 1992 it was 1.21 percent per year.[12] Beginning first in Great Britain and then spreading to other parts of Western Europe and the United States, the Industrial Revolution rose out of a variety of inventions and small improvements to existing technologies that replaced human and animal labor with inanimate machine power. In other words, vast improvements in economic productivity were driven by the improvement and rapid accumulation of **physical capital**, the machines and factories that can be used to produce goods and services. Engines driven by steam and fossil fuels powered machines that could carry out menial tasks and create consumer products such as cotton clothing in a fraction of the time that it had taken previously. The advent of telegraph and railroad technology dramatically increased the speed of transport. Incremental technological advances in farming, such as better plows, seeding tools, and fertilizers, boosted annual crop yields and created surpluses that farmers could sell to others. These advances also freed up former farmers to move to cities and work in manufacturing or service jobs that were wholly unrelated to food production. Improvements in medical knowledge and the increasing availability of education for the masses led to dramatic improvements in **human capital**—the skill, knowledge, and health of the labor force.

Thus began a long and steady economic divergence between the West and the rest of the world. This divergence created the gap, still in existence today, between the rich countries that initially adopted the technologies and organizational features of the Industrial Revolution and the less developed countries that did not until much later. Figure 1.1 depicts an example of this divergence by showing the trend between 1800 and 1950 in GDP per capita of one of these early Western developers: the United States.[13] Its trend is shown in comparison to GDP per-capita trends in the three countries that were the subject of this chapter's opening vignettes: China, DR Congo, and India. The figure depicts quite clearly the severity of the divergence. The United States did have a tiny head start as of 1800, but by any modern standards it was a poor country, with roughly the GDP per capita that African countries Cameroon or Senegal have today. A US$1,000 gap between the United States and China in 1800 grew into a $6,000 one by 1900, and by 1950 it was a US$15,000 gap. The United States, along with a small number of other Western countries, left the rest of the world behind between 1800 and 1950. In doing so, the West created not just the developed world but a lagging less developed world. During these 150 years, the ratio of incomes in the richest to poorest countries had grown from about three to one to about forty to one.

This bifurcation between a wealthy developed world and a set of relatively poor less developed countries and colonies persisted until the 1950s. To be sure, some industrialization and catching up did occur among non-Western nations before then. After 1870, Eastern Europe (including Russia/Soviet Union), parts of Latin America (Argentina, Brazil, and Mexico), parts of the Middle East, and Japan began developing a manufacturing base. Given their late starts, however, they still lagged well behind Western living standards in 1950, with average incomes typically less than US$2,500 per year. Economically speaking, it is only a slight oversimplification to say that the world featured two camps in 1950: a wealthy West comprising just 20 percent of the world's population, and the very poor rest of the world.

Modern Economic Growth in the Developing World

After 1950, modern economic growth finally occurred in many of the countries that had been left behind by the Industrial Revolution. Many have grown as fast as or even faster than the West during this era, complicating the simple distinction between developed and developing world. This wave of progress has been much more widespread in its geographical scope than the Industrial Revolution, reaching most of the non-Western 80 percent of humanity that had been left behind. Countries throughout Latin America, the Middle East, Southeast Asia, and East Asia have experienced dramatic increases in GDP per capita and average livelihoods. Most began the 1950s mired in desperate poverty, yet the vast majority of countries in these regions today have developed at least a minimal industrial base, lowered their rates of extreme poverty, and seen average incomes rise well past US$2,500 per person. As one scholar puts it, "Never in the history of the world have the incomes of so many people risen by so much over such a prolonged period of time."[14] The fraction of humanity living in extreme poverty fell from well over 50 percent in the 1950s to around 18 percent by early 2013,[15] and world GDP per capita rose from US$2113 in 1950 to over US$10,000.[16] The size of the middle class, defined as people who have enough income to meet basic needs and afford at least some luxuries, has risen in every world region. By some measures, it has more than tripled in size in Asia and almost doubled in Africa since 1990.[17] Today, according to public health expert Hans Rosling, "There is no such thing as a 'we' and a 'they,' with a gap in between. The majority of people are living in the middle."[18]

To be sure, this wave of modern economic growth has been extremely uneven in its timing throughout the developing world. It ranges from the East Asian "Tigers" of Hong Kong, Singapore, South Korea, and Taiwan, which skyrocketed from extreme poverty in 1950 to developed world status by 1980, to much of sub-Saharan Africa, where most economies have shown signs of life only in the last decade. In between these two extremes lies a myriad of patterns. For example, Latin America and

Figure 1.1 **The Economic Divergence between the West and the Global South, 1800–1950**

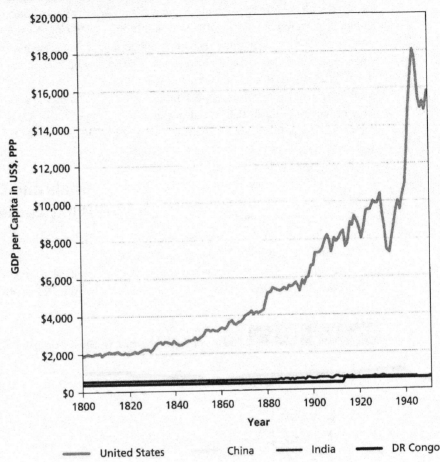

Source: Data compiled from Gapminder, www.gapminder.org/.

221

much of the Middle East enjoyed rapid industrial growth in the first three decades following World War II, only to collapse into economic stagnation for two decades before re-emerging in the new millennium. In sharp contrast, giants China and India were late bloomers, beginning their dramatic and ongoing economic expansions in the late 1970s and early 1980s. As a result of this unevenness, the developing world now features a much more diverse array of living standards than it did in the 1950s. Figure 1.2 exemplifies this diversity and some of these regional patterns by showing the post-1950 trends in prosperity levels for the four countries of Figure 1.1 plus two more, Brazil and South Korea.

Figure 1.2 demonstrates that living standards have improved outside the West since 1950, but it also exemplifies the large and ongoing gap between the West and the South. The West itself continued to grow during this time period, and its head start as of 1950 was vast, accrued over nearly two centuries.

Figure 1.2 depicts how far China, even after three decades of blazing economic growth, would have to go to ever catch up with the per-person incomes of the United States. Moreover, as exemplified by the DR Congo case, some LDCs have experienced little to no growth since 1950. Extremely poor countries, which economist Paul Collier categorizes as the "bottom billion,"[19] are almost exclusively in Africa, although they also include Afghanistan, Haiti, Myanmar, and North Korea. Because of these laggards, the ratio in incomes of the richest and poorest countries has ballooned to more than one hundred to one.

Goals and Organization: Who or What Causes Global Poverty?

This textbook has two primary goals. The first is to provide readers with a rich description of political, economic, and social life in the developing world. **Description** means the narration of a piece

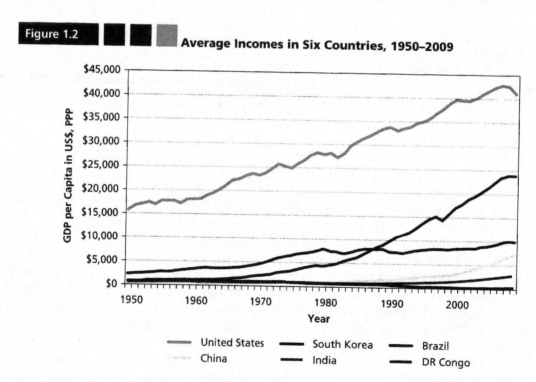

Figure 1.2 ▮ ▮ ▮ **Average Incomes in Six Countries, 1950–2009**

Legend:
United States   South Korea   Brazil
China   India   DR Congo

Source: Data compiled from Gapminder, www.gapminder.org/.

of reality to create an image and understanding of it in the reader's or listener's mind. To that end, this book defines and portrays various features of the global South that distinguish it from the developed world, giving empirical data—that is, facts, histories, summaries, and other observable information—that capture many important aspects of less developed countries. The second goal is to lay out the various explanations for why global income inequalities exist. Stated differently, the book focuses on the following question: Who or what caused less developed countries to be poor? This is thus a goal of **explanation**, meaning argumentation about how one factor causes or influences another one. Any well-reasoned argument about why and how a particular factor causes another one is called a **theory**.

Causes of Underdevelopment: A Framework

Many readers might consider social science theories to be overly complicated and abstract. In fact, however, people engage in theoretical thinking about cause and effect all the time. Consider the following example. In 1948, its year of independence from Japanese occupation, Korea had a GDP per capita of just US$660. In 1960, its year of independence, Nathalie's DR Congo had a higher GDP per capita of US$870. By 2009, however, South Korea had a GDP per capita that was sixty-seven times that of DR Congo's. Why did this reversal of economic fortunes occur? Even if they know little about South Korea and DR Congo, most people can surely think of some plausible possibilities to answer this "why" question. Perhaps there is something about the countries' natural resources, leadership, climate, culture, or treatment by foreign powers that caused the difference in average wealth to emerge. The many plausible answers to this question about cause and effect are examples of theory.

The West, the South, or the Natural World?

Decades of scholarship on economic growth and global poverty have yielded a huge number of theories about why global poverty and inequalities between wealthy and poor nations exist and persist. Scholars from numerous disciplines—economics, sociology, anthropology, political science, geography, history, genetics, archaeology, physiology—have weighed in on this important question, blaming poverty on everything from tropical diseases to the International Monetary Fund. To give readers some means to navigate this complex scholarly terrain, this book provides an easy-to-remember, threefold scheme for categorizing and understanding the various theoretical answers to the question "who causes global poverty?": the West, the South, and the natural world. This categorization is evident in the parts of this book and throughout most of the end-of-chapter case studies.

Did the West cause today's LDCs to be poor? This category attributes underdevelopment in the developing world to international factors, namely those originating in foreign lands and particularly in Western Europe and the United States. Through the international slave trade, colonialism, globalization, and foreign aid, the West may have created disadvantageous contexts for development or even directly impoverished other parts of the world. Alternatively, are factors indigenous to the South itself the cause of global wealth disparities? This category attributes underdevelopment to origins that are internal to LDCs. A large body of scholarship indicts the domestic factors that are part of an LDC's own leadership, institutions, or culture, such as economic policy, laws and customs, and degree of internal harmony. Scholarship within this tradition attributes underdevelopment to factors such as undemocratic rule, corruption, weak property rights, a failure to embrace free markets, poor treatment of women and girls, civil conflict and violence, state failure, and rigid identities. Finally, do factors in the natural world that are beyond human design explain global poverty? This third and final category attributes economic underdevelopment to various aspects of geography and the physical environment, such as climate, topographical terrain, land productivity, and disease burdens.

Thinking about Theory. In thinking about theory and the threefold classification scheme, several points are in order. First, readers should reject the temptation to conclude that a single theory could successfully explain why some countries are rich and why some are poor. Reality is far too complex to be monocausal. For example, the brief history of economic development given in the preceding section might indicate that the question of why some countries are poor today may need two answers. A country is an LDC today because (1) it was left behind by the rise of the West during the first Industrial Revolution and (2) it has failed to rise as quickly as South Korea in the post-1950 world. The causes behind the relative distancing in livelihoods between European and non-European countries in the nineteenth century may be different from those behind the failure of so many countries to replicate the South Korean skyrocket since 1950.

Second, readers must understand that no amount of logic, empirical observation, or sophisticated statistical manipulation will ever prove a theory to be accurate or inaccurate. There are always overlooked theories and factors that could be the source of the true impact on development. For example, one could attribute the differences in prosperity levels between DR Congo and Great Britain to the fact that one was colonized and the other was a colonizer. But the differences between the two do not stop there. Great Britain is far from the equator while DR Congo is on it. Great Britain is a democracy while DR Congo is not. Great Britain has a relatively unified national identity while DR Congo does not. In fact, the list of differences between the two is infinite, so isolating the one or ones exerting the causal effect is impossible. For this reason, readers should remember the adage that "correlation does not mean causation." That said, readers can certainly use their own logical and observational faculties to arrive at conclusions about which theories are more or less useful for understanding the causes of underdevelopment.

Third, as with any categorization, the threefold classification has oversimplifying imperfections. For example, one explanation for Africa's underdevelopment is that many of its countries have numerous ethnic groups that struggle to cooperate and get along. This seemingly attributes the cause of underdevelopment to the South, meaning a domestic factor. However, African countries' high levels of ethnic diversity are partly due to the West, an international factor. European colonizers drew the national borders for much of the continent and, in doing so, grouped together many ethnic groups that had little in common. Rather than getting overly hung up on whether the theory attributes ultimate cause to the South or the West, readers should simply think of the classification as a useful, albeit imperfect, tool that helps them more easily understand and remember the various theories.

Finally, this textbook will avoid the emotion and ideology that often accompanies debates over the causes of underdevelopment. In practice, millions find there to be much at stake in considering what causes global poverty, since the answer allows one to assign blame for impoverishment. For example, Zimbabwe's president Robert Mugabe repeatedly deflects blame for his leadership of a country in economic decline by retorting that the roots of its plight lie in the past sins of Western colonialism and white-minority rule. *Shaping the Developing World* stays away from explicitly making moral judgments or casting blame for global inequality, although readers will surely see the ethical implications of many of the theories discussed within.

Organization of the Book

The threefold classification scheme provides the organizing framework for this textbook. This chapter and the following two comprise Part I, which provides an introduction to human development and the costs of development. Part II: The West: International Contexts contains three chapters on the various arguments that claim that Western factors are the cause of global poverty. Part III: The South: Domestic Factors contains six chapters on the various aspects of the South that might be the cause of LDCs' plight. Part IV: The Natural World: Physical Geography contains two chapters on nature and the possible geographical and environmental sources of underdevelopment.

Each chapter is organized to first provide readers with important descriptive material about the topic at hand. Subsequently, in sections called "Causes of Underdevelopment," they convey theoretical arguments about how the just-described factor might have caused underdevelopment. Since every theory has its limitations, each chapter then presents challenges to these theories in sections entitled "Critiques." A concluding case study presents information on a single developing country to illustrate how the main theoretical arguments presented in the chapter might explain its underdevelopment. The case study introduces alternative theoretical explanations for the country's less developed status, providing one example each from the South, the West, and the natural world framework. The next section of this chapter illustrates this case study approach, although it is not until Part II of the book that case studies with this approach return. Since Chapters 2 and 3 provide more descriptive, not theoretical, material, their case studies do not present the threefold framework.

STUDY

WHY IS THE DEMOCRATIC REPUBLIC OF CONGO THE POOREST COUNTRY ON EARTH?

In 2009, the average citizen in Nathalie's Democratic Republic of Congo (DR Congo, named Zaire from 1971 to 1997) had a living standard equivalent to what a U.S. citizen would have if he or she had one dollar per day to spend. This figure made it the poorest country in the world and one of just a few countries whose living standards were lower in 2009 than they were in 1960.[20] All of this is true despite the fact that DR Congo is huge (it has the largest land area in sub-Saharan Africa), rich in topography (it contains the world's second-largest rain forest and Africa's second-largest river), and flush with natural resources (such as diamonds and the coltan found in most cell phones). In contrast, South Korea is tiny and poor in resources, and it was actually poorer than DR Congo as recently as 1950. Why is DR Congo, a country with so much potential, still so poor? Table 1.5 provides some possible answers that are described in greater detail in this case study.

case STUDY

WHY IS THE DEMOCRATIC REPUBLIC OF
CONGO THE POOREST COUNTRY ON EARTH?

Table 1.5 **Development Comparison: DR Congo and South Korea**

Indicator	DR Congo	South Korea
GDP per capita at PPP	US$329	US$27,541
Population in poverty	73 percent	<1 percent
Human Development Index	.286 (187th of 187)	.897 (15th of 187)
Number of languages spoken	216	1
Persons removed through Atlantic slave trade	~1,000,000	0
Malaria cases per 100,000 people, 2008	37,400	8

Source: Data compiled from the World Bank, World Development Indicators, 2011 and 2008, http://data.worldbank.org/sites/default/files/wdi-final.pdf; United Nations Development Programme, "Human Development Report 2010," http://hdr.undp.org/en/reports/global/hdr2010/, 161; Human Development Index; Ethnologue.com; and Nathan Nunn, "The Long-Term Effects of Africa's Slave Trades," *Quarterly Journal of Economics* 123, no. 1 (2008): 139–176.

The South: Kleptocracy and Cultural Fragmentation

One set of possible answers lies in DR Congo's political leadership and the makeup of its society. Five years after achieving independence from Belgium in 1960, a young army officer named Joseph Mobutu staged a successful coup d'état, installed himself as president, and remained in that post for thirty-two authoritarian years. In office, Mobutu, who later renamed himself Mobuto Sese Seko, established one of history's most corrupt regimes. Telling his state employees to "go ahead and steal, as long as you don't take too much,"[21] Mobutu himself followed only the first half of this advice. Mobutu treated state funds as his own, amassing numerous palaces and mansions, many of them in Europe and some containing 14,000-bottle wine cellars, discotheques, private zoos, and doors so large they required two men to open.[22] Mobutu also allowed his political allies and even opponents

to participate in the plundering, keeping them quiescent to his otherwise ineffective rule. The means to wealth were not talent and hard work, but theft of taxpayers. Under Mobutu, DR Congo was considered the paradigmatic kleptocracy: government by those who steal.

In the interest of Zaireanizing (based on his own renaming of the country) the economy and redistributing wealth from rich Europeans to Zairian citizens, Mobutu expropriated most of Zaire's foreign-owned firms and farms. He kept some of the assets for himself and handed the rest over to Zairian public officials and other elites. In doing so, he gave agricultural land and factories to individuals not because they were good farmers or industrial managers, but because they were his cronies or leaders of important ethnic groups. Economic collapse ensued. Prices rose and store shelves emptied because the new Zairian owners of many businesses were not knowledgeable or motivated enough to produce goods and services as productively as the previous owners. The experience of expropriation discouraged future investment by both foreigners and Zairians. Between 1973 and Mobutu's departure from power in 1997, the average income in Zaire declined by two-thirds.[23]

Another possible answer resides in the fact that Congolese citizens have little cultural unity. Congolese identify more with their ethnolinguistic group, of which there are more than 200, than they do with the DR Congo as a nation. There is little sense of national identity, with one set of scholars characterizing this reality by saying that "there is no Congo."[24] This lack of national unity has erupted on multiple occasions into violent conflict that has had major economic costs. For example, in its first year of independence in 1960, the Congo nearly disintegrated into four separate countries as three different regions declared their desire to secede based largely around ethnic nationalist claims. The Congolese military eventually reunified the country, but only after years of violently repressing secessionist movements. More recently, the Great War of Africa (1998–2003), the deadliest war in the continent's history, occurred on Congolese soil when militias claiming to represent disillusioned ethnic groups in the far eastern corner of the country attempted to march all the way to Kinshasa in the west to overthrow the incumbent government. The conflict killed an estimated 5.4 million people and cost billions of dollars in lost economic activity.[25]

The West: Stolen Aid, Colonial Abuse, and Slavery

Mobutu didn't act alone. The West was complicit in his kleptomania. Soon after independence, Belgian and American intelligence agencies intervened in Congolese politics to place Mobutu in power

U.S. president Ronald Reagan (1981-1989) shakes hands with Zairian president Mobutu Sese Seku (1965-1997). Despite years of inept and corrupt rule that impoverished his country, Mobutu received millions of dollars of aid from the United States and other Western countries simply because he was seen as a reliable bulwark against communism in Africa.

over other leaders they saw as overly friendly with the Soviet Union. In the interest of keeping him in power, the United States, France, and Belgium granted Mobutu $1 billion in foreign aid over his thirty-two-year reign. Much of the aid ended up in the Swiss bank accounts of Mobutu and his cronies, and little was actually used to build schools, health clinics, or roads. The International Monetary Fund also extended eleven different bailout packages to Mobutu despite knowing that the funds were misused and ineffective in stabilizing the economy. Amidst all of the theft, U.S. president Ronald Reagan still called one of the world's most prolific thieves a "voice of good sense and goodwill"[26] because of his anticommunist credentials.

The West's complicity in the plundering of the Congo did not begin with the rise of Mobutu.

WHY IS THE DEMOCRATIC REPUBLIC OF CONGO THE POOREST COUNTRY ON EARTH?

Nearly a century earlier, King Leopold II of Belgium initiated his own reign of terror in pursuit of what he called "a slice of this magnificent African cake,"[27] a reign that stripped the Congo of natural and human resources. Leopold, who from 1885 to 1908 was the sole proprietor of the Congo Free State, implemented a brutal system of forced labor and looting that contemporary Arthur Conan Doyle called "the greatest crime which has ever been committed in the history of the world."[28] Leopold's armed security apparatus, the Force Publique, required native villagers to periodically collect quotas of ivory or rubber that were to be exported to Europe. These quotas grew increasingly difficult to fill as nearby reserves became exhausted, and when villagers failed to deliver a sufficient amount, they were whipped with strips of dried hippopotamus hide, had their hands chopped off, or were shot. Under Leopold, the population loss in the Congo Free State was an estimated 10 million people, and countless hours of labor and troves of natural resources were taken with no compensation in return.[29] Leopold and other Western powers even bear some responsibility for DR Congo's deep cultural divisions, since it was they who arbitrarily drew the colony's and eventual country's borders. In drawing the borders at a conference in Berlin in 1884 and 1885, they consulted no Congolese citizens and paid no heed to the fact that they were uniting more than 200 different ethnic groups into a single political territory.

Leopold's colonization of the Congo actually occurred relatively recently in the history of Western contact with Africa. As early as the sixteenth century, men and women residing in the territory that is today the DR Congo were being captured and shipped across the Atlantic Ocean to become slaves in the New World. Slavery was devastating not just to the slaves themselves, but also to the African economies they left behind. Between 1400 and 1900, almost 1 million people were forcibly removed from DR Congo territory.[30] This dramatic loss of human capital, often in exchange for destructive or unproductive imports such as guns, clothing, and seashells, kept the Congo's population growth and density low in a time when other continents were developing urban centers that were hotbeds of productivity and innovation.

The Natural World: Geography and the Resource Curse

Clearly, Congolese leaders and Western personnel have ravaged both the human and natural richness of the Congo for centuries. Is it possible, however, that all of this exploitation has been just a sideshow to the ultimate cause of DR Congo's poverty: geography? Beneath its flashy mineral wealth and its superlative river and rain forest lies a natural context that is quite detrimental to economic growth. First, DR Congo is wet—too wet: The country has more thunderstorms than any other in the world. This leeches its soils of their minerals and makes it impossible to grow all but a few crops.[31] Second, DR Congo has the largest number of malaria cases in the world, and the disease is the country's top killer. Like Nathalie, the average Congolese child suffers six to ten bouts *every year*, and 200,000 Congolese children die from malaria annually.[32] At best, children heal in a few days, yet during that time they have missed out on some schooling, may have drawn an adult caregiver away from work, and have probably experienced stunted brain development.

Nature also may have cursed the DR Congo in a more paradoxical way: by endowing it with a vast quantity of valuable natural resources. Although perhaps done with some hyperbole, one source estimated DR Congo's underground mineral wealth to be worth $24 trillion, more than the GDP of the United States or Europe.[33] DR Congo has the world's largest deposits of cobalt and coltan, and it also contains rich underground stores of copper, diamonds, and gold. Yet instead of making it rich, this mineral wealth fuels DR Congo's recurring political violence and conflict. For example, some of the violent domestic and foreign militias that marauded DR Congo during the Great War looted mines and used their booty to finance themselves. Moreover, few investors care to build up DR Congo's industrial base since its minerals sector remains so attractive.

All told, this long list of explanations for DR Congo's underdevelopment would seem to suggest that the odds are stacked heavily against the world's poorest country. But are all of these explanations equally plausible, and is the picture this one-sided? This textbook will give readers the tools to answer these questions in an informed way.

Thinking Critically about Development

- Some of these explanations for the Congo's poverty focus on individual people, such as Mobutu and Leopold, while others stress broader and less ephemeral factors, such as culture and climate. Generally speaking, which approach is more convincing? In other words, if the Congo had had better-intentioned colonial and post-colonial leaders, would it be wealthier today, or would this not have mattered?

- Is it possible that some of the factors listed as sources of Congolese underdevelopment, such as deaths from malaria and number of languages spoken, are more a *result* of underdevelopment than its cause?

- Is the comparison between DR Congo and South Korea useful for deciphering cause and effect, or are the countries too different from one another?

 ## Key Terms

agricultural revolution, p. 15

description, p. 18

explanation, p. 19

gross domestic product, p. 10

human capital, p. 16

Industrial Revolution, p. 16

infrastructure, p. 9

less developed country (LDC), p. 5

physical capital, p. 16

• political regime, p. 13

theory, p. 19

underdevelopment, p. 6

 ## Suggested Readings

Banerjee, Abhijit Vinayak, Roland Benabou, and Dilip Mookherjee, eds. *Understanding Poverty.* New York: Oxford University Press, 2006.

Cameron, Rondo, and Larry Neal. *A Concise Economic History of the World: From Paleolithic Times to the Present.* New York: Oxford University Press, 2002.

Hochschild, Adam. *King Leopold's Ghost: A Story of Greed, Terror, and Heroism in Colonial Africa.* Boston: Mariner Books, 1998.

Smith, Dan. *The Penguin State of the World Atlas.* 9th ed. New York: Penguin Books, 2012.

Wrong, Michela. *In the Footsteps of Mr. Kurtz: Living on the Brink of Disaster in Mobutu's Congo.* New York: Harper Collins, 2001.

World Bank. *Atlas of Global Development.* 3rd ed. Washington, D.C.: World Bank Publications, 2011.

 Web Resources

Gapminder, www.gapminder.org

World Development Indicators, http://data.worldbank.org/sites/default/files/wdi-final.pdf

World Bank e-Atlas, http://data.worldbank.org/products/data-visualization-tools/eatlas

Endnotes

by Andy Baker

Chapter 1

1. The individuals described in these vignettes are fictional, although parts of their stories are compiled from nonfictional accounts.

2. All six of these regional categories are the designations used by the World Bank. The need to specify high income, instead of just OECD, is that the OECD now contains a few countries, such as Chile and Mexico, which are not strictly high income and are part of the traditionally defined developing world. The need for designating OECD, instead of just high income, in the category label is that there are a number of countries that only recently reached high-income status, such as Kuwait and Saudi Arabia, which are not part of the traditionally defined West or developed world. In the end, the "high-income OECD" category contains the following countries: Australia, Austria, Belgium, Canada, Czech Republic, Denmark, Estonia, Finland, France, Germany, Greece, Hungary, Iceland, Ireland, Italy, Israel, Japan, South Korea, Luxembourg, the Netherlands, New Zealand, Norway, Poland, Portugal, Slovak Republic, Slovenia, Spain, Sweden, Switzerland, United Kingdom, and United States.

3. Unless otherwise noted, regional averages are calculated using country population weights.

4. Matthew Ridley, *The Rational Optimist: How Prosperity Evolves* (New York: Harper, 2010), 22.

5. Branko Milanovic, *The Haves and the Have-Nots: A Brief and Idiosyncratic History of Global Inequality* (New York: Basic Books, 2011).

6. Statistics in this paragraph are from the World Bank's World Development Indicators, http://data.worldbank.org/data-catalog/world-development-indicators.

7. International Labour Organization, "Key Indicators of the Labour Market Dataset," October 16, 2011, www.ilo.org/empelm/what/WCMS_114240/lang--en/index.htm.

8. Abhijit V. Banerjee and Esther Duflo, *Poor Economics: A Radical Rethinking of the Way to Fight Global Poverty* (New York: Public Affairs, 2011), 160.

9. All data in this and the previous paragraph are from Gapminder, www.gapminder.org.

10. World Bank, *World Development Report 2008: Agriculture for Development*, 2007, http://siteresources.worldbank.org/INTWDR2008/Resources/WDR_00_book.pdf, 45.

11. William J. Bernstein, *The Birth of Plenty: How the Prosperity of the Modern World Was Created* (New York: McGraw-Hill, 2004), 193.

12. Angus Maddison, *Monitoring the World Economy, 1820–1992*. (Paris: OECD, 1995).

13. Gapminder, www.gapminder.org.

14. Milanovic, *The Haves and Have-Nots*, 102.

15. Benjamin M. Friedman, *The Moral Consequences of Economic Growth* (New York: Vintage Books, 2006), 354.

16. Charles Kenny, *Getting Better: Why Global Development is Succeeding—and How We Can Improve the World Even More* (New York: Basic Books, 2011), 19.

17. "The New Middle Classes Rise Up," *The Economist*, September 3, 2011, 23–24.

18. "Technology Quarterly: Making Data Dance," *The Economist*, December 11, 2010, 25.

19. Paul Collier, *The Bottom Billion: Why the Poorest Countries Are Failing and What Can Be Done About It* (Oxford: Oxford University Press, 2007).

20. Gapminder, www.gapminder.org.

21. Michela Wrong, *In the Footsteps of Mr. Kurtz: Living on the Brink of Disaster in Mobutu's Congo* (New York: Harper Collins, 2001), 99.

22. Ibid.

23. World Bank, World Development Indicators, http://data.worldbank.org/sites/default/files/wdi-final.pdf.

24. Jeffrey Herbst and Greg Mills, "There Is No Congo," *Foreign Policy*, March 18, 2009.

25. Joe Bavier, "Congo War-Driven Crisis Kills 45,000 a Month: Study," Reuters, January 22, 2008, www.reuters.com/article/2008/01/22/us-congo-democratic-death-idUSL2280201220080122.

26. Heidi Kriz, "When He Was King," Metroactive: News and Issues, May 22–28, 1997, http://www.metroactive.com/papers/metro/05.22.97/cover/mobutu-9721.html.

27. Thomas Pakenham, *The Scramble for Africa: White Man's Conquest of the Dark Continent from 1876 to 1912* (New York: Random House, 1991), 22.

28. Adam Hochschild, *King Leopold's Ghost: A Story of Greed, Terror, and Heroism in Colonial Africa* (Boston: Mariner Books, 1998), 271.

29. Ibid.

30. Nathan Nunn, "The Long-Term Effects of Africa's Slave Trades," *Quarterly Journal of Economics* 122, no. 1 (2008): 139–176.

31. World Lightning Map, Geology.com, http://geology.com/articles/lightning-map.shtml.

32. Miriam Mannak, "Malaria Remains Biggest Killer," Inter Press Service, October 27, 2008, http://www.ipsnews.net/2008/10/health-dr-congo-malaria-remains-biggest-killer/.

33. M. J. Morgan, "DR Congo's $24 Trillion Fortune," The Free Library, February 1, 2009, www.thefreelibrary.com/DR+Congo's+$24+trillion+fortune.-a0193800184.

Chapter 2

1. Amartya Sen, *Development as Freedom* (New York: Alfred Knopf, 1999), 4.
2. Martha Nussbaum, *Creating Capabilities: The Human Development Approach* (Cambridge: Harvard University Press, 2011), 152.
3. Sen, *Development as Freedom*, 33.
4. Charles Kenny, *Getting Better: Why Global Development Is Succeeding—and How We Can Improve the World Even More* (New York: Basic Books, 2011), 155.
5. United Nations Development Programme, *Human Development Report: The Real Wealth of Nations: Pathways to Human Development* (New York: Palgrave MacMillan, 2010); Kenny, *Getting Better*.
6. Kenny, *Getting Better*.
7. Greg Mortenson and David Oliver Relin. *Three Cups of Tea: One Man's Mission to Promote Peace … One School at a Time* (New York: Penguin, 2006).
8. William Easterly and Tobias Pfutze, "Where Does the Money Go? Best and Worst Practices in Foreign Aid," *Journal of Economic Perspectives* 22 (2008): 29–52.
9. John Krakauer, *Three Cups of Deceit: How Greg Mortenson, Humanitarian Hero, Lost His Way.* (San Francisco: Byliner, 2011).
10. All stats in this paragraph are from United Nations Development Programme, *Human Development Report: The Real Wealth of Nations*, 143–147.
11. World Bank. *Atlas of Global Development*, 2nd ed. (Glasgow: HarperCollins Publishers, 2009), 44–47.
12. Demographic and Health Survey, "Cambodia Demographic and Health Survey," 2010, http://www.measuredhs.com/pubs/pdf/GF22/GF22.pdf.
13. World Bank, *World Development Report 2006: Equity and Development* (Washington, D.C.: World Bank Publications, 2006), 30.
14. Abhijit V. Banerjee and Esther Duflo, *Poor Economics: A Radical Rethinking of the Way to Fight Poverty* (New York: Public Affairs, 2011), chapter 2. The Nutrition Puzzle," *The Economist*, February 18, 2012, 62–63.
15. Banerjee and Duflo, *Poor Economics*, chapter 2.
16. Jean Drèze and Amartya Sen, *Hunger and Public Action* (Oxford: Clarendon Press, 1989), 15.
17. "The Starvelings," *The Economist*, January 26, 2008, 58–59.
18. Dan Smith, *The Penguin State of the World Atlas*, 9th ed. (New York: Penguin 2012).
19. "The Nutrition Puzzle," *The Economist*, February 18, 2012, http://www.economist.com/node/21547771.
20. "Health: the Big Picture," United Nations Children's Fund, April 23, 2003, www.unicef.org/health/index_bigpicture.html. The fifth is malnutrition.

21. World Bank Health, Nutrition, and Population Statistics, http://data.worldbank.org/data-catalog/health-nutrition-population-statistics.
22. Ibid.; "Cholera and the Super-Loo," *The Economist*, July 30, 2011, 55.
23. Guy Howard and Jamie Bartram, "Domestic Water Quantity, Service Level and Health," 2003, http://www.who.int/water_sanitation_health/diseases/WSH03.02.pdf.
24. "Cholera and the Super-Loo," 55–56.
25. United Nations Development Programme, "Beyond Scarcity," 2006, http://hdr.undp.org/en/media/HDR06-complete.pdf, 112–113.
26. Banerjee and Duflo, *Poor Economics*, 46.
27. World Bank, *Atlas of Global Development*, 44.
28. United Nations Development Programme, *Human Development Report 2003: Millennium Development Goals: A Compact among Nations to End Human Poverty* (New York: Oxford University Press, 2003), 100.
29. World Bank, *Atlas of Global Development*, 52.
30. World Health Organization, "World Health Statistics 2010," *World Health Statistical Information System*, 2010, www.who.int/who-sis/whostat/2010/en/index.html.
31. Fernando Barros, J. Patrick Vaughan, and Cesar Victoria, "Why So Many Caesarian Sections? The Need for Further Policy Change in Brazil," *Health, Policy and Planning* 1, no. 1 (1986): 19–29.
32. World Bank, World Development Indicators, 2010 figures, http://data.worldbank.org/sites/default/files/wdi-final.pdf.
33. United Nations Development Programme, *Human Development Report 2003: Millennium Development Goals: A Compact among Nations to End Human Poverty* (New York: Oxford University Press, 2003), 99.
34. Nazmul Chaudhury, Jeffrey Hammer, Michael Kremer, Karthik Muralidharan, and F. Halsey Rogers, "Missing in Action: Teacher and Health Worker Absence in Developing Countries," *Journal of Economic Perspectives* 20 (2006): 91–116.
35. Quentin Wodon, *Access to Basic Facilities in Africa* (Washington, D.C.: World Bank, 2005).
36. Banerjee and Duflo, *Poor Economics*, Chapter 3.
37. "The Starvelings."
38. Ibid., 99.
39. Edward Miguel and Michael Kremer, "Worms: Identifying Impacts on Education and Health in the Presence of Treatment Externalities," *Econometrica* 72, no. 1 (2004): 159–217.
40. Dean Karlan and Jacob Appel, *More Than Good Intentions: Improving the Way the World's Poor Borrow, Save, Farm, Learn, and Stay Healthy* (New York: Dutton, 2011), 206.
41. Rodrigo R. Soares, "On the Determinants of Mortality Reductions in the Developing World," *Population and Development Review* 33, no. 2 (2007): 247–287.
42. Matthew Ridley, *The Rational Optimist: How Prosperity Evolves* (New York: Harper, 2010), 121.
43. Food and Agricultural Organization, "Food Security Statistics," 2010, http://faostat.fao.org/?lang=en.
44. Another commonly used and closely related measure is the gross enrollment ratio, which is the total number of people enrolled (regardless of age) expressed as a percentage of the total number of people in the relevant age group.

Required Readings Available Online

Odede, Kennedy. 2010. "Slumdog Tourism" *New York Times*, August 10, 2010. [link] and
http://www.nytimes.com/2010/08/10/opinion/10odede.html

Chimamanda Ngozi Adichie "The Danger of a Single Story"
http://www.ted.com/talks/chimamanda_adichie_the_danger_of_a_single_story.html

Additional Works Cited

Kovacevic, Milorad. 2010. "Review of HDI Critiques and Potential Improvements," Human Development Research Paper 2010/33. United Nations Development Fund.

Moyo, Dambisa. 2009. *Dead Aid: Why Aid Is Not Working and How There Is a Better Way for Africa*. New York: Macmillan.

Sagar, Ambuj D and Adil Najam. 1998. The Human Development Index: A Critical Review," Ecological Economics 25(1998): 249-264.

Sen, Amartya. 1999. *Development as Freedom*. New York: Anchor Books.

VI. MODULE SIX:

Culture and Identity

In keeping with the interdisciplinary approach of international studies, this module uses the humanities to understand issues of global significance. In the chapter on globalization, we began considering flows of goods, capital, and people, as well as responses to cultural flows like accommodation, resistance, and hybridity. We return to these themes in the last module, devoted to the study of culture and identity. Some of the questions we will consider include: How is culture transmitted? When intolerance becomes an issue, what are some promising responses toward improving xenophobia? Artists in particular have responded to identity-based hate crimes (often motivated by forms of intolerance or xenophobia) with public art. Artistic expression offers an opportunity for increasing cross cultural understanding and tolerance.

As the name suggests, the concept of culture is central to this module. The notion of "culture" emerged in eighteenth century Europe as an evolutionary concept that suggested a process of betterment and refinement. The idea was that peoples would develop in a uni-directional process that would make them more like Western Europeans. Anthropologists rejected this notion of culture in favor of seeing culture as an integrated pattern of human knowledge, belief, and behavior. The prevailing understanding was that culture is best understood as a set of shared attitudes, values, beliefs and practices that come to characterize a group of people. However, in the last two decades, anthropologists began to question whether there were ever discrete, isolatable cultures. They think of culture not as something that is "pure," or homogenous but as something that is hybrid and continually emerging.

Identity is another central concept throughout these readings. Identity is most simply defined as "the qualities, beliefs, etc., that make a particular person or group different from others."[10] The way we experience identity, is however much more complicated because of intersectionality – the fact that as individuals, we have religious, racial, ethnic, gender, sexual, and many other identities that result in patterns of privilege and disadvantage.

Political identities are notable for affording individuals access to resources and rights. For example, the refugee identity comes with a precise legal definition that specifies refugees to be persons fleeing well-founded fears of persecution and outlines specific criteria for their protection. There is a rigorous process of status determination by governments and international organizations. At the other end of the identity spectrum is another political identity category: indigenous people. In contrast with "refugee" there is no internationally agreed upon definition of indigenous peoples.

What does globalization, mean for the culture of indigenous people? Does it entail their homogenization? Or is it an opportunity for greater prosperity and more robust protection of their rights? This question returns us to the central problematic of globalization with which the volume began: understanding both the homogenizing tendencies that spread with globalization, and the continued cultural heterogeneity that is evident throughout the world at the local level.

---

[10] Merriam Webster Dictionary. http://www.merriam-webster.com/dictionary/identity

Readings

Denzin provides snapshots of three "formations" or ways the Native Americans have been represented. A telling moment is when Mayor Harrison of Chicago wrote to an artist requesting him to "paint the Indians darker" (page 16). In his work, which includes drama, Denzin aims to dismantle old stereotypes in order to create new understanding. This is an ambitious goal, considering, by his account, there are 500 years of colonial oppression.

Denzin describes himself as a cultural tourist. He seeks an escape from what he calls "white privilege," because it comes with a limited appreciation of Native Americans and the West. In his personal ethnography, he tell the story of how he inherited this understanding from the media, Hollywood, and his grandfather's dreams and fantasies about the West.

In the last pages of this volume, you will find two cartoons by **Richard Catè**. He is a Native American cartoonist who grew up on the Santo Domingo Pueblo in New Mexico. He describes how his cartoons are often criticized as insensitive to Native Americans - until readers realize he is a Native American (page 5). Catè suggests that the cartoons are not politically incorrect because he is "only drawing the funny side to what I know and experience as a Native American in this country" (page 5).

In "The Next Hot Sound," **Benjamin Shingler** introduces readers to a genre called "Powwow step" that mixes various musical genres like hip hop, reggae, and dub step into an original and hybrid form that includes traditional Native dance music. This is a classic example of the concept of hybridity. Shingler explores this hybridity through the work of A Tribe Called Red based in Ottawa. As indigenous artists, they feel it is important to speak out in favor of greater political self-determination for indigenous people. Shingler suggests that this band is working, by the means of the hybridity of their genre, to break down stereotypes, just as authors Saucedo (module one) Adichie (module five), and Odede (module five) have sought to dismantle other stereotypes.

In the Name of Identity:
Violence and the Need to Belong

by Amin Maalouf

How many times, since I left Lebanon in 1976 to live in France, have people asked me, with the best intentions in the world, whether I felt "more French" or "more Lebanese"? And I always give the same answer: "Both!" I say that not in the interests of fairness or balance, but because any other answer would be a lie. What makes me myself rather than anyone else is the very fact that I am poised between two countries, two or three languages and several cultural traditions. It is precisely this that defines my identity. Would I exist more authentically if I cut off a part of myself?

To those who ask the question, I patiently explain that I was born in Lebanon and lived there until I was 27; that Arabic is my mother tongue; that it was in Arabic translation that I first read Dumas and Dickens and *Gulliver's Travels;* and that it was in my native village, the village of my ancestors, that I experienced the pleasures of childhood and heard some of the stories that were later to inspire my novels. How could I forget all that? How could I cast it aside? On the other hand, I have lived for 22 years on the soil of France; I drink her water and wine; every day my hands touch her ancient stones; I write my books in her language; never again will she be a foreign country to me.

So am I half French and half Lebanese? Of course not. Identity can't be compartmentalised. You can't divide it up into halves or thirds or any other separate segments. I haven't got several identities: I've got just one, made up of many components in a mixture that is unique to me, just as other people's identity is unique to them as individuals.

Sometimes, after I've been giving a detailed account of exactly why I lay claim to all my affiliations, someone comes and pats me on the shoulder and says "Of course, of course — but what do you really feel, deep down inside?"

For a long time I found this oft-repeated question amusing, but it no longer makes me smile. It seems to reflect a view of humanity which, though it is widespread, is also in my opinion dangerous. It presupposes that "deep down inside" everyone there is just one affiliation that really matters, a kind of "fundamental truth" about each individual, an "essence" determined once and for all at birth, never to change thereafter. As if the rest, all the rest — a person's whole journey through time as a free agent; the beliefs he acquires in the course of that journey; his own individual tastes, sensibilities and affinities; in short his life itself counted for nothing. And when, as happens so often nowadays, our contemporaries are exhorted to "assert their identity," they are meant to seek within themselves that same alleged fundamental allegiance, which is often religious, national, racial or ethnic, and having located it they are supposed to flaunt it proudly in the face of others.

Anyone who claims a more complex identity is marginalised. But a young man born in France of Algerian parents clearly carries within him two different allegiances or "belongings," and he ought to be allowed to use both. For the sake of argument I refer to two "belongings," but in fact such a youth's personality is made up of many more ingredients. Within him, French, European and other western influences mingle with Arab, Berber, African, Muslim and other sources, whether with regard to language, beliefs, family relationships or to tastes in cooking and the arts. This represents an enriching and fertile experience if the young man in question feels free to live it fully   if he is encouraged to accept it in all its diversity. But it can be traumatic if whenever he claims to be French other people look on him as a traitor or renegade, and if every time he emphasises his ties with Algeria and its history, culture and religion he meets with incomprehension, mistrust or even outright hostility.

The situation is even more difficult on the other side of the Rhine. I'm thinking of the case of a Turk who might have been born near Frankfurt 30 years ago and who has always lived in Germany. He speaks and writes German better than the language of his ancestors. Yet for the society of his adopted country he isn't a German, while for that of his origins he is no longer completely a Turk. Common sense dictates that he should be able to claim both allegiances. But at present neither the law nor people's attitudes allows him to accept his composite identity tranquilly.

I have quoted the first examples that came to mind, but I could have used many others. For instance, that of someone born in Belgrade of a Serbian mother and a Croatian father. That of a Hutu woman married to a Tutsi, or vice versa. Or that of an American with a black father and a Jewish mother.

It may be said that these are special cases. I don't agree. The handful of people I've cited are not the only ones with a complex identity. Every individual is a meeting ground for many different allegiances, and sometimes these loyalties conflict with one another and confront the person who harbours them with difficult choices. In some cases the situation is obvious at a glance; others need to be looked at more closely.

Is there any citizen of present-day Europe who doesn't sense a kind of tug-of-war, an inevitably ever-increasing conflict between on the one hand his affiliation to an ancient country like France, Spain, Denmark or England, and, on the other, his allegiance to the continental entity that is in the process of forming? And there are many dedicated "Europeans," from the Basque country to Scotland, who at the same time feel a strong and fundamental attachment to a particular region and its people, its history and its language. Can anyone in the United States even today assess his place in society without reference to his earlier connections, whether they be African, Hispanic, Irish, Jewish, Italian, Polish or other?

That said, I'm prepared to admit that the first examples I cited are to a certain extent special. All the people concerned in them are arenas for allegiances currently in violent conflict with one another: they live in a sort of frontier zone crisscrossed by ethnic, religious and other fault lines. But by virtue of this situation — peculiar rather than privileged — they have a special role to play in forging links, eliminating misunderstandings, making some parties more reasonable and others less belligerent, smoothing out difficulties, seeking compromise. Their role is to act as bridges, go-betweens, mediators between the various communities and cultures. And that is precisely why their dilemma is so significant: if they themselves cannot sustain their multiple allegiances, if they are continually being pressed to take sides or ordered to stay within their own tribe, then all of us have reason to be uneasy about the way the world is going.

I talk of their being "pressed" and "ordered" — but by whom? Not just by fanatics and xenophobes of all kinds, but also by you and me, by each and all of us. And we do so precisely because of habits of thought and expression deeply rooted in us all; because of a narrow, exclusive, bigoted, simplistic attitude that reduces identity in all its many aspects to one single affiliation, and one that is proclaimed in anger.

I feel like shouting aloud that this is how murderers are made — it's a recipe for massacres! That may sound somewhat extreme, but in the pages that follow I shall try to explain what I mean.

My Identity, My Allegiances

A LIFE SPENT WRITING has taught me to be wary of words. Those that seem clearest are often the most treacherous. "Identity" is one of those false friends. We all think we know what the word means and go on trusting it, even when it's slyly starting to say the opposite.

Far be it from me to want to keep on redefining the idea of identity. It has been the fundamental question of philosophy from Socrates's "Know thyself!" through countless other masters down to Freud. To approach it anew today would call for more qualifications than I possess and for very much greater temerity. The task I set myself is more modest. I want to try to understand why so many people commit crimes nowadays in the name of religious, ethnic, national or some other kind of identity. Has it always been like this since time immemorial, or is the present era influenced by hitherto unknown factors? Sometimes what I say may seem rather simplistic. If so it's because I want to set my argument out as calmly, patiently and fairly as possible, without resorting to jargon or unwarranted shortcuts.

What's known as an identity card carries the holder's family name, given name, date and place of birth, photograph, a list of certain physical features, the holder's signature and sometimes also his fingerprints — a whole array of details designed to prove without a shadow of doubt or confusion that the bearer of the document is so-and-so, and that amongst all the millions of other human beings there isn't one — not even his double or his twin brother — for whom he could be mistaken.

My identity is what prevents me from being identical to anybody else.

Defined in this way the word identity reflects a fairly precise idea — one which in theory should not give rise to confusion. Do we really need lengthy arguments to prove that there are not and cannot be two identical individuals? Even if in the near future someone manages, as we fear they may, to "clone" human beings, the clones would at best be identical only at the time of their "birth"; as soon as they started to live they would start being different.

Each individual's identity is made up of a number of elements, and these are clearly not restricted to the particulars set down in official records. Of course, for the great majority these factors include allegiance to a religious tradition; to a nationality — sometimes two; to a profession, an institution, or a particular social milieu. But the list is much longer than that; it is virtually unlimited. A person may feel a more or less strong attachment to a province, a village, a neighbourhood, a clan, a professional team or one connected with sport, a group of friends, a union, a company, a parish, a community of people with the same passions, the same sexual preferences, the same physical handicaps, or who have to deal with the same kind of pollution or other nuisance.

Of course, not all these allegiances are equally strong, at least at any given moment. But none is entirely insignificant, either. All are components of personality — we might almost call them "genes of the soul" so long as we remember that most of them are not innate.

While each of these elements may be found separately in many individuals, the same combination of them is never encountered in different people, and it's this that gives every individual richness and value and makes each human being unique and irreplaceable.

It can happen that some incident, a fortunate or unfortunate accident, even a chance encounter, influences our sense of identity more strongly than any ancient affiliation. Take the case of a Serbian man and a Muslim woman who met 20 years ago in a café in Sarajevo, fell in love and got married. They can never perceive their identity in the same way as does a couple that is entirely Serbian or entirely Muslim; their view of religion and mother country will never again be what it was before. Both partners will always carry within them the ties their parents handed down at birth, but these ties will henceforth be perceived differently and accorded a different importance.

Let us stay in Sarajevo and carry out an imaginary survey there. Let us observe a man of about 50 whom we see in the street.

In 1980 or thereabouts he might have said proudly and without hesitation, "I'm a Yugoslavian!" Questioned more closely, he could have said he was a citizen of the Federal Republic of Bosnia-Herzegovina, and, incidentally, that he came from a traditionally Muslim family.

If you had met the same man twelve years later, when the war was at its height, he might have answered automatically and emphatically, "I'm a Muslim!" He might even have grown the statutory beard. He would quickly have added that he was a Bosnian, and he would not have been pleased to be reminded of how proudly he once called himself a Yugoslavian.

If he was stopped and questioned now, he would say first of all that he was a Bosnian, then that he was a Muslim. He'd tell you he was just on his way to the mosque, but he'd also want you to know that his country is part of Europe and that he hopes it will one day be a member of the Union.

How will this same person want to define himself if we meet him in the same place 20 years hence? Which of his affiliations will he put first? The European? The Islamic? The Bosnian? Something else again? The Balkan connection, perhaps?

I shan't risk trying to predict. All these factors are part of his identity. He was born to a family that was traditionally Muslim; the language he speaks links him to the Southern Slavs, who were once joined together in a single state, but are so no longer; he lives on land which belonged sometimes to the Ottoman and sometimes to the Austrian Empire, and which played a part in the major dramas of European history. In every era one or other of his affiliations swelled up, so to speak, in such a way as to eclipse all the others and to appear to represent his whole identity. In the course of his life he'll have heard all kinds of fables. He'll have been told he was a proletarian pure and simple. Or a Yugoslavian through and through. Or, more recently, a Muslim. For a few difficult months he'll even have been made to think he had more in common with the inhabitants of Kabul than with those of Trieste!

In every age there have been people who considered that an individual had one overriding affiliation so much more important in every circumstance to all others that it might legitimately be called his "identity." For some it was the nation, for others religion or class. But one has only to look at the various conflicts being fought out all over the world today to realise that no one allegiance has absolute supremacy. Where people feel their faith is threatened, it is their religious affiliation that seems to reflect their whole identity. But if their mother tongue or their ethnic group is in danger, then they fight ferociously against their own co-religionists. Both the Turks and the Kurds are Muslims, though they speak different languages; but does that make the war between them any less bloody? Hutus and Tutsis alike are Catholics, and they speak the same language, but has that stopped them slaughtering one another? Czechs and Slovaks are all Catholics too, but does that help them live together?

I cite all these examples to underline the fact that while there is always a certain hierarchy among the elements that go to make up individual identities, that hierarchy is not immutable; it changes with time, and in so doing brings about fundamental changes in behaviour.

Moreover, the ties that count in people's lives are not always the allegedly major allegiances arising out of language, complexion, nationality, class or religion. Take the case of an Italian homosexual in the days of fascism. I imagine that for the man himself that particular aspect of his personality had up till then been important, but not more so than his professional activity, his political choices or his religious beliefs. But suddenly state repression swoops down on him and he feels threatened with humiliation, deportation or death. It's the recollection of certain books I've read and films I've seen that leads me to choose this example. This man, who a few years earlier was a patriot, perhaps even a nationalist, was no longer able to exult at the sight of the Italian army marching by; he may even have come to wish for its defeat. Because of the persecution to which he was subjected, his sexual preferences came to outweigh his other affiliations, among them even the nationalism which at that time was at its height. Only after the war, in a more tolerant Italy, would our man have felt entirely Italian once more.

The identity a person lays claim to is often based, in reverse, on that of his enemy. An Irish Catholic differentiates himself from Englishmen in the first place in terms of religion, but vis-à-vis the monarchy he will declare himself a republican; and while he may not know much Gaelic, at least he will speak his own form of English. A Catholic leader who spoke with an Oxford accent might seem almost a traitor.

One could find dozens of other examples to show how complex is the mechanism of identity: a complexity sometimes benign, but sometimes tragic. I shall quote various instances in the pages that follow, some briefly and others in more detail. Most of them relate to the region I myself come from — the Middle East, the Mediterranean, the Arab world, and first and foremost Lebanon. For that is a country where you are constantly having to question yourself about your affiliations, your origins, your relationships with others, and your possible place in the sun or in the shade.

I SOMETIMES FIND MYSELF "examining my identity" as other people examine their conscience. As you may imagine, my object is not to discover within myself some "essential" allegiance in which I may recognise myself. Rather the opposite: I scour my memory to find as many ingredients of my identity as I can. I then assemble and arrange them. I don't deny any of them.

I come from a family which originated in the southern part of the Arab world and which for centuries lived in the mountains of Lebanon. More recently, by a series of migrations, it has spread out to various other parts of the world, from Egypt to Brazil and from Cuba to Australia. It takes pride in having always been at once Arab and Christian, and this probably since the second or third century AD — that is, long before the rise of Islam and even before the West was converted to Christianity.

The fact of simultaneously being Christian and having as my mother tongue Arabic, the holy language of Islam, is one of the basic paradoxes that have shaped my own identity. Speaking Arabic creates bonds between me and all those who use it every day in their prayers, though most of them by far don't know it as well as I do. If you are in central Asia and meet an elderly scholar outside a Timuride *medersa*, you need only address him in Arabic for him to feel at ease. Then he will speak to you from the heart, as he'd never risk doing in Russian or English.

This language is common to us all — to him, to me and to more than a billion others. On the other hand, my being a Christian — regardless of whether I am so out of deep religious conviction or merely for sociological reasons — also creates a significant link between me and the two billion or so other Christians in the world. There are many things in which I differ from every Christian, every Arab and every Muslim, but between me and each of them there is also an undeniable kinship, in one case religious and intellectual and in the other linguistic and cultural.

That said, the fact of being at once an Arab and a Christian puts one in a very special situation: it makes you a member of a minority — a situation not always easy to accept. It marks a person deeply and permanently. I cannot deny that it has played a decisive part in most of the decisions I have had to make in the course of my own life, including my decision to write this book.

Thus, when I think about either of these two components of my identity separately, I feel close either through language or through religion to a good half of the human race. But when I take the same two elements together, I find myself face to face with my own specificity.

I could say the same thing about other ties. I share the fact that I'm French with 60 million or so others; the fact that I'm Lebanese with between eight and ten million, if you include the diaspora; but with how many do I share the fact that I'm both French and Lebanese? With a few thousand, at most.

Every one of my allegiances links me to a large number of people. But the more ties I have the rarer and more particular my own identity becomes.

If I went into my origins in more detail I'd have to say I was born into what is known as the Melchite or Greek Catholic community, which recognises the authority of the Pope while retaining some Byzantine rites. Seen from a distance, this affiliation is no more than a detail, a curiosity; but seen from close to, it is a defining aspect of my identity. In a country like Lebanon, where the more powerful communities have fought for a long time for their territory and their share of power, members of very small minorities like mine have seldom taken up arms, and have been the first to go into exile. Personally, I always declined to get involved in a war that struck me as absurd and suicidal; but this judgemental attitude, this distant way of looking at things, this refusal to fight, are not unconnected with the fact that I belong to a marginalised community.

So I am a Melchite. But if anyone ever bothered to look my name up in the administrative records — which in Lebanon, as you may imagine, classify people in terms of their religious persuasion — they would find me mentioned not among the Melchites, but in the register of Protestants. Why? It would take too long to explain. All I need say here is that in our family there were two rival family traditions, and that throughout my childhood I was a witness to this tug-of-war. A witness, and sometimes even the bone of contention too. If I was sent to the French school run by the Jesuit fathers it was because my mother, a determined Catholic, wanted to remove me from the Protestant influence prevailing at that time in my father's family, where the children were traditionally sent to British or American schools. It was because of this conflict that I came to speak French, and it was because I spoke French that during the war in Lebanon I went to live in Paris rather than in New York, Vancouver or London. It was for this reason, too, that when I started to write I wrote in French.

Shall I set out even more details about my identity? Shall I mention my Turkish grandmother, or her husband, who was a Maronite Christian from Egypt? Or my other grandfather, who died long before I was born and who I am told was a poet, a freethinker, perhaps a freemason, and in any case violently anti-clerical? Shall I go back as far as the great-great-great-uncle who was the first person to translate Molière into Arabic and to have his translation staged in 1848 in an Ottoman theatre?

No, there's no need to go on. I'll merely ask: how many of my fellow men share with me all the different elements that have shaped my identity and determined the main outlines of my life? Very few. Perhaps none at all. And that is what I want to emphasise: through each one of my affiliations, taken separately, I possess a certain kinship with a large number of my fellow human beings; but because of all these allegiances, taken together, I possess my own identity, completely different from any other.

I scarcely need exaggerate at all to say that I have some affiliations in common with every other human being. Yet no one else in the world has all or even most of the same allegiances as I do. Out of all the dozens of elements I can put forward, a mere handful would be enough to demonstrate my own particular identity, different from that of anybody else, even my own father or son.

I hesitated a long time before writing the pages that lead up to this one. Should I really start the book by describing my own situation at such length?

On the one hand, I wanted to use the example with which I was most familiar to show how, by adducing a few affiliations, one could simultaneously declare one's ties with one's fellow human beings and assert one's own uniqueness. On the other hand, I was well aware that the more one analyses a special case the more one risks being told that it *is* only a special case.

But in the end I took the plunge, in the belief that any person of goodwill trying to carry out his or her own "examination of identity" would soon, like me, discover that that identity is a special case. Mankind itself is made up of special cases. Life is a creator of differences. No "reproduction" is ever identical. Every individual without exception possesses a composite identity. He need only ask himself a few questions to uncover forgotten divergences and unsuspected ramifications, and to see that he is complex, unique and irreplaceable.

That is precisely what characterises each individual identity: it is complex, unique and irreplaceable, not to be confused with any other. If I emphasise this point it's because of the attitude, still widespread but in my view highly pernicious, which maintains that all anyone need do to proclaim his identity is simply say he's an Arab, or French, or black, or a Serb, or a Muslim, or a Jew. Anyone who sets out, as I have done, a number of affiliations, is immediately accused of wanting to "dissolve" his identity in a kind of undifferentiated and colourless soup. And yet what I'm trying to say is exactly the opposite: not that all human beings are the same, but that each one is different. No doubt a Serb is different from a Croat, but every Serb is also different from every other Serb, and every Croat is different from every other Croat. And if a Lebanese Christian is different from a Lebanese Muslim, I don't know any two Lebanese Christians who are identical, nor any two Muslims, any more than there are anywhere in the world two Frenchmen, two Africans, two Arabs or two Jews who are identical. People are not interchangeable, and often in the same family, whether it be Rwandan, Irish, Lebanese, Algerian or Bosnian, we find, between two brothers who have lived in the same environment, apparently small differences which make them act in diametrically opposite ways in matters relating to politics, religion and everyday life. These differences may even turn one of the brothers into a killer, and the other into a man of dialogue and conciliation.

Few would object explicitly to what I've been saying. Yet we all behave as if it were not true. Taking the line of least resistance, we lump the most different people together under the same heading. Taking the line of least resistance, we ascribe to them collective crimes, collective acts and opinions. "The Serbs have massacred . . . ," "The English have devastated . . . ," "The Jews have confiscated . . . ," "The Blacks have torched . . . ," "The Arabs refuse . . . ." We blithely express sweeping judgements on whole peoples, calling them "hardworking" and "ingenious," or "lazy," "touchy," "sly," "proud," or "obstinate." And sometimes this ends in bloodshed.

I know it is not realistic to expect all our contemporaries to change overnight the way they express themselves. But I think it is important for each of us to become aware that our words are not innocent and without consequence: they may help to perpetuate prejudices which history has shown to be perverse and deadly.

For it is often the way we look at other people that imprisons them within their own narrowest allegiances. And it is also the way we look at them that may set them free.

Native Art, Identity, and Performance in the Postmodern West

by Norman Denzin

Historically, the role of the Indian artist has been primarily that of a performer, working from a script written by whites (Brody, 1971, p. 179, slight paraphrase).

It was primarily through the work of a group of 12 painters known as the Taos Society of Artists (TSA) that America began its 20th-century romance with the Southwest and its Indians (Peters, 1988, p. 1; see also Taggett and Schwarz, 1990, p. 3).[1] This romance built on an infatuation that had been established in the 19th century with the paintings of Native Americans done by George Catlin, Charles Bird King, Alfred Jacob Miller, Karl Bodmer, and John Mix Stanley.

Carter Henry Harrison (1860–1953): five-term Chicago mayor (1897–1905, 1911–1915), art patron to TSA artists, letter to Walter Ufer, member of the Taos Society of Artists:

> Walter, I can take a couple of your paintings this year. I want one of either the Santa Cruz or the Ranches of Taos Church. I would like an Indian on horseback crossing the sage brush with either mountains or a pueblo building showing in the background and painted towards dusk—no color except a suggestion of red in the horizon & turquoise blue in the upper sky.

> Walter, Please paint your Indians a little darker—the Chicago public does not know that the Pueblo Indians are not as dark colored as the ordinary Red Man and consequently think you off in your color. Another thing, paint in color that shows better under artificial light. Your yellows are beautiful by day, but look off at night in electric light. (Bickerstaff, 1955a, p. 142)

I've told this story before. Since an early age I have been a cultural tourist in the postmodern West. In the 1950s my brother Mark and I spent our summers, until we were young teenagers, with our grandparents on their farm south of Iowa City, Iowa. Saturday nights were special. Grandpa loved those "Cowboy and Indian" movies, and so did I. Every Saturday Grandma fixed an early supper. After supper, Grandpa and I, wearing going-to-town-clothes, drove to Iowa City to catch the first movie of a double-feature at the Strand Theatre starring John Wayne, or Glen Ford, or Henry Fonda, or Jimmy Stewart. It was a grand movie palace, Italian Renaissance style; a large canopy with yellow and red striped awnings extended from the building to the curb. Rich draperies and colorful movie posters adorned the lobby. The ceiling dome was finished in gold and silver leaf. Huge chandeliers hung from the ceiling. Grandpa and I always tried to get one of the box seats, the best seat in the house he said.

We'd time our arrival to town to allow for a stroll up and down Clinton and College Avenues, always seeing this neighbor or that neighbor, catching up on gossip, talk about rain, crops, the market price of beef or pork, whether corn would be shoulder high by the 4th. Then we'd hurry to get in line to buy our tickets to the movie.

Today, I dream myself back into those soft summer nights in cool darkness, nighttime dreams of cowboys, Indians, the cavalry, six-guns, stage coaches, barroom ladies, and school marms, and blonde-haired little boys running after a lonely rider on a horse. "Shane, Shane, Shane, come back." I still remember the names of the movies: *Stage Coach, Broken Arrow, Colt 45, She Wore a Yellow Ribbon, Winchester '73, High Noon, Naked Spur, Searchers, Far Country, Bend of the River,* and *Shane,* the only film I ever watched with my father. We'd leave by 6:00 and often not get back until after 11:00, especially if we stayed for the double feature. The house would be quiet when we got back home; Grandma and Mark would be in bed. And we'd whisper and tiptoe as we came up the stairs, so as not to awaken anyone.

It was always the same movie, bad Indians, good cowboys, dead Indians, dead cowboys. The Indians always looked the same: dark brown skin, bare chests, straight black hair, bows, arrows, bareback riders on swift horses, buckskin clothing, fancy headdresses, tom toms beating in the background, tipis, woman called squaws, happy little children playing along the river bank, barking dogs in the village. Always the same movie. Always the same Indians.

I wanted to be a cowboy when I grew up. So did Mark, I think. I don't know about Grandpa. He could be anybody he wanted to be. On Saturday mornings, while Grandma made hot doughnuts for us in the new deep-fat fryer in her big country kitchen, we watched "Cowboy and Indian" television shows: "The Lone Ranger," "Red Rider and Little Beaver," "Roy Rogers and Dale Evans," "Sky King." Mark and I had cowboy outfits—wide-brimmed hats, leather vests, chaps, spurs, little pistols, and gun belts. Grandpa bought us a horse. There is a picture of Mark and me in our cowboy outfits on the back of sway-backed Sonny, the horse who was deaf in the right ear. In fourth grade I was Squanto in the Thanksgiving play about the Pilgrims. When we played cowboys and Indians, sometimes I was an Indian—Tonto, or Little Beaver.[2] Sometimes I was the Lone Ranger or Red Rider. I could be anyone

I wanted to be. And this is the point, as Philip Deloria reminds us; I could be a hobby Indian, a white boy playing Indian (1998, pp. 128–129). I had that right. I could be Squanto, or Little Beaver, or Tonto, or Red Rider, or the Lone Ranger. At a moment's notice I could appropriate an Indian identity for myself.

In 1987 my wife and I spent three weeks vacationing in Red Lodge, Montana. We've returned every year, and in 1994 bought a small cabin 60 miles from Cody, Wyoming, and the Buffalo Bill Historical Center (BBHC). The BBHC became a research site in 1995 when I started focusing on the paintings of Native artists, including Fritz Scholder (Luiseno), Kevin Red Star (Crow), R. C. Gorman (Navajo), and T. C. Cannon (Kiowa, Choctaw) in the Whitney Gallery of Western Art. At the same time I was examining the exhibits devoted to Buffalo Bill, his Wild West Show and the presence of Lakota and Oglala Sioux in his show, including Sitting Bull.

In 2011 the Indianapolis Eiteljorg Museum of American Indians and Western Art in Indianapolis became a second research site because of the attention it gave to early 20th-century Southwestern Anglo Art, especially the paintings of Indians made by the Taos Society of Artists (see Appendix B). Of special interest were the ways in which these two museums located Western Art, Anglo painters, Native Americans, and the American West on a global stage. As I looked at many of the paintings of Indians in those two museums I saw versions of the same Indians I had watched as a young child in the Strand Theatre in Iowa City. It was as if I was back in my childhood. Time stood still. Indians everywhere.

This book, part performance text, part historical ethnodrama, part autoethnography, comes out of the intersection of these childhood memories with these repeated visits to the BBHC, and the Eiteljorg.[3] Hours spent looking at Indians and cowboys. How do I name these feelings; guilt, sadness, longing? Henhawk (2013, p. 519) cuts to the chase. He says these feelings represent another one of the ironies of white privilege and white guilt. Here I am, writing my way out of a past that was handed to me by the media, Hollywood, post-World War Two American culture, my grandfather, his dreams, his fantasies, and my own life as a critic of the West. But this life has taken me to the contemporary Postmodern West and its great regional museums where Indians and their identities still live. I linger here in these spaces of memory, Wild West Shows, and museums, performing my way out of a West I do not want to be part of.

This Project: Redfacing and Three Aesthetic Moments

So I write another chapter in an undoing of the past. *Indians in Color: Native Art,*[4] *Identity and Performance in the Postmodern West* continues my critique of the treatment of Native Americans[5] in art, museums, and Wild West shows in the contemporary West. It extends the project started in my 2013 book, *Indians on Display: Global Commodification of Native Americans in Performance, Art and Museums,* namely the examination of the commodification through performance and art of Native Americans in the colonial and postcolonial west. *Indians in Color* is a study in the politics of memory, art, race and performance.

Specifically, I examine the representations of Native Americans produced in three historical moments, by three groups of artists: the European-trained Taos Society of Artists (1898–1927); the 'tourist' paintings of three Indigenous Taos Pueblo Painters, who modeled for TSA painters (1920–1950); and the so-called Chapter Three Artists[6] (1960–): Fritz Scholder, R. C. Gorman, Kevin Red Star. The Chapter Three Artists taught in, or were trained in, the Institute of American Indian Art, Santa Fe (see Appendix B). The Chapter Three painters produced a radical postmodern artistic aesthetic that challenged the romantic Noble Savage created by the TSA. I co-mingle these moments and their images with scenes from the cowboy and Indian movies of my childhood.

These three artistic formations—modern, pre-modern, postmodern[7]— offer competing versions of America's 20th- and 21st-century Native American. It is necessary to revisit the history and politics behind these three discourses. Doing so permits a critical appraisal of how Native Americans should be represented today.

Reading Race

A complex argument organizes my reading of these three artistic movements.[8] The artistic representations of Native Americans have always been about colonial privilege, about race, about dark-skinned bodies, about how white and Native artists represent the bodies of persons of color—red, dark skin, brown, black, tan. It has always been about the uses of racialized visual languages grounded in popular culture and its codes and discourses, including film, music, literature, ethnography, paintings, Wild West minstrel shows, and Indianist reenactments (Kalshoven, 2015). This is what Raheja calls "redfacing," that is, the politics of creating and preserving images of a vanishing dark-skinned Indian and Noble Savage for a white audience, a form of privileged ethnic spectatorship (2010, p. xiii). Through the middle of the 20th century this visual language of color was used by Native and non-native artists alike. The same Indian, two sets of creators (see Dunn, 1968, pp. 362–368; Hoffman, 1986).

Indeed, until the emergence of the Institute of American Indian Art (IAIA)[9] in Santa Fe in 1962, modern Indian art was art primarily produced by Native Americans for white patrons using artistic techniques taught by white instructors (Brody, 1971; Eldredge, Schimmel, and Truettner, 1986; Sims, 2008a). After 1962 a new aesthetic emerged, a post-modern, postindian[10] Indian art, a radical art that celebrated Indian identity, even as it depicted Indians as victims of an oppressive white culture (Gibson and Leaken, 2014). This new art was consumed by a new generation of celebrity patrons,[11] elevating Native artists like R. C. Gorman and Fritz Scholder to the status of pop icons, Indigenous Andy Warhols.[12]

Production Sites

This Native art, its history, production and subject-matter, is anchored in Taos, the Taos Pueblo,[13] and Santa Fe, New Mexico, the home of IAIA. It must be read through the politics operating in these sites. The interpretation of this new art must also be written through the culture and rituals of the Taos Indians. They fiercely protected their sacred rituals, and did not allow the practice of their rituals to be witnessed by Anglo artists or anthropologists (Parsons, 1936, p. 4; 1962, pp. 1–2). Hence, an idealized Taos Indian was produced by Anglo painters, an Indian who would be un-done by the new generation of Native painters trained in Santa Fe at IAIA.

The subject of this new art is explicitly political. It is radically subjective. It raises key questions:

Whose racialized Indian is being painted?

Can white artists any longer claim any right at all, contested or not, to paint Native Americans?

Can the legacies of this art, which are now not so new, serve to advance an agenda of empowerment: can they function as an aesthetic pedagogy of liberation (Friere, 1992)?

These are the central questions I examine in this book.

Disneyland, Wild West Shows and Paintings of Indians

My narrative unfolds in five interconnected chapters plus this chapter.

The following quote from Ernest Blumenschein (1898), founding member of TSA, provides a segue to Chapter Two. Blumenschein's short article appeared in *Harper's Weekly* on April 30, 1898. He had attended a Buffalo Bill Wild West Show at Madison Square Garden. Before the show he mingled back stage with Indian performers. After the show he wrote:

Bedouins are whirling and tumbling through the dust and sunshine; scene-painters are retouching the marvelous blue mountains; Mexicans and Cubans and Cowboys lazily willing away the early morning hours. A young Indian writes a letter ... directed to Miss Alice Lone Bear, Pine Ridge Agency, South Dakota ... I enter a large room. Several ugly-looking bucks push me around while a few old men arrange feathers in a new war bonnet ... All connected with the show eat in a great room on the ground floor. Here in their working-clothes, or in the picturesque attire of their homes (for Cossack, Mexican and Indian refuse civilized costume) ... After dinner is over preparations for the evening performance begin.

With pigments, a good Indian type is made hideous in a short interval—bodies and limbs are painted half white, half green, or with circles, and crescents, and stars. The feathers come off the wall, sleigh bells jingle and tinkle, the squaws 'ti-ti' in their high shrill voices. A blast from a bugle starts them off to saddle their ponies on which they are soon mounted for the grand entry. The cowboy band starts up 'Hail, Columbia,' the bugle sounds again, the great canvas curtain is drawn, and the howling warriors dash wildly into the pubic gaze.[14]

Blumenschein would soon gravitate from writing short articles about Wild West shows to illustrating Indian stories by Stephen Crane and Hamlin Garland for *McClure's Magazine* and *Harper's Weekly* (Cunningham, 2008, pp. 26–27).[15] Sadly, the Buffalo Bill Wild West Show he described in 1898 is still going on in Paris in 2014.

Blumenschein's observations of Native Americans in Buffalo Bill's Wild West Show perfectly illustrates Raheja's (2010) arguments concerning "redfacing" and the intersection of art and performance in 20th- and 21st-century America:

Stemming from a long tradition of staged performances such as The Wild West shows that were themselves informed by American Literature's obsession with Native American plots and subplots, film and visual culture [art] have provided the primary representational field on which Native American images have been displayed to dominant culture audiences in the twentieth and twenty-first centuries. These representations have also been key to formulating Indigenous people's own self images.[16]

From the 19th century forward, the Wild West show, with its alignments with visual culture—advertising, art and painting, film—was the cultural engine that reproduced redfacing for American popular culture.

Chapter Two, "Disneyland Indians, Paris, circa 2014," starts with Graham Greene on a YouTube video reading the call for Native performers to audition for the Disneyland Buffalo Bill Wild West Show in Paris. Scenes of poverty from the Pine Ridge Reservation appear on the screen. It seems that when we talk about Native Americans, art, painters, and the West, we can never get too far from Buffalo Bill and his minstrel show. Disneyland lurks in the background (see Giroux and Pollock, 2010). Like in this recent advertisement.

Disneyland Paris Seeks New Recruits for Wild West Show, April 2014

Disneyland Paris is auditioning locally for Cowboys and Indians with exceptional horsemanship skills for the facility's new musical extravaganza, Buffalo Bill's Wild West Show ... with Mickey[17] and Friends. The western-themed spectacle, which still features Buffalo Bill, Sitting Bull, Annie Oakley, and a multitude of Cowboys and Indians, replaced the long running original production on April 4th last year at the grand premiere in Paris, France. This time around, Sheriff Mickey and a cast of Disney's beloved characters have joined the adventure.[18]

Wendy Red Star, Crow Indian cultural activist and performance artist, offers an alternative view, focusing on performances and artworks that contest images of the vanishing dark-skinned Indian.

I've created my own version of a Wild West Show. I call it *Wendy Star's Wild West & Congress of Rough Riders of the World*.[19] It will be held in the Fisher Pavilion, Seattle, August 30–September 1, 2014. My show combines performance, and art. I have Indian artists, painters, fancy dancers. I tell the story of the West from the Indian's point of view. We re-enact the Battle of Little Big Horn. Our show and artists challenge the representations of the west currently being staged by Wild West Paris Disneyland. It's time to stop this Disneyland travesty, even if Disney does hire Native Americans as performers.

This four-act historical ethnodrama critiques Paris Disneyland, the Buffalo Bill Wild West Show and its use of Native Americans as re-enactors of a Wild West that never was.[20] Drawing on Pirandello's *Six Characters in Search of an Author* (1921/1998a), the play uses the voices of Native Americans drawn from popular culture—Tonto, Pocahontas, Little Beaver, Minnehaha, Secagawea, Hombre. These characters are Indigenous activists, and they are asking for an author who will write a play that deals with real Indians and their plight. The activists, along with avatars, disrupt the performances that occur in the Disneyland Wild West Show. As the curtain comes down Count Basie's "April in Paris" (from the movie, *Blazing Saddles*, 1974) plays over the sound system. The Seventh Generation Performers join hands with the Indian activists and slowly dance around the stage. The theatre goes dark. The audience breaks out in cheers.

The play asks if new stories of the West can be performed, and if so, how. While the critique in this chapter is situated in Paris Disneyland, it could as easily be located in Disney Parks in Tokyo, London, or Rust, Baden-Wurttemberg, Germany. These global Wild West shows, with audience participation, enact recurring fantasies of colonial domination over Native Americans. By performing its own reflexive critique, my play is intended to mimic the Paris Wild West Show and expose this ideology. The criticisms are also intended to apply to Anglo paintings of Native Americans and mainstream Hollywood movies that represent Indians (see Hearne, 2012 a, b; Howe, 2013a).

Chapter Three, "Copper-Colored Primitives," contests the paintings of the twelve artists who were founding members of the Taos Society of Artists. This group produced a body of work (more than 400 paintings) that is popular and important to the present day (see Broder, 1980, pp. 312–321; Goodman and Dawson, 2008; Hassrick, 2008, 2009a, b; Lujan, 2003; Witt, 2003a, b). The TSA paintings of Taos Indians were presented to the public as accurate representations of an ancient, but dying culture. These paintings presented a unified Indian subject who was in danger of disappearing. The TAS painters helped turned Taos into a tourist site where their art and the material artifacts of Pueblo culture could be bought and sold.

Step back in time. Broder, the historian of art and the American West, locates the TSA project in its historical moment:

After the final defeat of the Indians at the Battle of Wounded Knee and the surrender of Sitting Bull in 1890, Indians no longer had to be feared.[21] Throughout the West they were confined to reservations. Many artists sentimentalized a defeated race and became interested in scenes of the ceremonial and daily life of aboriginals who lived peacefully with nature ... Several of the early Taos artists were romantics who wished to celebrate the idealized West of the past ... the idyllic life of the noble Indian living in harmony with nature. (1980, pp. 6–8, 215, paraphrase)

Walter Ufer, a member of the Taos Society of Artists, extends Broder and inserts a bitter irony into the situation:

The Society of Taos Artists refused to paint the Taos Indians as a people who had been defeated and Americanized and turned into passive, dejected people, second-class citizens living on the edges in the white man's world. Instead they romanticized the Taos Indian, creating a Noble savage at home in a western landscape. Ironically the Indians they turned into noble savages were in fact poor laborers, and servants working as models for TSA artists. (Walter Ufer, in Broder, 1980, p. 215, paraphrase)

The Atchison, Topeka and Santa Fe Railroad commissioned artwork by the TSA painters. They wanted Indians painted in a certain way. They turned these paintings into advertisements promoting tourism in the Southwest. The play sets up a critical dialogue between the TSA painters, who wanted to be recognized as true artists, approved by Anglo art critics, and members of the Taos Pueblo who served as models for the TSA artists and their commercial artwork and challenged the value of Western critics approving of TSA art.

Taos Pueblo Indians and Indigenous painters contest the way Taos Indians and Taos culture were represented by the TSA and by Elsie Parsons, a Columbia trained anthropologist. They critique Parsons, who criticized them for being too modern. Georgia O'Keeffe mediates an imaginary verbal dispute between Elsie and Albert Looking Elk Martinez. The play culminates in a play within a play, "A Protest on San Geronimo Feast Day, " performed by the Seventh Generation Performers (SGP),[22] Coyote, Ms. Coyote, the Forgotten Taos Painters, Carl Jung, and the San Geronimo Clowns. The fictional performance takes place in the Taos Pueblo on San Geronimo Feast Day, September 30, 2015.[23]

The work of the Taos Society of Artists is alive and well today. Their paintings hang in the Indianapolis Eiteljorg Museum of American

Indians and Western Art.[24] Indeed, the Eiteljorg has an entire room devoted to the work of the Taos Society of Artists, including paintings by Joseph Sharp, Bert Phillips, Ernest Blumenschein, E. I. Couse, Oscar Berninghaus, and Herbert "Buck" Dunton (see www.harwood-museum. org/collections/taos-society).[25]

The history of art in Taos, up until the present, has been written almost entirely through the eyes and works of white artists. The history inevitably starts with the stories of the founding members of the Taos Society of Artists, then moves to Georgia O'Keeffe and the post-war Taos Moderns, then to the work of contemporary Anglo artists, including Peter Parks, Agnes Martin, Jen Price, and Larry Bell (see Shipley and Weller, 1969; Weller, Donavan, et al. 1948–1963; Witt, 1992; also www.harwoodmuseum.org/collections/contemporary).[26]

Chapter Four, "Taos Indians on Canvas," challenges this official history by taking up three Indigenous Taos artists, Albert Lujan, Albert Looking Elk Martinez and Juan Mirabal, who until recently were not included in the story of Taos art scene. While they started out as models for TSA painters, they soon became artists in their own right. But their art was dismissed as the work of untrained primitives. The two Alberts and Juan responded by successfully marketing their own art. Their paintings challenged the work of the TSA painters and were an authentic Indigenous expression of the Pueblo and its values.[27]

In 2003 the Harwood Museum of Art of the University of New Mexico in Taos organized a three month exhibition of the work of three Indigenous Taos Pueblo painters: Albert Looking Elk Martinez, Albert Lujan, and Juan Mirabal (see Witt, 2003a, b). These three painters were anomalies in the history of Santa Fe and Taos art. They were excluded, until 2003, from the history of Southwest Indian painting. Their work was defined as unschooled and derivative and not worthy of white patronage or gallery sponsorship (see www.tfaoi.com/aa/3aa/3aa495. htm). Today, it is respected and collected for its naturalistic realistic style (see Baca, 2003; Lujan, 2003; Witt, 2003b).

Chapter Five, "Postmodern Indians on Canvas," focuses on the Institute of American Indian Art and the radical art of Fritz Scholder, R. C. Gorman, and Kevin Red Star, aka Third Chapter Artists. It re-visits the founding moment of the TSA, when Ernest Blumenschein, fresh from his experiences with the Buffalo Bill Wild West Show in New York City, made his way down the mountain to Taos after his wagon broke down. Here, he discovers his dark skinned subject in Taos, launching a history that is still alive today.

The Institute of American Indian Art, under the leadership of Lloyd Kiva New, created a space for a new art to emerge, what Gerald Vizenor (1999, 2008) would call "postindian"—a new radical Indian free of colonial trappings. This new art was framed in part by the energy of the anti-Vietnam war protests and the growth of the American Indian Movement. Fritz Scholder re-visited the tragedy of Wounded Knee and Custer's Last Stand and painted drunk Indians and vampires. Kevin Red Star worked with images from the pre- and post-reservation period, including tipis, warriors on horses, reservation policemen, fancy dancers wearing beaded leggings seen on pairs of Levi-Strauss blue jeans. He transformed these images and symbols into decorative postmodern collages of elegant, somber and joyous Indians outside time (Hoffman, 1986, p. 266).

T. C. Cannon's "Collector # 5 or Osage with Van Gogh" (woodblock print on rice paper) shows an elegantly dressed Osage in his wicker chair between a Navajo rug and Van Gogh's painting, "Wheatfield," which is hanging on the wall behind him (Hoffman, 1986, p. 267). Here two art worlds exist side-by-side—high modernist art and postmodern Native art. Cannon's painting says modern Indians make their own art and are comfortable moving through different art worlds (Hoffman, 1986, p. 267).

In April 2013 the Harwood Museum of Art celebrated the Third Chapter of the Taos Art Colony, honoring the work of Native artists Fritz Scholder, R. C. Gorman, and Woody Crumbo, and Anglo painter Jim Wagner (see www.harwood museum.org/news/view/4 5). This group of Native artists took control of the representation of Indians; they created a new postmodern Indian.

In 2008 an exhibition titled "Fritz Scholder: Indian/not Indian" was held concurrently at the Smithsonian Institution's National Museum of the American Indian and the George Gustav Heye Center in

New York City. A volume of the same name was published the same year (Sims, 2008). Scholder's Indian paintings could be interpreted as a direct challenge to the romantic Indian of the Taos Society of Artists. (See nmai.si.edu/exhibitions/scholder/biography.html.)

Chapter Five culminates in a one-act play, "Native Artists Attempt to Take Back the Day." The Seventh Generation Performers, along with the San Geronimo Clowns, praise the work of the Third Chapter artists. Supaman, a contemporary Crow nation musician, fancy dances across the stage. The play culminates in a dialogue about the exhibits of TSA art in the Eiteljorg Museum. R. C. Gorman, Fritz Scholder and Kevin Red Star lead a protest, calling for a new art that has yet to be imagined.

This art will no longer require, as art once did, the death of one kind of Indian painting and the death of one kind of Indian painter and the birth of a new painter who happens to be Indian (Highwater, 1986, p. 241). It requires only a commitment to the tradition already established by Scholder, Red Star, Cannon, Gorman and their heirs.

My themes all come back together in Chapter Six, "Indian Painters, Patrons, and Wild West Shows: A New Imaginary." The chapter begins with a dialogue over what is Indian Art and who has the authority to paint an Indian, and examines the three questions raised earlier in this chapter:

Whose racialized Indian is being painted?

Can white artists any longer claim the uncontested right to paint Native Americans?

Can the legacies of this art, which is now not so new, serve to advance an agenda of empowerment; can it function as a pedagogy of liberation?

The play unfolds as a series of imaginary dialogues between the Disney characters Mickey and Minnie, the Seventh Generation Performers, Buffalo Bill, Tonto, Johnny Depp, Coyote, Ms. Coyote, Ernest Blumenschein, Elsie Parsons, the two Alberts and Juan, Fritz, R. C., Kevin, Gerrald Vizenor, and contemporary Native artist, Wendy Red Star.[28] The characters review the ways in which 20th- and 21st-century painters and traveling Wild West minstrel shows turned Native Americans into commodities and sold them to a global audience.

Earlier themes are revisited: performance, colonialism, museums, Wild West shows, co-mingled fantasies, Mickey and Minnie Mouse, Buffalo Bill, Sitting Bull, global capital paying artists to paint only a certain kind of Indian. The TSA artists sold the West, or rather the Southwest, by painting a particular kind of Indian (Taggett and Schwartz, 1990). The Taos Indian was a marketable commodity. Ernest Blumenschein and his fellow artists hired Indians to pose as models and staged them in Western landscapes. Indeed, through their paintings the TSA school supplied the necessary imagery for the establishment of Taos and Santa Fe as national tourist sites.

They said they were doing more than railroad art. They said they were following in the footprints of Gauguin and Van Gogh; the Taos Indian was their primitive. But were they really anything more than railroad artists selling images of Indians to the highest bidder? Doesn't their Taos Indian get folded into new performative spaces, into new sites of consumption—advertisements for the AT&SF railroad, art galleries, art shows, museums, even Wild West shows where AT&SF railroad calendars and postcards were sold?

Vine Deloria, Jr., discusses the implications of representations such as these for how whites approach the lives of real Indians:

> Understanding Indians is not an esoteric art. All it takes is a trip through Arizona or New Mexico, watching a documentary on TV, having known *one* in the service, or having read a popular book on them.... Rarely is physical contact required. There is no subject on earth so easily understood as that of the American Indian. (1969/1988, p. 5, italics in original)

Chapter Six brings the work of contemporary aboriginal re-enactment artists up against these lingering colonial cultural formations. It seeks to chart a new beginning, a new way of thinking about how the West might have been painted, and hence won. I want to do more than found a new museum, one where whites are on exhibit and Native Americans are the tourists. I want to discover a wild Native art that finally breaks free of five hundred years of colonial oppression. I want a Native art that imagines its way into utopian spaces that have yet to be (Graves, 2014; Strong, 2013). The play ends with a new anthem, "Bury My Art at Wounded Knee"[29] (see www.tumblr.com/search/Radical Indigenous Survivance & Empowerment).[30]

A Coda, "Back to the Future," questions my place in this narrative while celebrating the concept of survivance (Vizenor, 2008) embodied in the work of the Forgotten Taos Pueblo Painters and the Chapter Three artists.

It's all here in these five chapters and coda: art worlds (Becker, 1982), performance, colonialism, museums, Native art, whites painting Indians, tourist consumption, Wild West shows, global capital constructing and selling 19th-century images of Indianness, Indians as hostile, blood thirsty savages, co-mingling fantasies, Mickey Mouse, Buffalo Bill, Sitting Bull, Wendy Red Star and her contested views of the Wild West.

Memory and Identity: Whose Indian?

There are tensions at work in these chapters. There is a tension between those Native Americans who perform in Wild West shows and those Wild West Paris Disney operators who keep the racist 19th-century minstrel representations of Indians alive (Graves, 2014; McNenly, 2012). There is a tension between the work of contemporary Native artists like Wendy Red Star, who wants to empower the Native American through art, and global corporations like Wild West Paris who continue to sell 19th-century images of Native Americans. There is a tension between the 20th-century Society of Taos Artists who painted a 19th-century pastoral Indian, fit for assimilation, and the Taos Three who modeled for these painters while painting their own images of Taos and its residents. There is a tension between the Society of Taos painters and the Chapter Three painters who resisted assimilation and inspired a new (Seventh) generation of scholars and activists who insist on honoring, managing and creating their own Indigenous cultural heritage (see Benally, 2013; also Aleiss, 2005; Allen, 2012; Nicholas, 2013).[31]

These tensions create a space for dialogue, a conversation about memory, identity, art, race and the West. But history repeats itself. What is the reader to make of the announcement earlier in this chapter concerning Disneyland Paris, 2014? In 1891 William Cody employed Lakota Sioux who were survivors of the Battle of Wounded Knee (located on the Pine Ridge Reservation) in his European Wild West Show (Denzin, 2013). In 2015 the great grandchildren of those survivors are still performing in a Wild West show. There is agency here, but what does it mean for a larger politics of representation? How do we untangle politics, performance, representation, intention, and meaning? Whose history? History for whom? Whose Indian? Whose West? Whose memory?

Performing History

I suture my texts into these contested historical spaces. Biegert calls this *committed documentation*, that is, the commitment to ground the narrative in the available historical record (see Biegert 1976, quoted in Peyer, 1989, p. 553; also Benjamin, 1983). However, the record is read through a 21st-century lens. I refuse to regard the representations of Native Americans by 20th-century artists (TSA) apart from my critical views on race, Native Americans and postmodern society. Of course this is a form of historical presentism (Fischer, 1970; Skinner, 2002), applying the standards of the present to the past. On this I follow Benjamin's advice about writing history under a white colonial regime. Benjamin's histories rip the present out of its present context, connecting it to its historical past and its ideological contradictions (Benjamin, 1983, p. 24; 1968, pp. 255–266). This is history turned inside out, meant to be read aloud, history that disturbs and moves back and forth across the seamless boundaries connecting the past, the present, and the future (Benjamin, 1983, p. 24).

In interpreting these performances and paintings, and the work of these painters, I am less interested in figuring out what each one means, or what each artist intended. I am more interested in figuring out my responses to them, and the consequences of these responses for further interpretations of the painting itself. A painting, a painter reaches you with a painting. His or her Indian looks you in the eye. You may try to forget the painting, but it won't let you; its imagery haunts you. So it is for me with the paintings and artists that I discuss in the chapters that follow. I cannot get them out of my head.

An artist of course is a performer who stages and creates a painting. A painting is a performance, a performance the painter performs for an imaginary audience. When I interpret a painting, my interpretation is a performance. The paintings I discuss are performances, dramas, stories of the white gaze, brown bodies turned into art, stories of conflict, and violence. To understand what they mean, I must again, following Benjamin, do more than locate them in their historical moment. I must read myself into them, as if I were looking in a mirror. With the exception of the paintings by the Forgotten Taos Three and the Third Chapter Native artists what I see in the TAS paintings are people—Taos Indians, Sioux, Navajo, Cheyenne, Crow, men, women, children—who are not free. They are trapped in an imaginary pastoral present, an imaginary landscape, players in a violent story they can't get out of. They could be part of a scene in *Broken Arrow, Stage Coach, Hombre, Little Big Man, Dances with Wolves*.

I have attempted to write myself into a shared space with the painters, and with you. If we can share this space long enough, perhaps we can imagine how this tragic piece of late 19th- and early 20th-century history could have been done differently. And if so, maybe, just maybe, such events will never happen again. That is my goal.

My thesis is simple: The TSA paintings and the Disney Wild West Shows function as paradigmatic images of First Nations people and their place in Western history. They represent 19th- and 20th-century Western American art in the service of official governmental history. As cultural documents, they reproduce prevailing racist views of Native Americans and their place in U.S. history and contemporary popular Western culture. In contrast, the paintings of the Indigenous Taos Pueblo painters and the Chapter Three artists offered a new politics of representation, a new Native American.

Except for this chapter, the chapters the chapters in this book are plays intended to be performed—that is, read aloud. A "Dramatis Personae" listing all the characters and their historical identities preceded this chapter. These characters appear throughout the text. Recurring characters are the Navajo tricksters, Mr. Coyote and Ms. Coyote (on Coyote see Valdez and Elsbree, 2005), the Seventh Generation Performers (SGP) (Benally, 2013), and Tonto, the fictional Indian sidekick to the Lone Ranger in the long-running television series.[32] The voices of Coyote, Ms. Coyote, Seventh Generation Performers and Tonto are meant to be disruptive.[33]

Borrowing from Anna Deavere Smith (2000, 2004), Kaufman et al. (2001, 2014), and Saldana (2011), I use the craft and techniques of theatre, performance autoethnography, and critical historical analysis.[34] I call this historical autoethnography. In each chapter I offer a performance text, a staged ethnodrama that is part myth, part critique, an experiment in [auto]ethnographic montage. These staged events are intended to bring the reader into a critical moral discourse. I organize citations, YouTube video clips, links to museum exhibits of specific art works, speeches, and other entries in ways that highlight critical, reflexive associations. My goal is to undo official history and to create a space for marginalized voices, alternative histories, new ways of writing the past so new futures can be imagined. Each play imagines a politics of resistance, a new politics of possibility, new ways of re-imagining the future and the past. Madison, after Dolan (2005), calls these utopian performatives. They are akin to Freire's pedagogies of hope (Dolan, 2005, p. 5; Freire, 1992; Madison, 2010, p. 26; 2012, p.182).

Each play revolves around specific acts of resistance and activism. These acts of resistance use performance as the vehicle for contesting official art history and the status quo. A double reflexivity is at work. The performance text as a play uses performativity as a method for making a slice of contested reality visible. The performance potentially brings the audience into a state of critical reflexivity concerning the events under discussion—somehow the world *can* be a better place (Dolan,

2005, p. 5). The act of witnessing a utopian performative is itself a performative, interpretive act. The coyote trickster leads us into this new space (Bhabha, 1994, pp. 46–49; Conquergood, 2013, p. 27; Haraway, 1991, p. 201). The intent is to create a counter-memory, an alternative history of the present.

Each play is based on imaginary and actual historical documents, interviews, reports. Each play constructs its own scenes of memory. I rearrange these scenes, suppressing, distorting, even inventing scenes, foregoing claims to exact truth or factual accuracy, searching instead for emotional truth, for deep meaning (see Blew, 1999, p. 7; Stegner, 1990, p. iv).

Each chapter contains the essential dramatic elements of a play: plot, storyline, script, dialogue and monologues, dramatic structure (acts, scenes, units), time line, characters, stage, and dramatic arc— beginning, middle, end, turning points (Saldana, 2005, p. 15). I arrange the speech of certain characters (Coyote, Ms. Coyote) in a poetic-like structure, attempting to convey a specific sense of character with this form (see Smith, 2000, p. 53). Each play is part mystory and part auto-ethnographic ethnodrama (Saldana, 2005, pp. 1–2, 15, 2011; Ulmer, 1989, p. 210).[35]

While there are often elaborate stage instructions in this text, costumes, stage sets, and props "can be as minimal or as ornate as one imagines" (Smith, 2004, p. 6). Actors can play several parts. "Gender and race do not need to match those of the characters played" (Smith, 2004, p. 7). Stage directions and props can be suggested, including the use of masks. If audio visual equipment is available, images and the text of some of the documents in the plays, such as timelines and letters, may be projected. While I use acts and scenes to mark movement through the play, I have been informed by Smith's notion of the frame as a way of marking a scene within an act (2004, p. 5) and Kaufman's concept of moment, to mark a unit of theatrical time, a play being a series of interconnected frames and moments (Kaufman et al., 2001, p. xiv; 2014, p. 102).

The act of reading aloud in a group, or co-performing, creates a shared emotional experience that brings the narrative alive in ways that silent reading cannot. The parts can be spoken going around in a circle of any number of readers or by two speakers. To simplify, I have identified each part as Speaker One or Speaker Two. Each speaker names his or her character before reading the character's lines. In writing the monologues and dialogues that appear in each play, I was guided by Walter Benjamin's argument (1969) that a critical text consists of a series of quotations, documents, excerpts, and texts placed side by side. This narrative strategy produces a de-centered narrative, a multi-voiced text with voices and speakers speaking back and forth, often past one another.

Unless indicated in quotations marks, quotations—words attributed to a speaker—are paraphrases of an original text that is cited. These are not the character's words but my interpretations of what they might say if they were persuaded to participate in this performance. This is especially true of those characters in the play who are currently alive; these are my hypothetical interpretations of their thoughts and not their own words. The caveat that appears on the copyright page of this book operates at all times:

> *This book is a product of my ethnographic imagination. Names, characters, places, events, and incidents are used fictitiously. Any resemblance to actual events, or locales or persons, living or dead is at least partially coincidental. The dialogue contained therein is intended as a stage play and should not be quoted or considered to be the actual words of the speakers unless a reference citation is given.*

In challenging these racist myths and cultural representations, I follow Hall (1997) and Smith (1997) who argue that it is not enough to replace negative representations with positive representations. The positive-negative debate essentializes racial identity, and denies its "dynamic relation to constructions of class, gender, sexuality [and] region" (Smith, 1997, p. 4). It takes two parties to do racial minstrelsy. Race is performative, contextual, and historical. Stereotypes of whiteness are tangled up in racial myth, in minstrel shows that re-play the Wild West, leading whites to look Western and Native Americans to look Indian (Dorst, 1999).

By unraveling these myths, and their meanings and origins, I point to the diversity and complexity of racial representations and racial performances in American popular Western culture. I seek to replace old stereotypes with new understandings. I want to show how historical discourse can in fact turn back on itself, revise its stance toward the past, and perform new, progressive representations of cultural difference.

I advance a critical performative pedagogy which hopefully allows us to dream our way into a militant democratic utopian space, into a space which also exposes and criticizes the racist politics buried deep inside the American democratic imagination. The challenge is to take up again Kittridge's (1996) and Limerick's (2001) charge to rethink Western history and mythology by starting out at the ground level, starting all over again. In bringing the past into the present, I insert myself into the past and create the conditions for rewriting and hence re-experiencing it. I want to invent a new version of the past, a new history. I want to create a chorus of discordant voices, memories, and images concerning art as a representational form. In so doing I contest current images of Western and Native artists, and the place of Wild West shows in our collective imagination.

This book completes a four-part series about Native Americans, art, painters, Wild West shows and the postmodern West. This book is about finding our way into these new performative spaces. I turn in Chapter Two to Native Americans performing in Buffalo Bill's Wild West Show in Paris, circa 2014. Imagine Wendy Red Star in the audience, sharing her critique of Buffalo Bill and Disney with anyone who will listen.

Endnotes

by Norman Denzin

Dramatis Personae

1   Ferlyn Brass, Kevin Dust, Kevin Mustus, Ernest Rangel, and Carter Yellowbird were all interviewed by McNenly (2012, pp. 140–165) and quoted in her chapter on Euro Disney's Wild West Show. Unless otherwise indicated, the words they speak in my play(s) are words I have given them.

Chapter One: Native Art, Identity and Performance in the Postmodern West

1   One of the largest collections of paintings by the Taos Society of Artists is in the Eiteljorg Museum of American Indians and Western Art in Indianapolis, Indiana (see www.eiteljorg.org/explore/collections). See Appendix B for a list of the TSA painters.

2   Attending a session at the International Congress of Qualitative Inquiry on "Cowboys and Indians," Henhawk asks, "What did I get myself into? I feel like I'm the only Indian in the room" (2013, p. 519).

3   As well as visits to art galleries in Taos and to the Museum of Indian Arts and Culture in Santa Fe.

4   By Indian art I refer to modern Indian painting not the full-range of Native American art, which, in addition to paintings, includes, among other forms, baskets, jewelry, pottery, sculpture, weavings, Zuni fetishes, and Hopi Kachina dolls, etc.

5   I acknowledge the misnomer "Indian" and the cumbersome "Native American" or equally cumbersome "Indigenous person," using wherever possible the name of a specific tribe: Lakota Sioux, Crow, Hopi, Navajo, etc. (see Yellow Bird, 2004).

6   I criticize the marketing concept of Third Chapter in Chapter Five.

7   Hoffman's 1986 discussion of Native American in the context of modern and postmodern art distinguishes three major movements—traditional/archetypal/premodern; modern (impressionism, expressionism, cubism, abstraction, magical realism), and postmodernism. J. J. Brody complicates the situation, outlining five chronological phases of 'modern' Indian painting: (1) Proto-modern (1885–1917): easel paintings; (2) Self-taught (1910–1930): stylistically similar easel painting by self-taught Pueblo artists sold to patrons; (3) Early Institutional (1928–1937): Indian artists trained by white instructors—two distinct styles, one at the University of Oklahoma and another at the Santa Fe Indian School Studio; (4) Later Institutional (1937–1962): Indian artists trained in segregated schools in the Santa Studio Style; (5) Idiosyncratic (1962–present): Indians trained by Indians at the Institute of American Indian Art (Brody, 1971, pp. 57–58).

8   See Brody (1971), Strong (2013), Deloria (1998, 2004), Raheja (2010), Cotter (2014).

9   The Institute of American Indian Arts (IAIA) was established in 1962 under the leadership of Dr. George Boyce and Lloyd Kiva New. It opened on the campus of the Indian School in Santa Fe, New Mexico. It was first a high school formed under the Department of Interior's Bureau of Indian Affairs. In 1975 it became a two-year college offering associate degrees in Studio Arts, Creative Writing, and Museum Studies. It became a congressionally chartered college in 1986 and in 2013 began offering a graduate program, a MFA in creative writing (see www.iaia.edu/about/history). The original faculty included Allan Houser, Fritz Scholder, Charles Loloma, Otelliee Loloma, and James McGrath (Gibson and Leaken, 2014, p. 36). The Institute was for talented Indian high-school art students who were recruited from schools across the country. Kevin Red Star, for example, was recruited in 1962 from Lodge Grass High on the Crow Reservation in Eastern Montana (Gibson and Leaken, 2014, pp. 31–32). This Santa Fe initiative had some parallels with the 1968 federally funded New Communicators program which was designed to train minority filmmakers. UCLA was the primary training ground for the new filmmakers (see Denzin, 2002, pp. 43, 90).

10   'Postindian' is Vizenor's term (1999, p. viii) which replaces the traditional racist term Indian. Indian is a primitive simulation, the product of colonial domination. Postindians embody survivance. They resist colonial domination and perform, paint, and tell stories of the new postmodern postindian.

11   Including Dennis Hopper, Robert Redford, Rod McKuen, and Andy Warhol (see Sims, 2008a, p. 19).

12 For a montage of Schlder's paintings see centerofthewest.org/explore/ western-art/research/fritz-scholder/

13 Taos Pueblo is an ancient pueblo belonging to the Taos speaking Native American tribe of Pueblo people. It is approximately 1,000 years old and lies about one mile north of the modern city of Taos, New Mexico. It is a UNESCO World Heritage Site (see whc.unesco.org/en/list/492). The Taos Indians and the Pueblo of Taos were the original subject matter of the Taos Society of Artists. More than 4,500 residents live on a reservation of over 95,000 acres. Residents speak Tiwa, English, and Spanish and practice a religion that is a blend of Catholicism and Tanoan. The Taos Pueblo revolted against the Church and Spanish colonizers in 1600, 1680, and 1847, killing priests and burning churches. See Parsons's (1936) anthropological study of the Taos Pueblo and Broder's (1980, pp. 4–6) review of the 19th-century painters who worked as official recorders for the 1846–1847 U. S. Survey expedition into the Taos Valley (also Brody, 1971, pp. 59–75; Eldridge, Schimmel and Truettner, 1986, pp. 17–42; Schimmel and White, 1994, pp. 141–143).

14 This would not be Blumenschein's last interaction with Cody's Wild West show. In June 1905 he married Mary Shepherd Green, an artist, in Paris. "He could not kneel during the wedding ceremony because he was recovering from a knee injury received while playing baseball with Buffalo Bill's Cowboys at the Bois de Boulogne" (Broder,1980, p. 71). On March 29, 1914, and November 8, 1915, he and Mary could have attended Buffalo Bill's Wild West Show in Albuquerque, where it did one-night shows.

15 Money from these assignments funded his first trip to Taos in 1898 (Cunningham, 2008, pp. 31–32).

16 Raheja (2010, p. ix) quotes Sherman Alexie who recalls watching western films on television as a child: "I hated Tonto then and I hate him now."

17 For the purposes of this project he is also known as William Red Cloud. His sister is Alice Red Cloud.

18 See photos of Buffalo Bill's Paris Disneyland at www. disneylandparis.co.uk/dining/disney-village/ buffalo-bills-wild-west-show-with-mickey-and-friends/

19 See pdxcontemporaryart.com/red-star. See Wendy Red Star's Wild West & Congress of Rough Riders of the World, bumbershoot.org/lineup/artist/wendy-red-stars-wild-west-congress-of-rough-riders-of-the-world/. The August 30–September 1, 2014, Bumpershoot event in the Seattle Fisher Pavilion was billed as a journey through the real Wild West. Shantel Martinez directed me to this site. We will meet Wendy again in Chapter Six.

20 A recurring feature of the Wild West show involved Indian attacks on white settler cabins and stage coaches. These attacks framed Indians as threats to white civilization. The inevitable defeat of the Indian, even with white losses, signaled the victory of civilization over barbarism, making the frontier safe for whites (Warren, 2005, p. 94–95). The participation of Native Americans in these performances can be read, in part, as a refusal to accept defeat at the hands of whites; that is, Native Americans steadfastly resisted white domination. Alternative non-violent racial narratives—assimilation, accommodation, separatism—could have been staged and performed but weren't.

21 Dates: Massacre at Wounded Knee: December, 29, 1890; murder of Sitting Bull, December, 15, 1890; and beginning February 27, 1973, American Indian Movement occupies the town of Wounded Knee for 71 days.

22 The SGP are fresh from their closing show in the Paris Disneyland Buffalo Bill Wild West Show with Mickey and Minnie Mouse, aka William and Alice Red Cloud.

23 San Geronimo Feast Day is the feast day for St. Jerome, the patron saint of the Taos Pueblo. The festival begins on day one with a sundown dance and evening vespers, followed, on the second day, by foot races in the morning, and in the afternoon 'clowns' wearing black and white body paint and black and white costumes compete in the pole climb. San Geronimo Feast Day is also a fall trading festival in which neighboring tribes participate in an Indian trade fair, offering Indians crafts and foods for sale. Clowns, dancers, cowboys, art dealers, magicians, showmen, persons selling Western memorabilia and Native American antiques, artists, and native Taos Indians, and Traveling Indian Medicine Show performers all co-mingle during the festival. The presence of the Traveling Medicine Show lends an air of minstrelsy to the festival (Denzin, 2013, pp. 25–27).

24 Quoting from the museum website, the paintings of the Taos Society of Artists were favorites of the museum's founder, Harrison Eiteljorg, and his collection is a core part of the museum and this gallery. See more at www. eiteljorg.org/explore/collections/western. Native American art is also represented in the Eiteljorg, again from the website: Native American art and artifacts at the Eiteljorg Museum represent all major culture areas of the Western Hemisphere, including tribes in the United States and Canada. The collection began with the personal holdings of founder Harrison Eiteljorg.

25 In 2013 the Denver Art Museum received a major gift of paintings produced by the Taos Society artists (see *New York Times*, August 14, 2013).

26 Beginning in 1948 and continuing through 1969 the College of Fine Arts at the University of Illinois produced "one of the most influential exhibition series in the country" (Witt, 1992, p. 18), privileging the work of 14

Taos Modern artists—O'Keeffe, Marin, Sterne, Rothko, and others. It was organized by C. V. Donavan and Allen S. Weller. No Native Taos or Native Santa Fe artists were included in these exhibitions.

27 Like the 1,000-year-old Taos Pueblo itself these artists embodied Vizenor's (2008, p. 11) concept of survivance, the active resistance and repudiation of colonial dominance, the creation of a positive presence that must be heard and witnessed, a formidable presence that is also an absence.

28 Shantel Martinez brought this work to my attention.

29 An obvious play on the title of Dee Brown's *Bury My Heart at Wounded Knee* (1971).

30 Radical Indigenous Survivance & Empowermen, or RISE. Established in 2010 by Demian Dine Yazhi, and drawing on Gerald Vivenor's (2008) aesthetics of survivance, RISE is a call to action yielding multiple tools, including photographs, paint, wheatpaste, clay, beadwork, dancing, words, and more. See www.facebook.com/RISEIndigenous http://burymyart. tumblr.com/. See also the recent art exhibit, "Bury My Art at Wounded Knee: Blood & Guts" which opened in the Stevens Studios of the Portland Northwest College Art School Industrial Complex, May 25, 2014.

31 Seventh Generation: From the great law of the Haudenoaunee people— how will the decisions made today benefit the children seven generations into the future (Benally, 2013). I have created a performance group, the Seventh Generation Performers. The theme of the 2015 Canadian Indigenous/Native Studies Association is "Survivance & Reconciliation: 7 Forward /7 Back" and borrows from the Seven Generations theme (see www.naisa.org/cfp-cinsa-2015-concordia-university-montreal.html).

32 Consider the irony of Johnny Depp, in redface, playing Tonto in Disney's 2013 film, *The Lone Ranger*. The 19th-century minstrel show tradition is alive and well in the Disney Studios.

33 I treat Mr. and Ms. Coyote as tricksters, as disruptive, critical, wise, laughing comic healers, liberators, mythic performers of postindian survivance stories (Vizenor, 1999, p. 89).

34 I introduce musical performances by Taos Pueblo drummers and flute players in Chapters Three, Four, Five, and Six. The music is intended to set a respectful mood, a soft ambience in the scene, and it can heard as Native muzak.

35 The mystory is simultaneously a personal mythology, a public story, a personal narrative, and a performance that critiques.

Without Reservations

by Ricardo Caté

Required Reading Available Online

Shingler, Benjamin. 2013. "The Next Hot Sound? Powwow step, aboriginal hip hop," Aljazeera America, November 28, 2013. http://america.aljazeera.com/articles/2013/11/28/the-next-hot-soundyouhearwillbepowwowstepaboriginalhiphop.html

---

i https://www.youtube.com/watch?v=SplxZiBpGU0&list=PLaCqVS0ceWqYR_ugpQfIeWivsWUBJD0jM

Image Credits

CPSIA information can be obtained
at www.ICGtesting.com
Printed in the USA
FSOW04n1801291216
29024FS